German
Expressionist
Plays

The German Library: Volume 66

Volkmar Sander, General Editor

GERMAN EXPRESSIONIST PLAYS

Edited by Ernst Schürer

CONTINUUM · NEW YORK

2005
The Continuum International Publishing Group Inc
15 East 26 Street, New York, NY 10010

The German Library
is published in cooperation with Deutsches Haus,
New York University.
This volume has been supported by Inter Nationes.

Printed in the United States of America

Library of Congress Cataloging-in-Publication Data

German expressionist plays / edited by Ernst Schürer.
        p.   cm.—(The German library ; v. 66)
Contents: Murderer the women's hope / Oskar Kokoschka—
Sancta Susanna / August Stramm—Ithaka / Gottfried Benn—
The bloomers / Carl Sternheim—The son / Walter Hasenclever—
From morning to midnight / Georg Kaiser—Masses and man /
Ernst Toller—Gas I and gas II / Georg Kaiser.
ISBN 0-8264-0951-2 (alk. paper).—ISBN 0-8264-0950-4
                (pbk. : alk. paper)
1. German drama—20th century—Translations into English.
            I. Schürer, Ernst. II. Series.
PT1258.G47   1997   96-37251
832'.912080115—dc21   CIP

Contents

Introduction

The theater has always played an important role in the spiritual, intellectual, and political life of the German-speaking countries. With medieval mystery plays, baroque and classical tragedies, naturalist comedies, and the documentary drama, playwrights have tried to entertain and enlighten their audiences. From its religious roots, the drama slowly grew during the sixteenth and seventeenth centuries, when it was used primarily for didactic religious or educational purposes; it blossomed during the eighteenth century when it was adopted by the politically disenfranchised middle classes and developed by the youthful and rebellious authors of the Sturm und Drang. It reached its zenith in the nineteenth century during the classical period of German literature, when Goethe and Schiller wrote and directed their plays at the Weimar court. Schiller considered the theater a moral institution that allowed politically impotent subjects to criticize their autocratic rulers and educate their fellow citizens morally and aesthetically. Maverick playwrights such as Lenz, Kleist, Büchner, and Grabbe produced plays that were so far ahead of their times that they came to be appreciated and performed only generations later. During the second half of the nineteenth century, dramatists followed in the footsteps of the masters Goethe and Schiller, and German drama stagnated. The classical plays, however, were performed on a regular basis on the stages of the numerous court and city theaters. After German unification under Bismarck, Berlin began to rival Vienna as a theater metropolis, and when in 1889 naturalism became the dominant literary movement, the plays of Gerhart Hauptmann were first performed in the imperial capital. The naturalist playwrights—inspired by Scandinavian and French dramatic innovations and theatrical experiments—brought a breath of fresh air to the stage, but in time the public grew tired of their often superficial reproduction of life, and neoromantic, neoclassical, and symbolist plays became the rage.

It was in this context that Expressionism and Expressionist drama made its entry. *Expressionism* is a term first used in the arts to signify a painting in which the emotive character of the subject, and especially color, is stressed at the expense of its representational, photographic function. The artists tried to capture the essence *(Das Wesen)* of their subject as it was revealed to them in a vision. Intuition, imagination, and dreams inspired this vision, which to them was more meaningful than experience and reality. Van Gogh, Cézanne, and Matisse were the models for young painters in Germany who formed circles such as "Die Brücke" (The bridge) and "Der blaue Reiter" (The blue horseman) in Dresden and Munich. They discussed "The Spiritual in Art," the title of a book published by Wassily Kandinsky in 1912, and argued passionately in *Der Sturm* (The storm), an avant-garde periodical founded by Herwarth Walden. There they discussed the aesthetics and the ethical and social mission of art in a world that they saw as morally decadent and shallow to the extreme. They revolted against the art establishment as well as against modern society and its values. Their prophet was the writer and philosopher Friedrich Nietzsche who had proclaimed the death of God and with it the loss of all metaphysical meaning for life. Nietzsche's prime call was for a reevaluation of all values. Many of these artists were multitalented; they painted, worked as sculptors, discussed their views in art journals and literary magazines, and published poems, plays, and prose pieces.

Their cry of protest was taken up by writers and philosophers who were searching for new values in a complacent society, a world that in their opinion was ruled by soulless, rationalistic, and dangerous technological progress, crass and superficial materialism, greedy and corrupt capitalism, and saber-rattling, chauvinistic nationalism. They looked upon educational institutions and state churches as servants of the dominant ideology, more interested in maintaining the status quo than in helping the downtrodden and disadvantaged, the tragic victims of industrialization and so-called progress. Following the perceived loss of all transcendental values in the wake of modern science, the Expressionist artists were searching for a new meaning in life, new spiritual values. They saw themselves as the prophets of a new spirituality. A good example is the youthful protagonist of Reinhard Sorge's autobiographical play *Der Bettler* (The beggar, 1912), a budding playwright. In contrast to his mad scientist father who harasses the family and wants to subjugate nature, he is desperately searching for meaning and love in life, not only for himself but also for the masses of city dwellers whom he wants to redeem. He envisions a new theater for the people in which they will find solace and salvation. Human beings are basically good, the Expressionists agreed; they only need to overcome the restrictions and negative influences of society in order to realize their true potential. And if revolution and war were necessary to achieve this goal, the Expressionists were ready to go along.

Expressionism was the Sturm und Drang period of the twentieth century, carried by young artists born between 1880 and 1890. Like the characters of Walter Hasenclever's *Der Sohn* (*The Son*, 1912) they formed a "League of the Young against the World." Older writers such as August Stramm (1874–1915), Georg Kaiser (1878–1945), and Carl Sternheim (1878–1942) were swept along by the enthusiasm of the youthful members of the movement who published their views and works in periodicals with such telling names as *Die Aktion* (The action, 1910), *Der Sturm* (The storm, 1910), *Revolution* (1912), and *Neue Jugend* (New youth, 1916). They were searching for new values in art and life, and they saw as their primary mission the creation of a new individual. Once this "new man" came into being, he would transform society. As Georg Kaiser expressed it: "What is the vision? There is only one, that of the regeneration of the human individual!" "Vision" is also the key concept in Kasimir Edschmidt's famous manifesto "Concerning Poetic Expressionism": "For the Expressionist artist the whole world becomes a vision. He does not observe, he envisions. He does not portray, he experiences. He does not reproduce, he creates. He does not take, he seeks. . . . Man no longer exists as an individual, tied to duty, ethics, society, and family. In this art he becomes nothing but the highest and lowest: a human being."

Aesthetically, the Expressionist playwrights rejected the conventions and principles of naturalism. They were not interested in the psychology of their characters but saw them as essential human beings solely defined by their family relationships or professions. Therefore, they are described only as "The Son," "The Cashier," "The Daughter," "The Billionaire Worker," and "Chief Engineer."

They are not fully developed personalities but rather types or figures. In *Gas II,* Kaiser carries this typification to its extreme when he designates the opposing camps simply as Yellow Figures and Blue Figures. The speech of their characters also becomes more and more abstract: from the colloquial, dialect-filled conversation *(Sekundenstil)* in naturalist drama it slowly develops into a diction stripped down to its bare essentials, the so-called telegraphic style *(Telegrammstil)* in which adjectives are used sparingly, and verbs and articles are often omitted. This language appears also in the poetry of Gottfried Benn, August Stramm, and Georg Trakl, in which traditional syntax has been drastically reduced. Evocative nouns, newly coined verbs, and autonomous metaphors create a new reality of art that aims at a strong emotional impact and the evocation of cultural, mythological, and literary associations. The ultimate reduction of language results in the *Scream (der Schrei)* as the pure expression of intense feeling. It goes without saying that this language is difficult to understand and even harder to translate, since it does not primarily serve rational discourse, but rather proclamation and provocation. When produced on the stage, the setting of Expressionist plays and stage props take on a symbolic meaning, and serve to underline the spoken word and the message of the drama. The innovations of Adolphe Appia and Gordon Craig in stage design, their use of lighting devices and stage props, new developments in opera productions, especially for the operas of Richard Wagner and his concept of *Gesamtkunstwerk,* as well as the new film medium, all influenced the often revolutionary productions of Expressionist plays in experimental and regular theaters in Berlin and in the provinces.

Most Expressionists also rejected the traditional structure of the well-made play in five acts. Influenced by the plays of Frank Wedekind (1864–1918) and especially August Strindberg (1849–1912), whose dramas portray the frustrated and isolated individual on his way through a hostile world, they developed the station play *(Stationendrama),* which shows the protagonist, often a thinly disguised self-representation of the author, his ego, on his way in a world that is viewed only through the eyes of the main character. In consequence, it is a highly subjective portrayal. Peter Szondi correctly remarked that the "I-drama of Expressionism paradoxically does not lead to the description of the lonely individual, but to the shocking exposure of especially the cities and their places of amusement." The metropolis in all its manifestations and industry as the focus of Expressionist criticism of the modern world occupies a central position in the discourse of Expressionist writers.

Before World War I, most Expressionists found an outlet for their feelings and sentiments in the fine arts and in lyric poetry. Therefore, it is small wonder that the first three authors represented here are famous more for their paintings and poetry than their work as playwrights. When Oskar Kokoschka (1886–1980) wrote *Mörder, Hoffnung der Frauen (Murderer the Women's Hope)* in 1907, he had been a student in the School of Arts and Crafts *(Kunstgewerbeschule)* in Vienna since 1903 and was active in progressive art circles in the city. Sigmund Freud and Otto Weininger whose study *Geschlecht und Charakter* (Sex and character, 1903) had made headlines some years earlier, are godfathers to Kokoschka's portrayal of the battle of the sexes. Actually, the text is rudimentary; it is rather the theatrical production with its use of symbolic colors, innovative lighting, and stylized movements that captured the attention of the audience. The violent action culminates in the spiritual victory of the super hero who strides across the stage killing women intent on capturing and enslaving him. Kokoschka's production of the spectacle at the 1909 Art Exhibition in Vienna caused a riot, which resulted in his expulsion from the Academy. Fortunately, he was offered private financial support that allowed him to continue writing new plays and revising his old ones; they greatly influenced the theater of Expressionism. He also became active in the *Sturm* circle in Berlin, had a love affair with Alma Mahler-Werfel, the *femme fatale* among Expressionist artists, and was severely wounded during World War I. The modern composer Paul Hindemith used Kokoschka's play as a libretto for an opera with the same title. It was produced in 1927 with the assistance of the playwright.

Like Kokoschka's play, August Stramm's *Sancta Susanna* (1914) focuses on sexuality, in this case the repressed sexuality of nuns in a convent. His one-act play is noteworthy for its linguistic innovations, reminiscent of his poetry. Although the stage directions are quite detailed, the dialogue is fragmentary, consisting of exclamations, incomplete sentences, and long silences. As with Kokoschka, the stage settings and lighting are highly evocative and symbolic, but it is Stramm's pioneering use of dramatic dialogue that influenced the development of Expressionist drama. He, however, did not experience that development since as an officer fighting in Russia he was killed in combat in 1915, another victim of World War I. *Sancta Susanna* was first produced in 1918 by Lothar Schreyer at the Berlin *Sturmbühne,* an experimental stage supported by Herwarth Walden and his *Sturm.* Since Stramm worked as a postal clerk, it has been suggested that his telegraphic style of writing was a *deformation professionelle.* But he obviously worked very hard at it, even inventing new words in his attempt to revise the language to make it more expressive and evocative.

Gottfried Benn (1886–1956) was a medical doctor, as was Expressionist novelist Alfred Döblin. Both had their practice in the working-class section of Berlin. Benn experimented with language in his poetry, but it was not his linguistic innovations, but rather the clinically graphic and often simply disgusting subject matter presented in aesthetically beautiful form that shocked even the rather blasé Berlin society. His play *Ithaka* (1914), on the other hand, is of interest because it portrays the youth revolt and Benn's nihilistic, anticivilizatory view of the universe. Benn had studied theology and philosophy before turning to medicine, and he writes about the fragmentation and alienation of the modern individual, his total loss of all transcendental values, and his existence in an utterly meaningless world. He calls for a return to a mystical past and a natural primeval existence that is evoked by such key words as *blood, dream, myth, ecstasy,* and *Dionysos.* The title of the play encompasses the positive ideal, which is opposed by the ideas of scientific progress and humanitarian values that are encoded in concepts such as *intellect, brain, knowledge,* and *logic.* The author is clearly influenced by Nietzsche, who extolled instinct above intellect, vitality above spirit, and stressed the Dionysian element of passion and fate.

Benn served as a medical doctor in both wars and because of his nihilism he was briefly attracted to the National Socialist ideology of blood and soil, of folk community and a new mythical age. His dream was short-lived, however, since he soon realized that their real aim was not creative innovation but conformity and subservience to their political goals and reactionary values. Thereafter, Benn devoted himself exclusively to his profession and his poetic labors (cf. The German Library, volume 73). At the time of his death, Benn was considered the preeminent Expressionist poet.

Carl Sternheim also read Nietzsche. He started with neo-romantic plays, but only achieved success with his tetralogy dealing with "the heroic life of the bourgeoisie": *Die Hose* (*The Bloomers,* 1911), *Der Snob* (The snob, 1913), *1913* (published 1914), and *Das Fossil* (The fossil, 1922). In these comedies, he illustrates the rise of the "Maske" family from bourgeois middle-class roots to the heights of aristocracy. In *The Bloomers,* Theodor Maske is only a minor clerk, but in *The Snob* and *1913,* his son Christian succeeds in becoming a partner in industrial firms, acquires an ammunition factory, and earns a fortune. By marrying the daughter of a count, he climbs still higher up the social ladder. Finally, his ambitions are crowned when he is knighted after having attained a dominant position in industry. The name *Maske* is symbolic, for under the mask of bourgeois respectability, the Maskes ruthlessly further their ambitions for material wealth and social advancement.

Sternheim's satire and caricature expose the selfishness and vulgarity of the upper-middle class, but they are always mixed with a great deal of admiration for the self-assured bourgeois, a tyrant in his own household, interested only in his own smug comfort and having no use for literature, philosophy, or politics. He is the ruthless superman who triumphs over the effeminate aesthete Scarron and the opera-lover and Wagner-aficionado Mandelstam, who both ascribe to social Darwinism, the survival of the fittest, and social domination by the strongest, but are no match for the prosaic and down-to-earth giant Maske.

Sternheim's most powerful weapon in his attack against the bourgeois way of life was his language, which he cut down to essentials in his "fight against the metaphor." By thus distorting everyday speech, he uncovers its real meaning. Sternheim also extensively used, or rather misused, proverbs and quotations, thus exposing the pretense and hollowness of idealistic, romantic, or sentimental clichés. Sternheim's characters are not well rounded; they represent social strata and prefigure the abstract types of Expressionistic drama. Yet Sternheim's comedies are very effective and the best of them are still successful on the stage today.

Walter Hasenclever's (1890–1940) *The Sohn* has as its topic the *Generationskonflikt*—the rebellion of the sons against the fathers and the adult world in general. Although many plays in the repertoire of the German theater focus on this topic, among them Schiller's *Die Räuber* (The robbers, 1781), the first modern treatment was Frank Wedekind's *Frühlings Erwachen* (Spring's awakening, 1891). Wedekind called his play a tragedy of adolescence caused by the bigoted, bourgeois attitude and hypocrisy of both parents and teachers. Instead of guiding youth through this often painful adolescent period, he shows them merely suppressing any stirrings of independence and all natural instincts—especially the sexual urge at the time of puberty.

Wedekind's play was not only pioneering a new topic but a new style as well. The language of the students is poetical, but they are represented realistically. On the other hand, the teachers are mercilessly caricatured. But at the end, the realistic plane is left behind altogether; the apparition of his dead friend tempts a student to follow him by committing suicide, whereupon an allegorical figure, a masked man representing life, appears and persuades the boy that he should continue to live. Wedekind seeks to draw the attention of the audience to society's sores by grossly exaggerating and distorting them. The structure of the play is also revolutionary: like Georg Büchner's *Woyzeck* (1879), it consists mostly of short scenes following each other in rapid succession.

Hasenclever's play was semiautobiographical with the son as the protagonist who sees and judges everything from his own point of view. He is imprisoned and treated as a child by his father who only wants the best for his son but has no feeling for his desire to be on his own. Instead of studying for his exams, the son wants to go out and experience life in all of its manifestations. Only slowly he realizes that he must set himself a spiritual goal. In an assembly he passionately pleads for freedom from paternal oppression. When his friend gives him a revolver and he is taken home by a sympathetic police officer, he threatens his father who conveniently dies of a heart attack. The son is now free to go into the world, and proclaims his desire to live his own life and fight for freedom. He does not espouse a specific political program but simply calls for revolutionary action to change society.

Hasenclever's play and Reinhard Sorge's *The Beggar* have much in common thematically. Together with Georg Kaiser's *Von morgens bis mitternachts* (*From Morning to Midnight*, 1916) they rank among the earliest Expressionist plays. *The Son* was first published in 1914 and performed on stage in late 1916. Ernst Deutsch, a youthful actor gave such a brilliant performance in Dresden that he swept the audience off its feet with his expressive and fiery acting style, which was then copied by other famous directors for productions of Expressionistic dramas. Both the playwright Hasenclever and the actor Deutsch were celebrated as brothers in revolutionary spirit. Hasenclever was at that time doing military service and was wounded in Macedonia. He recovered in a Dresden sanatorium where he wrote *Antigone* (1917) a historical drama directed against World War I. In the 1920s, Hasenclever wrote successful comedies, but was forced into exile in France in 1933 when the Nazis came to power. Interned by the French authorities at the beginning of World War II, he committed suicide when German troops approached the camp.

Georg Kaiser maintained that he wrote *From Morning to Midnight,* a play in two parts, in 1912, but he probably continued working on it until its date of publication in 1916. Even before this play and shortly before the war, Kaiser's *Die Bürger von Calais* (The citizens of Calais, 1914) was published. It did not attract much attention at that time, as a fever of patriotism swept across Europe. Only three years later, as the warring nations began to tire of the savagery and waste of trench warfare, and started to comprehend the horror and futility of war, was this play discovered and proclaimed a powerful denunciation of war, and a call for "the new man." The director of the Frankfurt Neues Theater, Arthur Hellmer, produced the play in the presence of Kaiser, on January 27, 1917. This premiere had the same importance for Expressionism that the first performance of Hauptmann's *Vor Sonnenaufgang* on October 20, 1889, had for naturalism. The play ushered in a new epoch in the history of German drama and started the so-called Frankfurt Expressionism.

From Morning to Midnight is a prime example of the Expressionist play of regeneration *(Wandlungsdrama)*. At first thought, this seems to be a misnomer, since the Cashier never undergoes such a regeneration. But most plays of this type end in failure. In the center of a *Wandlungsdrama* stands one person, in this case the Cashier, through whose eyes all characters and events are viewed. He has become dehumanized in the service of the bank and lives imprisoned behind the bars of the teller's window. Sexually aroused by the visit of a beautiful Italian lady and the suggestive monologue of the manager, he comes to life, embezzles sixty-thousand marks, and leaves. Frustrated by his empty and mechanistic existence, he goes in search of a meaningful ecstatic life, first in his hometown of W.[eimar], then in the big metropolis B.[erlin]. But in spite of his riches and the financial rewards he offers, he cannot find it in the private sphere with the Italian lady, the Salvation Army girl who betrays him, or with his conventional bourgeois family, nor can he find it in the public sphere of sports, amusement, politics, and religion. In the end, he commits suicide and dies leaning against a cross with the words "Ecce homo" on his lips. His end is not so much an allusion to the passion of Christ as to Nietzsche's autobiographical work *Ecce homo* (1888). By attempting to reach Dionysiac ecstasy and a full life, the Cashier emulates Nietzsche's ideal and not Christ's. However, he does not achieve his goal but remains imprisoned by his past. He follows his accustomed thought patterns by trying to buy pleasure instead of completely rejecting the kind of society that enslaves him. When he finally recognizes that he has been chasing illusions all along, he takes his own life since he is faced by nothingness and sees no other way of escape.

The language of the play is as reduced as the figures themselves. The Cashier, however, uses metaphors and imagery in his monologues as well as highly symbolic speech. The present translation does not always capture the punctuation, which is of great importance in Kaiser's plays since it underscores the dynamic qualities of his style. It is also indicative of the kind of acting, gesturing, and pantomime demanded of the actor. Otto Falckenberg, the director of the Munich Kammerspiele, premiered the play with great success on April 28, 1917, in the presence of the author. This success was repeated during the following years on many stages in Germany and abroad. *From Morning to Midnight* is generally considered Kaiser's best play, and provides a challenge to good actors and imaginative directors.

Gas I (1918) and *Gas II* (1920) are part of Kaiser's *Gas* trilogy, which begins with *Die Koralle* (The coral, 1917). The principal characters of the trilogy belong to four generations of the Billionaire's family. The play covers a time span of about sixty-five-to-seventy years. The events in *Die Koralle* take place around the turn of the century, but it would be a mistake to place them into a realistic setting. Nevertheless, it might be surmised that the capitalist prewar society of Wilhelminian Germany is portrayed in *Die Koralle*. The rich are getting richer, the poor poorer, and strikes are suppressed with the help of the military. The Billionaire is still an old-fashioned capitalist, while his son belongs to the new generation that is rebelling against the social irresponsibility of the fathers. He improves the lot of the workers but also speeds up the economic and technological progress. The explosion in *Gas* can be looked upon as World War I, which many intellectuals considered a result of industrial development, caused by forces beyond human control. The strike of the workers can be compared to the strikes in the German armament plants in 1917 and 1918; they were put down, and the industries were taken over by the state and geared exclusively to military programs. *Gas* was finished before the signing of the armistice and was already performed on November 28, 1918, at the Frankfurt Neues Theater and the Düsseldorf Schauspielhaus.

In *Gas II*, the end of World War I is depicted; industrial systems were strained to the breaking point, and the war of attrition had progressed to a stage where the opposing camps were bleeding to death and facing total destruction. The German military wanted to fight to the finish—Hindenburg's all-or-nothing plan was carried out when Ludendorff mounted the final gigantic German offensive on March 21, 1918. The war ends in act 2, when the workers, their resources exhausted, refuse to produce any longer. The call for peace they send out is patterned after the Bolshviks' proclamations and cables "To all" during the revolution and peace negotiations at Brest-Litovsk, a call not taken up by the rest of the world, although a call for brotherhood was issued by intellectuals and pacifists in many nations. They had been encouraged by Wilson's Fourteen Points but were cruelly repelled by the victorious Allied politicians, who were more interested in punishment of Germany, territorial annexations, and payment of reparations than in securing a permanent peace. In this frame of mind, they drew up the Treaty of Versailles, which was partly responsible for World War II that followed twenty years later. Kaiser foresaw this in the last act of *Gas II*. The occupation of the factory at the beginning of the play may allude to the occupation of parts of the Rhineland by French troops to ensure the payment of reparations.

Gas II can also be looked upon as the symbolic expression of the death of the Expressionist hopes for the regeneration of man and the dawn of a new era. The storm of World War I had blown across Europe and had left destruction and chaos in its wake. But the masses were still selfish and unregenerate, and humanity was not ripe for salvation and therefore had to be annihilated. Structurally, the *Gas* plays are not *Stationendramen*, but follow the model of the well-structured play. They are prime examples of a play typical for Kaiser called a *Denkspiel*, or play of ideas. The idea, or thesis, is opposed by its antithesis. Kaiser, however, does not arrive at a synthesis of opposing ideas, but pits them against each other until one is vanquished. Concepts that in reality appear in many combinations and allow for many solutions, are pictured as exclusive opposites unable to exist side by side, such as man and machine, or civilization and nature. These simplified ideas are portrayed in dramas with a rather simplified structure. Kaiser did not write these plays in order to portray reality, but rather shows the development of an idea, and the principles of parallelism, counterpoint, and symmetry in the structure of the play are designed to this end.

Symbolism is found in every aspect of the plays: the syntactical structure and the style of the dialogue are symbolic of man's mechanization and specialization as a cog in the machine of technological society. This isolation and alienation of the characters are expressed through the content and vocabulary of their speech. While the world of industry and technology is presented for the first time in Kaiser's plays, the stage settings are highly symbolic, as well. The author also employs color symbolism extensively, though in a rather conventional manner. He uses the traditional symbols and metaphors of the Christian faith to express his vision of the earth's salvation in terms the audience can understand. Christian teachings helped Expressionists in preaching a secularized gospel of man's regeneration.

Ernst Toller (1893–1939) is generally considered the most politically inspired and active of the Expressionist authors. The son of wealthy German-speaking Jewish parents in the Polish-speaking parts of Prussia, he early recognized the social injustices in the world, and developed a feeling of being an outsider in Wilhelminian German society. Nevertheless, when in 1914 he heard that war had been declared, he rushed back from France where he was studying to volunteer for military service and prove himself a true patriotic German. But the horrors of combat in the trenches and mechanized warfare soon led him to question his nationalism. After being hospitalized in 1916, he began to reeducate himself and to oppose the war. In early 1918, he participated in a general

strike in Munich directed especially against the ammunition factories. Out of his experiences grew his semiautobiographical play *Die
Wandlung* (The transformation, 1919).

Following the armistice and the revolution on November 9,
1918, Bavaria became a republic. Its provisional government, however, proved reactionary, and in April 1919, a group of idealists,
among them Toller, formed a Central Revolutionary Committee
and proclaimed a Bavarian Soviet Republic in Munich. Toller was
elected its president, but was soon pushed aside by the communists
who raised an army to defend themselves against the troops of
the deposed provisional government, the Free Corps and the
Reichswehr. Toller was put in command of the Red Army which,
however, was crushed by the counter-revolutionary forces. Toller
had unsuccessfully tried to prevent the execution of members of a
reactionary society by the revolutionaries, and these murders were
followed by mass executions of captured workers by the victorious
and vengeful white troops. Toller escaped certain death by hiding;
when he was later arrested he was sentenced to five years in prison.
He was deeply shocked and disturbed by the atrocities committed
by both sides, and in prison he agonized over his decisions and
actions during the revolutionary period. By following his ethical principles and by not ruthlessly exterminating the counter-
revolutionaries, had he helped the conservative forces to victory
and the consequent murder of his comrades, the workers, and pro-
letarians to whom the play is dedicated? He also critically examined the ideas and goals of the revolution and the means used to
attain those aims. In October 1919, he started to write *Masse
Mensch (Masses and Man)* in which the use of violence as a means
of changing society is discussed. The title of the play refers to the
opposition of the individual against society, of his ethical responsibility toward another human being against the social demands of
the oppressed masses. Toller himself referred to the "duality between man as an individual and man as a social being." Is it possible that the bourgeois idealistic Expressionist hero in this play,
Sonja Irene L., can help establish a communist, egalitarian society
without being liquidated by either side in the conflict, or must
she become guilty by participating in killing the class enemy, her
husband, in order to save her revolutionary friends? How can she
escape this tragic dilemma, which had been explored previously by
Georg Büchner in *Dantons Tod* (Danton's death, 1835)? Is it simply

inevitable that anybody taking part in political action will be burdened by guilt? It seems that the existing societal forms cannot survive without resorting to force and suppression, but does this fact justify the use of counter-force to establish a new society that in the long run can also be sustained only by force? Are non-violence and pacifism viable options in this militaristic and aggressive world?

In contrast to most Expressionist dramatists, Toller wrote his play in verse, and used alternating realistic scenes *(reale Bilder)* and dream scenes *(Traumbilder)* to show on the one hand the actual political events based on his experiences during the days of the Bavarian Soviet Republic, on the other the ethical struggle within the protagonist of the play. Toller explained it as follows:

> All action is separated into external and internal action, which are of equal importance, equally strong as motivating forces. . . . Only a few [of the critics] recognized that the struggle between the individual and the masses occurs not only in the external world, but that in everybody's mind the individual and the masses coexist. As an individual, a man acts according to the ethical principle which he has recognized as being just. He wants to live according to this principle, even though the world might perish as a consequence. As part of the masses, a man is driven by social impulses and situations; he wants to reach that goal, even if he must relinquish the moral principle. For a political activist, this contradiction cannot be solved today. [In this play,] I wanted to show especially the fact that no solution is possible.

Toller's play stands between the drama of Expressionism and the later *Agitprop*-plays of the authors of the BPRS, the League of Proletarian Revolutionary Writers. It was highly successful and controversial on stage and was translated into several languages. Toller's revolutionary Expressionism, his idealism and pacifism, however, made him unwelcome in both the capitalist and communist camps, and he suffered a harsh fate.

The golden age of Expressionism on the stage lasted for only a decade from about 1916 to 1925. With the stabilization of the Weimar Republic in 1924, the public grew tired of the call for revolution and the utopian ideals of the Expressionist drama. It had endured over four years of war, another four years of revolution, civil unrest, and a disastrous inflation, and the anticipated realization of neither nationalistic aspirations nor the later proclaimed renewal of mankind and universal brotherhood had come about. Now the audiences rejected the enthusiasm, pathos, and intensity of Expressionist plays as well as their idealistic and utopian goals. And the playwrights themselves realized that their work had become too abstract, too subjective, and too idealistic. They were looking for new ways of expressing themselves. Hasenclever, Kaiser, and even Toller turned to comedy and were quite successful in this genre. Nevertheless, German Expressionist drama exerted a lasting influence on modern drama and film. Wedekind, Sternheim, and Kaiser were early models for Bertolt Brecht and Carl Zuckmayer, and their influence can also be detected in the plays of Swiss dramatists Max Frisch and Friedrich Dürrenmatt. Expressionism also made a lasting impact on the American stage, as several studies have shown. Following the revival of interest in Expressionism in Germany after the Nazi period, when most Expressionists were driven into exile or even to suicide, their plays have been critically examined and restaged, and Expressionist dramatists have even become the topic of modern plays, as in *Toller* (1968) by Tankred Dorst. In conclusion, it may be asserted that although Expressionism as an avant-garde movement was shortlived, its drama still exerts a powerful influence on the modern stage and mass media.

E. S.

Oskar Kokoschka

Murderer the Women's Hope

Characters

Man
Woman
Chorus: Men and Women

Night sky. Tower with large red iron grille as door; torches the only light; black ground, rising to the tower in such a way that all the figures appear in relief.

THE MAN *in blue armor, white face, kerchief covering a wound, with a crowd of men—savage in appearance, gray-and-red kerchiefs, white-black-and-brown clothes, signs on their clothes, bare legs, long-handled torches, bells, din—creeping up with handles of torches extended and lights; wearily, reluctantly try to hold back the adventurer, pull his horse to the ground; he walks on, they open up the circle around him, crying out in a slow crescendo.*

MEN: We were the flaming wheel around him,
  We were the flaming wheel around you, assailant of locked
    fortresses!

Hesitantly follow him again in chain formation; he, with the torch bearer in front of him, heads the procession.

MEN: Lead us, pale one!

While they are about to pull his horse to the ground, women with their leader ascend steps on the left.

WOMAN, *red clothes, loose yellow hair, tall.*

WOMAN, *loud:* With my breath I fan the yellow disc of the sun, my eye collects the jubilation of the men, their stammering lust prowls around me like a beast.

FEMALE ATTENDANTS *separate themselves from her, only now catch sight of the stranger.*

FIRST FEMALE ATTENDANT: His breath attaches itself to the virgin!

FIRST MAN *to the others:* Our master is like the moon that rises in the East.

SECOND GIRL, *quiet, her face averted*: When will she be enfolded joyfully?

Listening, alert, the CHORUS *walks round the whole stage, dispersed in groups;* THE MAN *and the* WOMAN *meet in front of the gate.*

(*Pause.*)

WOMAN *observes him spellbound, then to herself*: Who is the stranger that has looked on me?

GIRLS *press to the fore.*

FIRST GIRL *recognizes him, cries out:* His sister died of love.

SECOND GIRL: Oh the singing of Time, flowers never seen.

THE MAN, *astonished; his procession halts:* Am I real? What did the shadows say?

Raising his face to her.

Did you look at me, did I look at you?

WOMAN, *filled with fear and longing:* Who is the pallid man? Hold him back.

FIRST GIRL, *with a piercing scream, runs back:* Do you let him in? It is he who strangles my little sister praying in the temple.

FIRST MAN *to the girl:* We saw him stride through the fire, his feet unharmed.

SECOND MAN: He tortured animals to death, killed neighing mares by the pressure of his thighs.

THIRD MAN: Birds that ran before us he made blind, stifled red fishes in the sand.

THE MAN *angry, heated:* Who is she that like an animal proudly grazes amidst her kin?

FIRST MAN: She divines what none has understood.

SECOND MAN: She perceives what none has seen or heard.

THIRD MAN: They say shy birds approach her and let themselves be seized.

GIRLS *in time with the men.*

FIRST GIRL: Lady, let us flee. Extinguish the flares of the leader.

SECOND GIRL: Mistress, escape!

THIRD GIRL: He shall not be our guest or breathe our air. Let him not lodge with us, he frightens me.

MEN, *hesitant, walk on,* WOMEN *crowd together anxiously. The* WOMAN *goes up to* THE MAN, *prowling, cautious.*

FIRST GIRL: He has no luck.

FIRST MAN: She has no shame.

WOMAN: Why do you bind me, man, with your gaze? Ravening light, you confound my flame! Devouring life overpowers me. Oh take away my terrible hope—and may torment overpower you.

THE MAN, *enraged:* My men, now brand her with my sign, hot iron into her red flesh.

MEN *carry out his order. First the* CHORUS, *with their lights, struggle with her, then the* OLD MAN *with the iron; he rips open her dress and brands her.*

WOMAN, *crying out in terrible pain:* Beat back those men, the devouring corpses.

She leaps at him with a knife and strikes a wound in his side. THE MAN *falls.*

MEN: Free this man possessed, strike down the devil. Alas for us innocents, bury the conqueror. We do not know him.

THE MAN, *in convulsions, singing with a bleeding, visible wound:* Senseless craving from horror to horror, unappeasable rotation in the void. Birth pangs without birth, hurtling down of the sun, quaking of space. The end of those who praised me. Oh, your unmerciful word.

MEN: We do not know him; spare us. Come, you singing girls, let us celebrate our nuptials on his bed of affliction.

GIRLS: He frightens us; you we loved even before you came.

Three masked men on the wall lower a coffin on ropes; the wounded man, hardly stirring now, is placed inside the tower. WOMEN retire with the MEN. The OLD MAN rises and locks the door, all is dark, a torch, quiet, blue light above in the cage.

WOMAN, *moaning and revengeful:* He cannot live, nor die; how white he is!

She creeps round the cage like a panther. She crawls up to the cage inquisitively, grips the bars lasciviously, inscribes a large white cross on the tower, cries out.

Open the gate; I must be with him.

Shakes the bars in despair.

MEN *and* WOMEN, *enjoying themselves in the shadows, confused:* We have lost the key—we shall find it—have you got it?—haven't you seen it?—we are not guilty of your plight, we do not know you—

They go back again. A cock crows, a pale light rises in the background.

WOMAN *slides her arm through the bars and prods his wound, hissing maliciously, like an adder:* Pale one, do you recoil? Do you know fear? Are you only asleep? Are you awake? Can you hear me?

THE MAN, *inside, breathing heavily, raises his head with difficulty; later, moves one hand; then slowly rises, singing higher and higher, soaring:*

Wind that wanders, time repeating time, solitude, repose and
   hunger confuse me.
Worlds that circle past, no air, it grows long as evening.

WOMAN, *incipient fear:* So much light is flowing from the gap, so much strength from the pale as a corpse he's turned.

Once more creeps up the steps, her body trembling, triumphant once more and crying out with a high voice.

THE MAN *has slowly risen, leans against the grille, slowly grows.*

WOMAN *weakening, furious:* A wild beast I tame in this cage; is it with hunger your song barks?

THE MAN: Am I the real one, you the dead ensnared? Why are you turning pale?

Crowing of cocks.

WOMAN, *trembling:* Do you insult me, corpse?

THE MAN, *powerfully:* Stars and moon! Woman! In dream or awake, I saw a singing creature brightly shine. Breathing, dark things become clear to me. Who nourishes me?

WOMAN *covers him entirely with her body; separated by the grille, to which she clings high up in the air like a monkey.*

THE MAN: Who suckles me with blood? I devour your melting flesh.

WOMAN: I will not let you live, you vampire, piecemeal you feed on me, weaken me, woe to you, I shall kill you—you fetter me—you I caught and caged—and you are holding me—let go of me. Your love imprisons me—grips me as with iron chains—throttles me—let go—help! I lost the key that kept you prisoner.

Lets go the grille, writhes on the steps like a dying animal, her thighs and muscles convulsed.

THE MAN *stands upright now, pulls open the gate, touches the woman—who rears up stiffly, dead white—with his fingers. She feels that her end is near, highest tension, released in a slowly diminishing scream; she collapses and, as she falls, tears away the torch from the hands of the rising leader. The torch goes out and covers everything in a shower of sparks. He stands on the highest step; men and women who attempt to flee from him run into his way, screaming.*

CHORUS: The devil! Tame him, save yourselves, save yourselves if you can—all is lost!

He walks straight towards them. Kills them like mosquitoes and leaves the fire behind. From very far away, crowing of cocks.

Translated by Michael Hamburger

August Stramm

Sancta Susanna

Characters

Susanna	Choir of Nuns
Clementia	A Spider
A Maid	Nightingales, Moonlight,
A Servant	Wind, and Blossoms

(The Convent Church. Trembling streaks of moonlight; in the rear of the high altar, the eternal light. A large candle is burning in a wall niche to the left in front of a larger-than-life image of Christ on the Cross. SUSANNA lies in prayer in front of the flower-adorned altar of the Virgin, which stands in a niche at a right angle to the crucifix altar. Her forehead rests on the lowest step, her arms are spread over the upper steps.)

CLEMENTIA: *(A few steps behind SUSANNA.)* Sancta Susanna! . . . *(She lays her hands on SUSANNA's shoulders. SUSANNA gets up.)* Night has begun! . . .

SUSANNA: *(Her spirit far away.)* It sounds . . . a tone . . .

CLEMENTIA: The organ re-echoes! . . .

SUSANNA: To me it is . . . like the ringing . . . of bottomless depths . . . heavenless heights . . .

CLEMENTIA: You come from there . . . You were with God! . . .

SUSANNA: *(Meditating.)* I . . . was . . .

CLEMENTIA: You are sick . . . you pray . . . you scarcely live on this earth any longer . . . you have a body, too! *(SUSANNA gets up, stares at her terrified. CLEMENTIA puts her arm around her.)* Come! *(The belfry clock strikes one clearly, the night wind*

rattles the windows, the branches rustle. To herself.) Ave
Maria! . . .
SUSANNA: *(Startled.)* Who is speaking?! . . .
CLEMENTIA: The night wind flings the blossoms against the win-
dows . . .
SUSANNA: Something called . . .
CLEMENTIA: The belfry clock struck . . . I spoke the Ave . . . *(A
window opens, the night wind enters, singing in a tone that dies
away; leaves and branches rustle and whisper down to a
murmuring.)*

*(SUSANNA turns with hands stretched down, away from her body
toward the dark choir, silently, rigidly.)*

CLEMENTIA: A window opened! . . . I will close it!
SUSANNA: Let it . . . *(She breathes heavily.)*
CLEMENTIA: The great lilac bush, do you smell its blossoms? *(She
inhales.)* . . . They smell sweetly even here! It blooms in white
and red clusters . . . oh . . . such clusters. . . ! I will have it up-
rooted . . . tomorrow . . . if it disturbs you!
SUSANNA: It is not disturbing . . . it blooms! . . . *(A woman's voice
chokes in moaning desire.)*
CLEMENTIA: The meadow ridge below the blossoms! I will close
the road . . .
SUSANNA: *(Listening.)* . . . she . . . is . . . not . . . alone . . . ! (CLEM-
ENTIA *crosses herself.* SUSANNA *breathes heavily, starts making
the sign of the cross, but her motion freezes.)* Will . . . she . . .
perhaps . . . come?!
CLEMENTIA: Who?! . . .
SUSANNA: . . . (CLEMENTIA, *frightened, folds her hands.)*
SUSANNA: *(Her hands heavy on the pew.)* I . . . will . . . appeal . . .
to . . . her conscience . . . (CLEMENTIA *folds her hands, bows her
head, and goes away. A catch door rattles softly.)* The . . . *(The
terrified scream of a woman dies away; branches rustle. Winc-
ing.)* Lilac . . . blooms! . . . *(The catch door rattles softly with a
wafting echo; softly shuffling steps approach. The* MAID, *behind*
CLEMENTIA, *trembles with timid glances, her hands folded.)*
SUSANNA: Ave Maria! . . . *(The* MAID *sinks to her knees, bowing
low to the ground.)* Child! . . .
MAID: *(Lifts her head helplessly, staring at her.)* I . . . I . . . don't
know! *(She breaks out in frightened crying and, with folded
hands, slides toward the middle pillar to hide behind it.)*

SUSANNA: I am not angry with you . . . you . . . were . . . under . . . the . . . lilac?! . . .

MAID: *(Becoming very quiet, stares at* SUSANNA.*)* I . . . I . . . nothing . . . ! . . . he . . . he . . . wants . . . *(She hangs her head very low.)*

SUSANNA: *(Gravely.)* He . . .?!

MAID: *(Lifts her head and stares at her, then bursts out laughing loudly.)* My Bill . . . holy . . . *(She pauses in fright, bowing shyly, the laughter and the words resound from the vaults . . . twice . . . three times . . . in a jumble . . . in a vanishing ghostly echo.)*

SUSANNA: *(Looks at her motionless; then she is shaken by a sudden, silvery laughter that encompasses her whole figure; the laughter dies away in the vaults as if in small silver bells and dissolves in trembling vibrations. She goes toward the* MAID, *puts a hand on her shoulder, lifts up her head, and looks into her face.)* Get up! . . . *(The* MAID *gets up with hands folded.)* Do you love him?

MAID: *(Twists her fingers, shy, laughing quietly, bashful.)* Oh . . . holy mother . . . Oh . . .

SUSANNA: I . . . would like . . . to . . . see him . . . *(*CLEMENTIA *raises her hand.)*

(The MAID *stares at* CLEMENTIA *and shudders. A loud knock at the door in the choir . . . three times . . . and a voice calling. All are frightened.* CLEMENTIA *lets her arm fall.)*

MAID: *(In relieved, restrained rejoicing.)* That's him!

*(*CLEMENTIA *goes into the choir; a key turns heavily; a door opens creakily and falls shut with a dull sound; a man's repressed voice speaks angrily. Heavy steps try in vain to tread softly.)*

A SERVANT: *(Young, stocky, turning his cap in one hand, in the nave between the pillars, his eyes looking downward, with shy defiance.)* I want to fetch my girl!

*(*CLEMENTIA *emerges from behind him out of the darkness.* SUSANNA *stares at him, then turns abruptly and walks to the altar. Complete stillness. The* MAID *sneaks toward the* SERVANT *who puts his arm around her; both exit with shyly thundering steps, followed by* CLEMENTIA. *The key turns. The door creaks. A gust of wind whisks blusteringly between the pews. The door falls shut with a*

loud thud. The key cries out. The candle in front of the crucifix
goes out with a sudden flare and shiver.)

SUSANNA: *(Stares, startled, into the darkness where, between the*
pews, the white face of CLEMENTIA *now floats closer. She*
screams.) Satanas! . . . Satanas! . . .

CLEMENTIA: *(Remains motionless for a moment as if paralyzed,*
then rushes forward and, with hands convulsively twisting,
stands before SUSANNA.) Susanna!!! *(*SUSANNA *puts her hand on*
CLEMENTIA's *shoulder and bows her head, exhausted.)*

CLEMENTIA: *(Shocked.)* Sister Susanna!! . . . Sister! . . . You must
rest . . . *(She tries to lead her away.)*

SUSANNA: *(Sits down on the steps of the altar.)* Light the
candle! . . .

CLEMENTIA: . . .

SUSANNA: Light it . . . *(*CLEMENTIA *takes a wax taper out of the*
niche and goes into the choir. She turns around in her confused
haste, the eyes behind her.)

SUSANNA: What is . . .?! . . .

CLEMENTIA: *(In panting fear.)* I . . . can . . . not! . . . *(She presses*
quite close to SUSANNA. SUSANNA *rises and gazes into the*
darkness.)

CLEMENTIA: *(Sits on the steps of the altar.)* I do not . . . know . . .
it blows . . . it moves . . .

SUSANNA: The night wind. . . .

CLEMENTIA: It hums . . . it taps. . . .

SUSANNA: The organ . . . the blossoms . . . *(Takes the wax taper*
away from her.)

CLEMENTIA: Sancta Susanna . . . *(Cowers and convulsively claps*
her hands in front of her face. SUSANNA *walks slowly forward*
between the pews and vanishes in the darkness; the eternal light
goes out behind her. Out of the darkness, a light approaches
slowly at the same height: the light of the wax taper SUSANNA
carries before her. She lights the candle.)

CLEMENTIA: *(Leans her head in one hand.)* There was a night . . .
there was a night . . . like this . . . thirty, forty years ago . . . it
was a night like this. *(She stands up staring, looks into the void,*
and raises her hand imploringly. SUSANNA *turns around, stares*
at CLEMENTIA *under her sway.)*

CLEMENTIA: The night wind sang . . .

SUSANNA: The . . . night wind . . . sang . . . ?

CLEMENTIA: The . . . blossoms . . . tapped . . .

SUSANNA: The . . . blossoms . . . tapped . . . ?

CLEMENTIA: And I was young . . .

SUSANNA: Young . . . ?

CLEMENTIA: Dedicated to the Lord . . . *(SUSANNA lets her head sink on her breast.)* Here I was lying on my knees just as . . . you do . . . *(A nightingale warbles. She cries out hoarsely.)* Beata! . . . *(She covers her face with her arms in terror and lets her arms fall again. SUSANNA raises her head, staring at her with large, fearful eyes. CLEMENTIA speaks with a choking voice, staring into the void.)* Pale . . . without breast veil or headband . . . naked . . . thus, she came . . . *(A nightingale calls from far away.)* Thus . . . *(Her rigid arm pointing to the right.)* She mounted the steps . . . and saw me not . . . she ascended the altar . . . and saw me not . . . *(In hot haste.)* She pressed her naked, sinful body against the crucified image of the Redeemer . . . and saw me not . . . she embraced Him with her white-hot arms . . . and kissed His head . . . and kissed . . . and kissed . . . *(The two nightingales rejoice near and far, loud and persistently. Crying out.)* Beata . . . I called . . . I only called . . . ! *(Weary.)* Then she fell down . . . fell down . . . *(Suddenly, the nightingales fall silent.)* We carried her away . . . *(In horror, the upper part of her body half turning toward the image of the crucifixion and stretching out her hands as if warding off something.)* Ever since the light is burning . . . eternally . . . the candle for atonement . . . ever since the cloth girds the loins . . . the loins . . . there . . . *(Points to the darkness behind the crucifix.)* There they have her . . . flesh and blood . . . imbedded her . . . in a stoned wall . . . *(Hoarsely.)* Do you hear her?! . . . do you hear . . . ?! I have . . . heard her . . . for a long time . . . always . . . just before . . . *(Points to the darkness around the high altar.)* . . . there . . . just now. *(Clasps her hands in front of her face.)* . . . Almighty Father in Heaven! . . . the candle has gone out!

SUSANNA: *(Rigidly.)* I have lit it again! . . . *(She leans with her hand on the altar.)*

CLEMENTIA: *(Lets her hands sink slowly and stares at her. A spider the size of a fist creeps forth out of the darkness behind the altar. Terrified, she goes down on her knees, pointing to the insect.)* The . . . spider!

SUSANNA: *(Turns her head toward the spider and remains standing, paralyzed and trembling. The spider runs across the altar and disappears on the other side behind the crucifix. After a while she turns to* CLEMENTIA; *trembling and shuddering, she lifts her hand mechanically from the altar, hands stretched from her body toward the floor, stiff with terror.)* Do you hear her . . . ?!

CLEMENTIA: *(Terrified.)* Do . . . you . . . hear . . .

SUSANNA: Do . . . you . . . hear . . .

CLEMENTIA: . . .

SUSANNA: The voice . . .

CLEMENTIA: I . . . hear . . . nothing . . .

SUSANNA: . . .

CLEMENTIA: *(Attempts to scream, but remains hoarse with terror.)* I hear . . . nothing!

SUSANNA: *(Speaking in the same ghostly voice.)* Confess . . . confess . . . *(She stands with her back turned to the cross.)* Does . . . he say . . . something?! . . .

CLEMENTIA: *(In utmost terror.)* . . . ?! *(*SUSANNA *motions with her head toward the crucifix.)*

CLEMENTIA: *(Folds her hands, stammering.)* Ave . . . Maria . . .

SUSANNA: Does he say nothing . . .?! . . . *(*CLEMENTIA, *in dumb terror, shakes her head.* SUSANNA *extinguishes the wax taper with her hand and puts it on the altar, performing all motions mechanically; then she descends from the altar . . . step by step . . . silently . . . remains standing close in front of* CLEMENTIA. *She bursts out laughing happily and silver-clear . . . a tender, many-voiced echo mingles with the dying song of the wind and the rustle of the branches. She tears off her veil, kerchief, and band; her long hair falls over her naked shoulders.)* Sister Clementia . . . I am beautiful . . .! . . . *(The wind pushes hard; the branches rustle mightily and the nightingales warble together.* CLEMENTIA, *her folded hands raised high, sinks to her knees.)*

SUSANNA: Sister Clementia . . . I am beautiful . . .

CLEMENTIA: Sancta Susanna . . .

SUSANNA: Sister Clementia . . . I am . . .

CLEMENTIA: *(Rises stiffly and rigidly, with each word becoming more resolute.)* Chastity . . . poverty . . . obedience . . .

*(*SUSANNA *stares at her silently, her hand heavily on a pew.* CLEMENTIA *passes her firmly to go into the darkness; the window slams*

shut; the jubilant song of the nightingales, the rustle of the trees, and the song of the wind all die suddenly. She returns.)

SUSANNA: *(Jumps up and grabs her.)* Open the window! . . . the window . . .

(CLEMENTIA raises the great cross of the rosary against her.)

SUSANNA: *(Reels back, staring at the cross, step by step back to the altar.)* I . . . I . . . see the . . . shining body . . .! . . . I see . . . Him stooping down . . . I . . . feel Him spread his arms . . .

CLEMENTIA: *(Holding the cross high.)* Chastity . . . poverty . . . obedience . . .

(Each word re-echoes clearly in the vault. In the end, all three words coalesce into one and die out.)

SUSANNA: *(Screaming and staring around her.)* Who speaks here?! . . .

CLEMENTIA: I!

SUSANNA: I . . . I . . . I . . . never said that!! . . . *(CLEMENTIA holds up the cross in front of her. SUSANNA rips off the loin cloth from the great crucifix in one single pull.)* Thus, my savior helps me against yours . . . ! *(She sinks on her knees and looks up to Him. The spider falls down behind the arm of the cross and into her hair. She screams shrilly and hits the altar with her forehead. The spider creeps across the altar and disappears behind it. The hour bell sounds shrilly through the vault, recording the hollow strokes of the twelfth hour. She rouses herself, runs her hands wildly through her hair, and creeps on all fours down the altar steps, fleeing in horror from herself. With the last stroke of the hour, the bell dies down.)*

CLEMENTIA: *(Lets the cross sink.)* Ave Maria! . . . a new day! . . . *(SUSANNA crouches with a vacant look on the first altar step. Soft steps shuffle and prayers are murmured. A procession of nuns enters.)*

PRECENTRESS: Kyrie eleison . . .

CHORUS: Kyrie eleison . . .

PRECENTRESS: Regina coeli sancta . . .

CHORUS: Ora pro nobis . . .

PRECENTRESS: Virgo virginum sancta . . .

CHORUS: Ora pro nobis . . .

(The moonlight that fell in clear streaks through the windows and cast a bluish light on the pews disappears; it becomes completely dark. The nuns come forward to the holy water font, but stop when they catch sight of CLEMENTIA, *who stands immobile in the nave between the pillars and looks at* SUSANNA. *The prayer ends; the nuns assemble in a wide semi-circle around* SUSANNA, *moving silently; finally they all stand still, motionless in mute awe.)*

OLD NUN: *(Silently makes a step forward.)* Sancta . . . Susanna! . . . *(*SUSANNA *jumps up straight as a bolt.)*

OLD NUN: *(Bows her head.)* Sancta Susanna . . . !

SUSANNA: There are stones behind the yard . . . *(The* OLD NUN *looks up.)*

SUSANNA: *(In a firm voice.)* You must get the wall ready for me! . . . *(The* OLD NUN, *spreading her arms, slowly sinks on her knees. The* CHORUS *follows her,* CLEMENTIA *stands rigidly, staring at* SUSANNA.)*

SUSANNA: *(Suddenly forceful.)* No! . . . *(The* OLD NUN *jumps up; the* CHORUS *follows her. The* OLD NUN *holds the cross of the rosary over her head. The* CHORUS *follows her.)*

OLD NUN: Confess! . . .

SUSANNA: . . . *(*CLEMENTIA *raises the cross.)*

CLEMENTIA AND OLD NUN: *(Severely urgent.)* Confess!!!

SUSANNA: No!!! . . .

CLEMENTIA, OLD NUN, AND CHORUS: *(Shrill.)* Confess!!! *(The word echoes three times in the vault; the church windows are shaking; the storm howls outside.)*

SUSANNA: No!!! *(The echo of the word is submerged in the earlier echoes.)*

OLD NUN: *(Ecstatically.)* Satana!!!

OLD NUN AND CLEMENTIA: Satana!!!

OLD NUN, CLEMENTIA, AND CHORUS: Satana!!! *(Shrill, confused echo.)*

*(*SUSANNA *draws herself up to full height, in untouched dignity. All stand quiet and motionless.)*

Translated by Henry Marx

Gottfried Benn

Ithaka

Characters

Albrecht, a professor
  of pathology
Dr. Rönne, his assistant

Medical students
Kautski, a student
Lutz, a student

*(In the professor's laboratory. At the end of a course. The professor
and medical students.)*

PROFESSOR: And now, gentlemen, to the special surprise I have
saved for you as a final treat. As you see here, having stained
pyramidal cells from the cornu ammonis in the left hemisphere
of the cervical cortex of a fourteen day rat of a special strain,
what do we find—they are stained not red but pink with a tinge
of brownish violet, just verging on green. A most fascinating
observation. You are aware that not long ago the Graz Institute
brought out a paper disputing this, notwithstanding the detailed
nature of my own investigations on this subject. Far be it from
me to make any general comment on the Graz Institute, but I
must say that the paper in question struck me as immature in
the extreme. And now, as you see, I have the proof here in front
of me. The possibilities this opens up are quite staggering. One
would be able to tell rats with long black hair and dark eyes
from those with short rough hair and light eyes by the additional
means of this sensitive color-index, given that the rats are similar
in age, fed on candy-sugar, that they play for half an hour daily
with a puma kitten and defecate spontaneously twice nightly at

a body temperature of 37 to 36 degrees celsius. Naturally, the fact that similar phenomena have also been observed under other conditions must not be ignored, but even so this observation seems to me worth publishing in full—indeed, I would almost regard it as a new step toward the understanding of the vast complex of forces which control the universe. And so, good evening, gentlemen, good evening.

LUTZ: And supposing, Professor, that one does examine this preparation carefully, can one say anything more than: I see, so this is not red, but pink, tinged with brownish violet, verging on green?

PROFESSOR: Gentlemen, please! In the first place there is the three volume encyclopedia by Meyer and Müller on the staining of rats' brains. As a first step one would have to go through that.

LUTZ: And supposing that was done, would it be possible to draw any conclusions? To come up with practical consequences?

PROFESSOR: Conclusions! My good man, we are not Thomas Aquinas, ha ha ha! Have you never heard of the new age of conditionalism which has dawned for our science? We establish the conditions in which something happens. We vary the conditions which make certain changes possible. Theology is a different case entirely.

LUTZ: And supposing one day your whole student audience got to its feet and bellowed at you that it would prefer mysticism of the blackest hue to the dusty creakings of your mental acrobatics, suppose they sent you flying from the rostrum with a kick in the backside, what would you say to that? *(Enter* DR. RÖNNE.*)*

RÖNNE: Here is your book on the perforation of the peritoneum in infants. I have no interest whatsoever in describing the state of an abdominal cavity as found on autopsy to an audience of people I do not know, already trained in what to expect. And my brain revolts at this game, this wish to destroy, to break up the simple, self-contained naiveté of an individual case.

PROFESSOR: Your reasons are foolish in the extreme, but as you wish, give it to me. There are plenty other gentlemen interested in the paper. If you were rather less short-sighted than you seem to be in my opinion, you would understand that it's not a question of this individual case. On the contrary, with every particular examination the systematization of all knowledge, the organization of experience—in a word, science itself is at stake.

RÖNNE: Science had its rightful place two hundred years ago when it could prove God's wisdom from the perfection of organs and the extent of His intelligence and goodness from the mouths of locusts. But in two hundred years from now, Professor, will it not seem just as ludicrous that you spend three years of your life establishing whether the stain to be used on a particular type of fat is osmium or Nile blue.

PROFESSOR: I have not the slightest intention of discussing general principles with you. You do not wish to do this piece of work. Right, I shall give you another one.

RÖNNE: Nor do I wish to describe the result of the catheterization of Frau Schmidt's uterus—whether the intestinal coils passed through the gap in question in the sixth or the eighth month. Nor to tell them how much the diaphragm of a drowned man was distended next morning. The collection, the systematization of knowledge—is the most puerile brainwork imaginable! For a century now you have been encouraging the stupidity of the population to the point where the plebs will gawk in respectful silence at any old B.F. who knows how to work an incubation chamber, but in so doing, you have yet to come up with as much as a grain of thought of less than total banality. Get one lot hatched after another; keep your thoughts on the navel and don't forget the placenta—that's all you can think of—you bunch of moles and ape-brains—you make me spew, the lot of you!

LUTZ: What are you really doing? Now and again you grab up a fact, so called. In the first place it's been discovered already, but not published, by a colleague ten years ago. Another ten years and it'll all be in the dustbin. And what do you really know? That earthworms don't need knives and forks and ferns don't get sores on their backsides. That's the extent of your achievements. Is there anything else you know?

PROFESSOR: In the first place, it is completely beneath my dignity to reply to the tone of your remarks.

LUTZ: Dignity? Whose dignity? Who are you? Go on, answer.

PROFESSOR: I'll frame my reply to suit the occasion. Right, gentlemen, you talk disparagingly about theories, that's no concern of mine. But in a subject of such eminently practical implications, you must admit that serum and salvarsan are not just speculation?

LUTZ: Are you trying to argue that what you're working for is to let Frau Meier do her daily shopping for two months longer or to let Krause, the chauffeur carry on at the wheel for another two months? Anyway, if that is what you enjoy, the fight to keep these nobodies alive, you carry on. And just to forestall you, Professor, don't bring up the argument about the universal human drive. There are whole civilizations where the people lie in the sand all day playing bamboo flutes.

PROFESSOR: And humane values? Saving a child's life for its mother or a breadwinner's for his family? The gratitude shining in their eyes.

RÖNNE: Let it shine, Professor! Infant mortality and every other kind are as much a part of life as winter is of the year. Don't let us reduce life to trivialities.

LUTZ: Anyway these practical aspects are of very superficial interest. The question which we want to hear answered is this: where do you get the courage to introduce youth to a science which you know to be incapable of any greater insight than a confession of its own ignorance? Just because it suits your shit-like lump of a brain to work out the statistics of bowel-blockages when you're not hard at it fucking? What kind of brains do you think you've got in front of you?

PROFESSOR: . . .

RÖNNE: . . . OK! OK! The commanding heights of the intellect! A thousand years of optics and chemistry! OK! OK! There are not so many color-blind people in the world, so you have a certain advantage. But let me tell you, I've stomached your lies till they make me sick—if you dare to come out with them just once more I shall strangle you with my own hands. I've chewed the whole cosmos to pieces inside my head. I've sat and thought till I slavered at the mouth. I've been so out and out logical I nearly vomited shit. And once the mists had cleared, what was left? Words and the brain. Over and over again this same terrifying, everlasting brain. Nailed to this cross. Caught in this incest. In this rape of things—if you only knew my existence, this torment, this terrible sense that we're at an end, betrayed before God by the beasts, and God and beast alike destroyed by thought and spewed out, a random throw in the mists of this land, I tell you you would resign quietly without fuss and be glad that you are

not being called to account for the brain damage you have
caused.

PROFESSOR: I am extremely sorry if you should be feeling unwell.
But if your degeneracy or neurosis or for all I know these medieval mists of yours are causing you to go to pieces, what has that
got to do with me? Why get worked up at me? If you really
haven't got the strength to join us on the road to the new knowledge, why not just stay behind? Give up your anatomy. Go in
for mysticism. Use formulae and corollaries to calculate the loca-
tion of the soul; but leave us out of it. We are spread out over
the world like an army: heads to rule with and brains to conquer
with. The force that cut axes from stone, that kept fire alive,
that gave birth to Kant, that created machines—is ours to con-
serve. The prospects ahead are infinite.

RÖNNE: The prospects ahead infinite; an enormous cervical cortex
with a fold in the middle takes a little stroll; fingers stand up
like calipers; teeth have grown into computers—mankind will
turn into a maw with a machine on top, systematizing—what
perspectives! What infinite perspectives ahead! For all I care we
could have stayed jellyfish. For me the whole history of evolution
is useless. The brain is a blind alley. A bluff to fool the middle-
classes. Whether one walks vertically or swims horizontally is
all a matter of habit. The totality of life, its overall structures
have been destroyed for me by thought. The cosmos roars past
on its way. I stand on the bank: gray, steep, barren. My branches
hang down into the living water; but their gaze is turned inward,
on the waning flow of their blood and the numbing chill in their
limbs. I am set apart, myself. I make no move now.

Where, where will it lead? Why make the long journey? What
center is there for us to gather round? When I stopped thinking
for a moment, surely my limbs fell off?

Something finds associations inside one. Some process takes
place inside one. All I can feel now is my brain. It lies on my
skull like a lichen. It gives me from above a feeling of nausea. It
lies everywhere ready to pounce: yellow, yellow, brain, brain. It
hangs down between my legs . . . I can feel it distinctly knocking
against my ankles.

Oh, if I could return to the state of being a grassy field, sand
dotted with flowers, a vast meadow. With the earth bearing

everything to one on waves that are warm or cool. No forehead left. A state of being lived.

KAUTSKI: But can you not see the dawn all around our bodies? There since eternity, since the primal stage of the world? A century is at an end. A sickness is conquered. A dark journey, the sails straining; now the music of home is heard across the sea.

Who is to say what has driven you away? A curse, the Fall, or something else. For thousands of years there were no more than mere beginnings of it. For thousands of years it lay hidden. But then, a century ago it suddenly exploded and like a pestilence engulfed the world 'til nothing was left but that animal, large, greedy, and power-hungry: the man of intellect; he stretched from heaven to heaven, he conjured the world out of his mind. But we are older. We are blood; from the warm seas, the mothers who gave birth to life. You are a small channel of this same sea. Come home now. I call you.

PROFESSOR: Don't let Rönne mislead you. All this thinking with no clearly defined objective has crushed him. Such casualties will be inevitable on our path.

RÖNNE: The Mediterranean was there; from primeval times; and it is there still. Perhaps it is the most human thing there has ever been? What do you think? . . .

PROFESSOR: *(Continuing)* But, gentlemen, all these strange feelings and the other things you talked about—myth and knowledge, could it not be that these are age-old poisons in our bloodstream, which will be cast off in the course of evolution, just as we no longer possess a third eye looking backwards to warn us of enemies. In the hundred years during which the sciences and their application have existed, how life has changed! Has not Man's mental activity largely abandoned speculation and the transcendental to concentrate entirely on the shaping of material things, to satisfy the needs of a self-renewing soul? Is it not already possible to talk about a homo faber instead of a homo sapiens as hitherto? Is it not right that in the course of time all Man's speculative-transcendental needs will be refined and purified out of existence? Could scientific research and the teaching of knowledge not be justified from that point of view?

KAUTSKI: If you want to produce a race of plumbers, certainly. But there was a country once: full of the whirring of doves' wings, with the thrill of marble from sea to sea, dream and ecstasy . . .

RÖNNE: . . . Brains, soft and rounded; dull and white.

A rosy flush spreading and rustling groves of blue.

Forehead soft and blooming. All tension eased in yearning towards shores.

The banks piled high with oleander, then lost to view in fragrant, gentle bays.

. . . Blood now seems ready to burst. Temples to surge with hope.

In my forehead, the coursing of waters about to take flight.

Oh, the rush of ecstasy like a dove to my heart: laughing, laughing—

Ithaca!—Ithaca! . . .

Oh stay! stay! Don't send me back! Such a path to tread, homeward at last, as the blossom falls sweet and heavy from all the worlds . . .

(Goes up to the PROFESSOR *and takes hold of him.)*

PROFESSOR: Gentlemen, what are you trying to do? I am more than willing to meet your wishes. You have my assurance that in the future I shall invariably give out in my lectures that we in this faculty cannot teach ultimate wisdom and that lectures in philosophy should be followed at the same time. I shall not fail to emphasize that the nature of our knowledge is open to question . . .

(Shouting.) Listen to me, gentlemen! After all, we are all scientists, we must avoid fantasy. Why should we get involved in situations which the structure of modern society is—let's say—not equipped to cope with . . . We are doctors after all, don't let us overdo questions of belief. No one will ever know what took place here!

Murder! Murder!

LUTZ: *(Also taking hold of him.)* Murder! Murder! Fetch some shovels. Back to the ground with this lump of clay! Lash this scum with our foreheads!

PROFESSOR: *(Choking.)* You callow youths! You murky dawn! Your life blood will be shed and the mob will feast in triumph over it! Go on, trample the north under foot! Logic will triumph! On every side the same abyss: Ignorabimus! Ignorabimus!

LUTZ: *(Smashing him repeatedly with his forehead.)* Ignorabimus! Take that for your ignorabimus! Your researches weren't deep enough! Go deeper into things if you want to teach us! We are the young generation. Our blood cries out for the heavens and the earth and not for cells and invertebrates. Yes we're trampling the north underfoot. The hills of the south are swelling up already. Oh soul, open wide your wings; soul! soul! We must have Dream. We must have Ecstasy. Our cry is Dionysos and Ithaca!

Translated by J. M. Ritchie

Carl Sternheim

The Bloomers

Characters

Theobald Maske, *civil servant*
Louise Maske, *his wife*
Gertrud Deuter

Frank Scarron
Benjamin Mandelstam, *a barber*
A Stranger

The Scene throughout is the Maskes' living room
Time: 1900

Act 1

SCENE 1

Enter THEOBALD *and* LOUISE.

THEOBALD: Maddening!

LOUISE: Put the stick away.

THEOBALD: *(strikes her.)* A scandal to be bandied about by the whole district. Frau Maske loses her bloomers!

LOUISE: Ouch! Oh!

THEOBALD: In the street, in public, before the King's very eyes, so to speak. And me a civil servant!

LOUISE: *(screaming.)* Stop!

THEOBALD: Isn't there plenty of time to fasten ribbons, button buttons at home? Excess, dreams, fantasies on the inside, slovenliness and neglect on the outside. That's you.

LOUISE: I'd tied a firm double bow.

THEOBALD: *(laughs scornfully.)* A firm double bow! Good God, listen to this contemptible cackling. Firm—here's a firm double clip on the ear for you. The consequences, the consequences! I don't dare think of them. Dishonored, deprived of livelihood, hunted out of the service.

LOUISE: Do calm down.

THEOBALD: Furious . . .

LOUISE: You're not to blame.

THEOBALD: I'm to blame for having a wife like you, a slattern like you, a trollop and stargazer. *(Beside himself.)* Where's the real world? *(He grabs her head and strikes it against the table.)* Down here, in the saucepan, on your dustcoated living-room floor and not up there in the sky, do you hear? Is this chair polished? No—filth. Has this cup a handle? Wherever I lay my hand, the world is splitting apart. Crack after crack in an existence like yours. Horrible! Oh woman, just think! Fate in its providence gave me a post which brings in seven hundred Taler. *(Shouts.)* Seven hundred Taler. On that we can afford a few rooms, eat well, we're able to buy clothes and heat the place in winter. We can rise to a ticket for a play, good health saves us the expense of doctor and chemist—heaven smiles benignly on our existence. Then up you come with those ways of yours and destroy the blessings we could have in life. Why isn't the fire lit yet? Why is this door open, that one shut? Why not the other way round? Why isn't the clock going? *(He winds it.)* Why do the pots and pans leak? Where's my hat, where did that important file get to, and how can your bloomers fall down, how could they?

LOUISE: You know, you knew me when I was a young girl.

THEOBALD: So?

LOUISE: And you liked me dreamy.

THEOBALD: For a young girl there's nothing better considering the unlimited free time she has. It's her lot, because she's not allowed contact with reality. But you've got that, now the dreaming's over.

LOUISE: Yes.

THEOBALD: Louise, look how deeply affected I am.

LOUISE: I can see you are, dear.

THEOBALD: On the street, in public.

LOUISE: There's just no accounting for it.

.

THEOBALD: Laughing and leering, urchins, loafers. It'll drive me mad!

LOUISE: You're off again.

THEOBALD: My heart stood still. Hate attracting any kind of attention, as you know. Do I allow you a fashionable frock or hat? Why do you have to dress so unbecomingly? Because your pretty face is much too striking for my modest position, your bosom, your eyes too provocative. If I could only make you grasp the fact that all the trouble in the world comes when two factors forming one entity are incongruous.

LOUISE: Stop; I can't bear it any longer.

THEOBALD: *(loudly.)* Two factors forming one entity, do you understand? My position and your appearance are incongruous.

LOUISE: I can't help it, God made me like this.

THEOBALD: Not God. It's all the fault of a shameless upbringing which waved and rolled your hair and forced out with stays a bosom harmless enough in itself. A plague on all matchmaking mothers!

LOUISE: My mother was a respectable woman.

THEOBALD: What if I should lose my post!

LOUISE: Why ever should you?

THEOBALD: They say His Majesty wasn't far away. Egads!

LOUISE: Theobald!

THEOBALD: A twitch of his brow, I sink in the dust, never to rise again. Misery, shame, and hunger; the end of a life full of toil.

LOUISE: You're torturing me.

THEOBALD: *(his head in his hands.)* Oh, oh—oh.

LOUISE: *(after a pause.)* Will a leg of lamb and green beans be all right?

THEOBALD: In the street, in public. It's lucky there's still no child to share the consequences that threaten us.

LOUISE: I was thinking of raspberries for dessert.

THEOBALD: And His Majesty!

LOUISE: Father writes, he's sending some new wine.

THEOBALD: How many bottles is he going to send?

LOUISE: Fifteen.

THEOBALD: Do we still have some?

LOUISE: Five bottles.

THEOBALD: Hm. Leg of lamb. And properly salted. Woman, demons are active in our soul all the time. If we don't enslave them with the whole power of our will—there's no telling how far they'll go. Raspberries and cream. But where will you get cream from at such short notice?

LOUISE: The Deuter woman will let me have some.

THEOBALD: Do you think so?—Frivolity! yes, yes—*(He sits down in an armchair by the window and takes up a newspaper.)*

(LOUISE busy at the cooking stove.)

THEOBALD: There now—they say the sea serpent has reappeared in the Indian Ocean.

LOUISE: Good heavens, would you believe it!

THEOBALD: It's in *The Courier* in black and white.

LOUISE: Dear, dear.

THEOBALD: Thank God the country there is sparsely populated, if at all.

LOUISE: What does an animal like that live on?

THEOBALD: Well—the experts don't agree about that. It must be a dreadful sight. I much prefer being in safe surroundings, in my little town. One should limit oneself strictly to one's own, hold on to it and watch over it. What have I in common with that serpent? Doesn't it at most excite my imagination? What's the point of all that? *(Gets up.)* One has one's little rooms. Everything familiar, gradually acquired, dear and cherished. Is there any need to dread that our clock will spit fire, the bird rush greedily at the dog from its cage? No. Six o'clock will strike, when, as for the last three thousand years, it is six o'clock. That's as it should be. That's how we like it, that's the way we are.

LOUISE: Certainly.

THEOBALD: How could you spoil my day off with excitement like that? Pray that we're left with what we have, and see that the roast is well cooked. I'll just go and find out what kind of talk is going the rounds about this damnable business.

LOUISE: Have you forgiven me?

THEOBALD: When I thought over how well-off we've been till now, God moved me. And remember the tulips need watering. Pray, Louise. *(He goes; through the door he can be seen disappearing downstairs.)*

LOUISE: *(has followed him to the landing and looked after him. Now she calls.)* Fräulein Deuter!

DEUTER: *(from below.)* Is it you, Frau Maske? Good morning.

LOUISE: Have you heard about my accident yet?
DEUTER: *(appears upstairs.)* It can't have been all that serious.
LOUISE: Are you coming in for a moment?
DEUTER: I don't mind if I do.

SCENE 2

Enter LOUISE *and Fräulein* DEUTER.

DEUTER: The Kieswetter woman said they were pure linen and looked quite proper and respectable.
LOUISE: That's true—
DEUTER: But fancy having your initials on them in red—nowadays everybody wears white. Anyway hardly anybody noticed the incident, because the King was driving in the neighborhood and everybody was looking out for him. I suppose your elastic broke?
LOUISE: As I was stretching to see the coachman.

*(*DEUTER *laughs.)*

LOUISE: A pretty kettle of fish. Suddenly the white showed below my dress. I didn't dare to move.
DEUTER: Your husband beside himself?
LOUISE: Completely. And the usual outburst about our slovenliness.
DEUTER: I hear you looked charming.
LOUISE: Who told you that?
DEUTER: Frau Kieswetter. You must have had some of the gentlemen cricking their necks.
LOUISE: I got out of the affair with decorum. First a careful step out of the elastic, then down like lightening and under my cloak with it.
DEUTER: By tomorrow they'll be saying the whole thing was a well thought out piece of coquettishness.
LOUISE: Evil tongues.
DEUTER: Anyone who looks like you can laugh at the world.
LOUISE: My husband can't stand talk at any price.
DEUTER: Your husband will get used to a lot of things.
LOUISE: Why, Fräulein Deuter?
DEUTER: Because sunshine makes people want to walk in it.
LOUISE: What?

DEUTER: My dear Frau Maske, I don't like your husband at all.

LOUISE: Dear Theobald.

DEUTER: Oh God!

LOUISE: No really!

DEUTER: All right.

LOUISE: But Fräulein Deuter! Could you possibly spare me a little bowl of cream?

DEUTER: For you—always. Isn't it about a year just now since you got married?

LOUISE: A year the day after tomorrow.

DEUTER: And nothing stirring? No prospect of the patter of tiny feet?

LOUISE: Alas.

DEUTER: Surely that can be no accident? If I know my Herr Theobald—

LOUISE: Do be quiet.

DEUTER: You shall have your cream. *(Exit.)*

SCENE 3

After a moment SCARRON *comes very quickly upstairs from below.* LOUISE *who had remained on the landing, utters a cry.*

SCARRON: Have I startled you? Do you know me?

LOUISE: Whom do you want to see?

SCARRON: I am in the right place.

LOUISE: This is where I—

SCARRON: Who else?

LOUISE: My husband will be back directly.

SCARRON: By then everything must be said.

LOUISE: But sir!

SCARRON: May I utter a metaphor, lady? Bluntly dare a great word? No. Forgive me. I am much too excited, too little master of my soul, which I still had a moment ago, and which has now been torn from me and dances through this hall.

LOUISE: Someone's coming, mustn't see us together.

(SCARRON disappears upstairs.)

SCENE 4

DEUTER *returns with a bowl in her hand:* There! Clothes, above all your underclothes, are extremely important. But a lot can be done with a ribbon, a little bow as well. I could certainly show you a thing or two. And how to please is not always a question of clothes. You have sweet eyes. We'll talk about it another time. Today we'd better not let ourselves be caught, you little coquette. (*She runs downstairs again laughing.*)

SCENE 5

SCARRON *appears.*

LOUISE: Is there something you want?
SCARRON: Yes, madam, if you want to know, something did bring me here.
LOUISE: Briefly—?
SCARRON: This morning in the main boulevard at the Tiergarten.
LOUISE: Heavens!
SCARRON: Suddenly enchantment penetrates my every limb. A young lady—

(LOUISE *turns away.*)

SCARRON: I believe in miracles, for months I've been rushing hungrily through the city in search of one, turning a hundred street corners at lightning speed in pursuit, and lo it appears under a linden. Bathed in sun, brown forged to the light green trunk, beneath eyes filled with confusion a helpless body. A stupid greedy crowd and an enchanting martyrdom. A brilliant joke of the Almighty. Life pulsed through me! What I suffered with you in three minutes until you reached for the ground, diverted my heart from what yesterday I thought I loved and turned it to you. I still don't speak your language, much remains not yet fully understood between us, but how soon I can learn from gesture, glance and word what it pleases you to hear.

(LOUISE *makes a gesture.*)

SCARRON: I know, your way of thinking does not permit such emotional breathlessness, since it is not legitimized by any length of acquaintance. But silence is worship. (*A moment of silence,* SCARRON *sits with closed eyes.*)
LOUISE: Sir!
SCARRON: You don't know who I am?

LOUISE: I think I have seen you.
SCARRON: When?
LOUISE: This morning.
SCARRON: Nowhere else? Are you sure?
LOUISE: Certainly not. I don't go to the sort of places you frequent. My life runs its course within these walls.

(SCARRON *steps close to her.* LOUISE *retreats.*)

SCARRON: Hear my destiny.
LOUISE: I'm frightened.
SCARRON: From today I must desire you with all the strength of my soul. It's such bliss for me to say this, that I do not even ask what you think. Whether you wish me to the devil or ask me back.
LOUISE: Unparalleled boldness. Get up.
SCARRON: So much certainty surged through my limbs that I cannot. Kill me, but let me remain seated.
LOUISE: ˙For Heaven's sake! What if my husband were to come suddenly.
SCARRON: You are truly chestnut-brown. I'll rent the two rooms which you advertise in the window. You are glowing like a chestnut over coals. Let's regard it as settled. The preliminary negotiations have already taken place.
LOUISE: A fine gentleman like you staying with us. Who'll believe that?
SCARRON: As soon as I've gone away again—I promise never to come here except dressed as the simplest of citizens.
LOUISE: You plunge me into deepest confusion.
SCARRON: And you me into confusion as deep as a bottomless pit.
LOUISE: Rent the rooms—
SCARRON: I will.
LOUISE: If he comes—
SCARRON: Simply introduce us.
LOUISE: Herr?
SCARRON: Scarron. Between the first sound of his key in the lock and his entry there are still seconds in which to stand up.
LOUISE: You living here?
SCARRON: Where?
LOUISE: A bedroom, a livingroom, oh God!

SCARRON: These simple words: oh God! They say all there is to say. Why are you trembling?

LOUISE: Please—

SCARRON: I am a church bell. My rope is hanging limp. If you strike me, I shall echo your throat's clear cries. Enough. I'm going. When shall I return?

LOUISE: He must be back soon.

SCARRON: You'll be waiting for me?

(LOUISE is silent.)

SCARRON: You'll be waiting for me!

LOUISE: Yes.

(They are standing in front of the ladder. SCARRON rushes out.)

SCENE 6

LOUISE *climbs the ladder as if in a dream, then Fräulein* DEUTER *enters.*

DEUTER: The door open? Good gracious, what are you doing up there?

LOUISE: The curtains—

DEUTER: Even with the longest arms you won't reach the curtains. By the way, you're losing your you-know-whats—no I'm joking. But the ribbon is hanging down again and you'll trip over it as you climb down. You really are, as I've long thought, an extremely luscious creature.

LOUISE: Don't make fun of me.

DEUTER: What *do* you believe, you little darling? You've known for a long time that I'm not the sort of neighbor who murders people's reputations. Shall I say boldly what I want from you?

LOUISE: Help me down.

DEUTER: Stay there for a bit. It suits what I'm going to say. I'm endowed with a tremendous lust for life, which my face doesn't match. But you are so visibly favored in appearance, that all my wishes would be bound to come true if I could hear or see at close quarters what you can have if you want it.

LOUISE: I don't understand.

DEUTER: Do you like me?

LOUISE: Certainly.

DEUTER: You know without more ado that I'll stand by you?
LOUISE: You'll not do me any harm.
DEUTER: What did he want?
LOUISE: Just think!
DEUTER: A nobleman! I'd give ten years of my life. What was the pretext?
LOUISE: There was a real reason. He saw me this morning.
DEUTER: In all your glory?
LOUISE: Yes.
DEUTER: How wonderful! You are a person who gives many people pleasure. He leaped at it like a tiger?
LOUISE: He was very impetuous.
DEUTER: Shook the tree of life and overwhelmed you.
LOUISE: He's renting our rooms.
DEUTER: Splendid! Now I understand your expedition to the heights.
LOUISE: Catch me. *(She jumps down.)*
DEUTER: *(kisses her.)* I'll make such a job of fitting you out that the old Cinderella will still be there on the outside for Herr Theobald. But underneath will be a white dream, with a few brightly colored bows in memory of this day. At the knee a rose-red one like a barricade. Listen quickly. Six meters of fine cambric will make six. I'll borrow a spanking brand new pair to see how they're made, and I can probably find out a lot by asking. Plus four meters of fine lace edging for the frills.
LOUISE: What are you thinking of! I'm an honest woman.
DEUTER: But he's a hero! A stormer of barricades.
LOUISE: Oh—You're a proper matchmaker.
DEUTER: Of course. If one is left outside by oneself in the cold facing a black wall there's nothing better.
LOUISE: What silly ideas. You know yourself my husband will wring his neck if he as much as looks at me.
DEUTER: Such naiveté. A husband can have a dozen eyes. If the wife wants to, she'll throw sand in them all.
LOUISE: I'll decline.
DEUTER: Too late. In your domestic grayness there's already too much longing leaning at the window looking out. Why, dearest girl, hasn't the master of the house used the year he's had. Why hasn't he distended your veins with new life. Why aren't you

going round padded out, lisenting to things stirring inside you? What became of God's blessing in this marriage?

LOUISE: We have to save. We can't afford a child on our salary.

DEUTER: But you've begun to sit in judgment on him for his eternal evasions of duty.

LOUISE: It's only by a hair's breadth that I'm not standing in front of you today a virgin. He wanted me to stay that way.

DEUTER: The barbarian!

LOUISE: "On seven hundred Taler"—that was what he kept muttering every day.

DEUTER: Raise your eyes to God on high. Every human being has a right to happiness. Now we can both work to that end with a clear conscience. Give me your hand.

LOUISE: Heaven knows, I agree with you.

DEUTER: Hoho, husband Theobald will have to be quite a fellow now to avert disaster.

LOUISE: For heaven's sake! The lamb!

DEUTER: Who?

LOUISE: The lunch, I mean.

DEUTER: Are you having lamb today like me?

LOUISE: I haven't got it; gone clean out of my mind with all this talking.

DEUTER: Wait. My joint will wander into your pot. With the lamb you must have beans. May I include them?

LOUISE: You angel. What about yourself?

DEUTER: Fried egg. Back in a second. *(She runs out.)*

LOUISE: *(goes to the window and takes down the advertisement. Then she lights a fire in the fireplace, meanwhile humming the Mörike song.)*

> Early, when the cocks crow
> Before the stars disappear
> I must stand by the hearth
> Must light the fire.

(Then she goes to the mirror and looks at herself, goes back to the hearth and goes on humming.)

DEUTER: *(returns with a pot.)* Onto the stove quickly. It's just about ready. Add a touch of butter, a soupçon of salt.

LOUISE: How much do I owe you?

DEUTER: Listen. I've often wanted to say this to you. Your husband is a machine. If you get in his way you'll be flattened. But since, like all pile drivers, he announces his coming, it's easy to avoid him. For complete safety, however, I offer my services as signalman waving a red flag. If I lower it he'll stop. That will give you time to hoist your signal mast for an unimpeded journey.

LOUISE: How freely I feel my soul stirring, you've removed my last scruples. Yes, I *will* get away from all this endless duty, these reins and fetters, that warning finger. Help me escape to freedom!

DEUTER: Only if you take to heart what I advised. You lucky little simpleton. Let your common sense be a reliable manager of the many opportunities you'll have during your husband's working hours between nine and three, then in his free time you fulfil your duty, and things can't go wrong. But get the nobleman to fix his alleged business activities for the time when your husband is at home. In that way you'll prevent their meeting and escape a thousand embarrassments. Enough for now. And may I do that shopping?

LOUISE: But bring roses instead of violets and reckon on eight meters not six.

DEUTER: Theobald will have to be a cyclops to escape his fate. A real giant. Something still on your mind?

LOUISE: Don't condemn me.

DEUTER: I've never been capable of condemning. For me there were always only desires, for each one unfulfilled two new ones to take its place.

LOUISE: It's as if someone had lifted a ton weight off my mind.

DEUTER: As if one were a child again.

LOUISE: And all the doors were still open—

DEUTER: Just a young girl walking along.

LOUISE: Dreaming—

DEUTER: Longing—

LOUISE: No telling what—*(They take each other's hands and dance in a ring.)*

Ring-a-ring of roses
A pocket full of posies

A tishoo, A tishoo
We both fall down.

(Fräulein DEUTER *hurries away laughing.)*

LOUISE: Quick! Raspberry, stop hiding. I wonder what his first
name is? Two spoonfuls of sugar. He's something out of a different world! I remember a picture: in the foreground a woman
lying swathed in a veil, the man bends over her, her feet move
apart. Father must give me a present of some shoes. But now to
set the table: past three. *(She laughs.)* Hoist the mast.

SCENE 7

THEOBALD *enters with* MANDELSTAM: What disgraceful tomfool-
ery is this; where's the notice in the window?
LOUISE: The rooms, if you're agreeable, are taken.
THEOBALD: Oho! *(to* MANDELSTAM.) What do you say to that?
But meanwhile don't worry, you have my promise. Admittedly
a critical situation. *(To* LOUISE.) For?
LOUISE: Fifteen Taler.
THEOBALD: Inclusive?
LOUISE: Without.
THEOBALD: *(to* MANDELSTAM.) Just think: fifteen Taler without.
MANDELSTAM: I don't understand.
THEOBALD: Without coffee. This could literally make one's hair
stand on end. If only I hadn't gone out. *(to* LOUISE.) If only your
little pranks hadn't driven me into going. Misfortunes always
come in twos, and you see how unfortunate this all turns out to
be. *(to* MANDELSTAM.) Avarice is alien to me, the person of the
tenant can sway the balance just as much as the amount in-
volved, but—you're a barber, Herr?
MANDELSTAM: Mandelstam.
THEOBALD: Semite?
MANDELSTAM: Certainly not.
THEOBALD: Turn to the light.
MANDELSTAM: With one M. S—t—a—m.
THEOBALD: I am a German. No question of anti-Semitism or anything like that, but the Red Sea between them and me would be
best as I see it.

MANDELSTAM: Entirely my opinion.

THEOBALD: *(shakes his hand.)* Bravo! To business: You were prepared to pay five Taler for the smaller room?

MANDELSTAM: With coffee.

THEOBALD: Now here's someone who can use both rooms for fifteen Taler. I'll carry out the following manoeuvre: I transform myself into Herr Mandelstam and I ask you, Herr Maske: what do you propose, what must you do in your own and your family's interest?

MANDELSTAM: Your calculations, I can see, favor the other person, but I have your word and I rely on your sense of honor. Being young a disappointment in this respect would come as a bitter blow.

THEOBALD: Friend, whither? Can I, a son of the people which bore a Schiller, be faithless?

MANDELSTAM: Are you fond of Schiller?

THEOBALD: Young man, I am naturally not a very good judge.

MANDELSTAM: Wagner, not Schiller, is the man of our epoch.

THEOBALD: To remove your last doubt, I speak one name: Luther.

MANDELSTAM: Good.

LOUISE: Can I serve lunch?

THEOBALD: Eat a bite with us.

MANDELSTAM: Since you ask me, I don't mind if I do.

(They sit down.)

THEOBALD: Give me your hand. You seem a good sort and you aren't to blame for the predicament you've created.

MANDELSTAM: I lost my parents at an early age, I live by the labor of my hands.

THEOBALD: But you manage to make ends meet?

MANDELSTAM: I've been with the same employer for three years.

THEOBALD: That's good.

MANDELSTAM: In the evenings, every penny I save, everything for Wagner. I've seen *Lohengrin* three times.

THEOBALD: Good Lord!

MANDELSTAM: It's like being in paradise.

THEOBALD: But good long walks too, stretch your legs. Health.

MANDELSTAM: Health—there I must admit—

THEOBALD: What does that mean? Pass me the beans again—out with it.

MANDELSTAM: What is there to say? You've already guessed. Not that there's any precise illness I could put my finger on.

THEOBALD: But?

MANDELSTAM: My mother was delicate, probably undernourished like me. My father was fond of a glass more than was good for him.

THEOBALD: Good heavens!

MANDELSTAM: Had I been born with a completely healthy body, believe me, I'd have considered rather different prospects for myself in life.

THEOBALD: Do you hear that, Louise?

LOUISE: Yes.

THEOBALD: It's true, health, strength above all else. Feel that thigh, the biceps.

MANDELSTAM: Gigantic.

THEOBALD: My boy, with those I ride life so to speak. I can lift a hundredweight. Believe me, I could lift you into the air with one arm. If anybody comes up against my muscles, he knows about it. We'll have to coddle you a little, poor fellow. How would it be if we were to feed you and look after you?

MANDELSTAM: If it doesn't cost more than I can afford I'd like that.

THEOBALD: What do you think, Louise? Don't you feel sorry for him? What should we charge him?

LOUISE: That can't be worked out in a minute.

THEOBALD: I've no say in this, my boy. That's my wife's business. Discuss it with her, I'll raise no objections. (*to* LOUISE.) Give me a cigar in honor of the occasion.

LOUISE: You were going to buy some. There's not a single one left.

THEOBALD: Forgotten naturally in all the upset. I'll just run across. Can we expect the other tenant to make do with one big beautiful room?

LOUISE: He's coming at a quarter past three. Speak to him.

THEOBALD: If it was for a longer period, we could buy a screen and make two rooms as it were; a lot could be done with a curtain too. But what if he's not willing?

MANDELSTAM: I have your word.

THEOBALD: Good God, you have your room, Mandelstam of Aryan stock. I'll be back directly. (*Exit. A moment's silence.*)

MANDELSTAM: Excuse me—

LOUISE: I'm surprised you haven't even asked to see the room. It must be very important for you to live in this particular house. Do you work across the road with Master Lämmerhirt?

MANDELSTAM: No. I work in Lindenstrasse.

LOUISE: Fifteen minutes away. That's strange. Wouldn't it be wiser—?

MANDELSTAM: I have reasons.

LOUISE: Are you shortsighted? You're looking at me as if you were.

MANDELSTAM: Oh, Frau Maske!

LOUISE: What's wrong? You've gone red all over.

MANDELSTAM: Don't think badly of me. If I seem strange.

LOUISE: Your secrets don't concern me.

MANDELSTAM: Since this morning, I have one only, and it would be a release to unburden my soul.

LOUISE: Confide in my husband.

MANDELSTAM: He must be the last to know. His sympathy would suddenly disappear. Nothing dishonorable, something which hardly concerns me, something much more to do with you.

LOUISE: Me? How me? *(She has got up.)*

MANDELSTAM: *(rises.)* Forgive me.

LOUISE: Tell me.

MANDELSTAM: Through no fault of my own—

LOUISE: Please!

MANDELSTAM: I've never been in a situation like this. But, but— I must say it: Your bloomers—

LOUISE: What—?

MANDELSTAM: Today—your—

LOUISE: Quiet!

SCENE 8

THEOBALD: *(comes back.)* The decision?

LOUISE: I want to talk to you about it.

THEOBALD: Good. For the time being you'll move in. Would you like a cigar?

MANDELSTAM: I don't smoke.

THEOBALD: Lungs played out? Have you noticed my chest? Plenty of room for everything in there. Come here, stand in front of

me. Arms outstretched. Trunk bent backwards. Slowly. Lower.
Listen, we'll have to have a serious talk about this.

MANDELSTAM: I'm exhausted.

THEOBALD: You're puffing like a bellows.

(The bell rings. THEOBALD goes to the door.)

LOUISE: *(quickly to MANDELSTAM.)* It was unspeakable of you
to come.

MANDELSTAM: Don't scold.

LOUISE: Go away!

SCENE 9

SCARRON: *(enters.)* I had the honor of putting my request to
madam.

THEOBALD: My wife has told me you need two rooms. Now sir,
the situation has arisen that, without knowing of your offer, I
have given the smaller of the rooms to Herr Mandelstam here;
who incidentally is of a good German family.

SCARRON: Oh!

LOUISE: Herr Mandelstam was just saying—

MANDELSTAM: Not at all, I'm determined to stay.

THEOBALD: Yes, we know that. There remains the quite plausible
possibility that you'll be satisfied with the beautiful big room
that's left. It measures six and one half meters by five. Will you
please look at it thoroughly and give us your considered decision.

(He leads him to the door and into the room.)

LOUISE: *(to MANDELSTAM.)* Your behavior is unworthy. I shall
report it to my husband.

MANDELSTAM: I can't prevent you. But I ask you not to, for otherwise I shall have to draw Herr Maske's attention to the following: what induces the aristocratic Herr Scarron to look for
quarters in a house like this, if not—

LOUISE: You know him?

MANDELSTAM: I twice had the honor of dying his hair.

LOUISE: What a slander!

MANDELSTAM: He'll certainly not remember me, but I know all
about him.

LOUISE: And what makes you behave like this?

MANDELSTAM: This morning I reread *The Flying Dutchman*. Do you know Senta, Frau Maske? You're as dreamy as she is. I was still reading when I saw you coming with your husband, when you passed only two steps away from where I was lying on the ground. Suddenly—

LOUISE: Only two steps! Disgraceful. But when all's said and done your whole behavior is no concern of mine. I utterly despise you—that's all.

SCENE 10

THEOBALD *and* SCARRON *come back.*

THEOBALD: Herr Scarron is agreeable. He appreciates the room's merits and will pay twelve Taler. By the way he intends normally to use it for only a few hours during the day.

SCARRON: That is so.

THEOBALD: For something important which he cannot carry out in the uproar of the busy street where he lives.

SCARRON: That is so.

THEOBALD: I was able to assure him that we would exert ourselves to make his stay pleasant. My wife, worthy sir, possesses the skill, tact and civility of a person from the better classes and our deep rooted awareness of a decent background gives us a certain pride; nevertheless we, my wife especially, is not averse to doing favors.

SCARRON: I am very pleased, indeed.

THEOBALD: Finally, to touch on the question of the neighboring rooms, Herr Mandelstam, who by the way is of good German stock—as I already stated—is kept out of the house all day by his business. So we can divide our whole attention between you, during the day it can be devoted unreservedly to Herr Scarron, for the rest of the time to Herr Mandelstam. Another thing occurs to me: on this side there's an alcove with enough light from a window in our bedroom for Herr Scarron to keep anything there that he doesn't want to take into his room. We'll hang up a little curtain for him, so that we can't look in. And the convenience, gentlemen, on the half-landing. Really now everything's settled beautifully. Here are the keys for the street door and the flat for each of you. Nothing now hinders you from regarding the flat as yours at all times. May I, purely as a matter of form, Herr Scarron, ask you, this work which you intend doing in our house isn't of a subversive nature or likely in any way to contravene law and order? I am a civil servant.

SCARRON: Not at all, sir. I give you my word of honor.

THEOBALD: I accept it and feel as man to man that the word *honor* still has for you the tremendous significance that it has for every German.

MANDELSTAM: Till tomorrow morning then.

THEOBALD: (*to* SCARRON.) And the agreement for a year.

SCARRON: Certainly.

THEOBALD: Till tomorrow.

SCARRON: Madam!

THEOBALD: Till tomorrow.

(SCARRON *and* MANDELSTAM *off.*)

LOUISE: That barber is an unpleasant lout.

THEOBALD: Because he doesn't smell of scent like the other one.

LOUISE: He'll bring his disease into the house with him and thousands of nasty things with it.

THEOBALD: He doesn't really have any disease. He's tired, weak, he hasn't any marrow or sap if you like. From living in hostels and among hand to mouth existences. That'll improve. For the rest, my dear Louise, you're to behave quietly today and for the next few days and spare us any of your lip otherwise I'll beat your behind so thoroughly that you'll not be able to speak at all for a long time. Thank God that your slatternliness today doesn't seem to have had any evil consequences. I hope you're now fully aware of how very lucky you are. And it must have dawned on you when you saw the pitiful figure of that hollow-cheeked barber how important inherited good health is. But also if you take a closer look at the middle-aged gent with his impeccable clothes and well-brushed hair, you'll not fail to see how imperfectly his pretended purposefulness masks the fact that his will is sapped. Believe me, my dear, my few words about honor and conscience met a character incapable of such considerations. All the same he has taken a year's lease.

(LOUISE *bursts out sobbing.*)

THEOBALD: *(laughing loudly.)* This is priceless! Why tears, don't you agree he's rather comical? *(He chucks her under the chin.)* Shall I really beat you? Laugh, you silly goose. Go on, laugh. These two inferior specimens of manhood that God has sent into our house have put me in a really good mood again. Wasn't it too funny for words, the way he stood there saying Madam! To my Louise who can't even keep her bloomers up. (LOUISE *sobs more violently.)*

THEOBALD: And then: that is so! That is so! That is so! like a nutcracker. *(He shakes with laughter.)* In the other corner that angel of the soapsuds gasping for breath. Anyone not helpless with laughter here just has no feeling for the divine humor of it all. *(They laugh and weep in unison.)*

Act 2

SCENE 1

THEOBALD: *(comes from the alcove.)* That's the little curtain up then.

MANDELSTAM: *(at the coffee table.)* Why haven't you fixed it on your side?

THEOBALD: He must have the feeling that nobody can stick their nose into his affairs.

MANDELSTAM: As long as he has the same intention there'll be no objection.

THEOBALD: His laconic answers, his reserve toward me allow me to suppose so.

MANDELSTAM: The arrogance of a superior social position.

THEOBALD: Would he move here if that were the case? He could find the quiet room he wants for his work in the house of people better situated than we are.

MANDELSTAM: What's the man really doing?

THEOBALD: Why do you avoid the term gentleman? As far as I could make out from what he said, he wants to write about an experience he feels strongly about.

MANDELSTAM: An affair!

THEOBALD: An experience, he said. Watch this tendency of yours to switch terms. Write about an experience he feels strongly about.

MANDELSTAM: Well, well; an experience!

THEOBALD: If you say it like that, you're missing the point again.

MANDELSTAM: You're very precise.

THEOBALD: Naturally. I have to be. From nine in the morning till three in the afternoon I have official documents in front of me. What if I were imprecise there!

MANDELSTAM: Well yes, people do sometimes just talk. I have to entertain my clients when I'm shaving them, see that they don't notice a cut, the shaved-off end of a mustache. No time for long reflection there, one just throws words about. Main thing is to keep talking.

THEOBALD: So you're a victim of your profession! *(He laughs.)*

MANDELSTAM: An experience! Probably a love affair.

THEOBALD: Possibly. Don't you have to put in an appearance before eight on Saturdays?

MANDELSTAM: That's the way I work it. The boss doesn't come till then either, and the apprentice deals with the riff-raff.

THEOBALD: Hm. Well at least go for a walk in the early morning. If I were as uncertain of my body as you are, I'd go all out to strengthen it.

MANDELSTAM: Long walks are too strenuous for me.

THEOBALD: At first. I'd like to make you realize your condition really clearly.

MANDELSTAM: Why?

THEOBALD: So that you know what's what.

MANDELSTAM: If my means don't permit adequate attention— what use is the truth?

THEOBALD: Good Heavens, man, what use is self-deception?

MANDELSTAM: Heavens above, in the end everything all around is deception.

THEOBALD: You're a queer fellow, hohoho. A pessimist. Everything deception, downright deception?

MANDELSTAM: Don't laugh. I'll prove it to you.

THEOBALD: *(laughing.)* Good. Where?

MANDELSTAM: Wherever you like, everywhere, everybody.

THEOBALD: *(laughing.)* Yourself?

MANDELSTAM: *(furious.)* Certainly.

THEOBALD: Herr Scarron?

MANDELSTAM: Also.

THEOBALD: *(roaring.)* My wife?

MANDELSTAM: Especially.

THEOBALD: Me?

MANDELSTAM: Surely.

THEOBALD: *(uproariously.)* You're the life and soul of the party, a miracle, good value. And you are not a barber at all really? A baron in disguise maybe, my wife's lover who's wormed his way in?

MANDELSTAM: *(in a towering rage.)* Herr Maske!

THEOBALD: A power house of explosive virility with innards like powderkegs.

SCENE 2

LOUISE *comes from the bedroom.*

THEOBALD: Louise, leave your cooking smells behind. Mandelstam is a baron. Your lover, hohoho, and the world is deception and there's an end to it.

MANDELSTAM: Herr Maske, now I must seriously object—

THEOBALD: Oh no, my dear fellow. What my eyes see is as sure as the fact that you remove people's beards and aren't quite firm in the saddle, that I think of nothing but getting my columns to agree, that Herr Scarron writes love stories and my wife belongs to me. Certainly the only deception is something you dream up. And that comes from your liver or your lungs or your stomach. I won't rest till you've realized it. Are you coming with me?

MANDELSTAM: No thanks. In ten minutes.

THEOBALD: Don't be angry with me. Think your hour will come and you'll convince me? Never, my good chap; but let's not be enemies because of that. Well, I'm going. You don't want to?

MANDELSTAM: No thanks.

THEOBALD: Good. Au revoir. *(Exit.)*

MANDELSTAM: He makes it really easy.

LOUISE: *(looks him up and down.)* He does?—Who for?

MANDELSTAM: He really is most ridiculously credulous.

LOUISE: He knows who he can trust.

MANDELSTAM: He's going to have his eyes opened in no uncertain manner.

LOUISE: About people whom he takes into his house.

MANDELSTAM: My opinion entirely.

LOUISE: Who uses a transparent pretext.

MANDELSTAM: Which a child could see through! Writing a love story far from the noise of the streets!

LOUISE: If you mean to insult me, I'll call my husband back.

MANDELSTAM: Call him: He's still on the stairs. Don't provoke me, I'm still not in complete control of myself. Why does he keep laughing at me, why the contemptuous pity in his voice? What cause have you to despise me? I—I say it freely—I have a feeling for you, which however is far removed from approaching you other than respectfully.

LOUISE: No one will prevent you from doing that.

MANDELSTAM: You yourself. Do you think I'll watch calmly while another man conquers you for himself, bear living through what's in the wind, tolerate it as an accessory? I swear by this table: I'll prevent it with any means I can think of.

LOUISE: When do you have to go to work on Saturdays?

MANDELSTAM: You're underestimating me, Frau Maske. Someone took an oath then. May God be my witness, you shall not attain your goal!

LOUISE: *(slowly.)* You're a child.

MANDELSTAM: I'm a highly strung human being. Heaven knows.

LOUISE: A real child. Getting excited about nothing, nothing at all.

MANDELSTAM: I won't have people despising me.

LOUISE: Getting quite breathless. Have another cup of coffee. I'll spread you a roll with honey.

MANDELSTAM: When one has no one in the world.

LOUISE: Help yourself to lots of sugar.

MANDELSTAM: One just has no one in the world.

LOUISE: That's my father's honey. He has a little house in the country a couple of miles from here.

MANDELSTAM: If one had known one's parents better.

LOUISE: Usually I'm grudging with it.

MANDELSTAM: One is so inanely alone. No roots at all, nothing to lean on, nothing to hold on to.

LOUISE: We'll have to look after you a bit. A lot of it's nerves. Only you're so excitable.

MANDELSTAM: No.

LOUISE: I can't help despising violent natures. Docility and submissiveness are what I like. Good children.

MANDELSTAM: When a person doesn't have a mother, that's his one wish.

LOUISE: Yes, yes—his one wish! I've heard that before.

MANDELSTAM: Frau Maske, I swear by the memory of my dead mother who is looking down on us at this moment: I will never pass beyond any line you draw for me.

LOUISE: Not that I have anything against you.

MANDELSTAM: What I saw yesterday wasn't my fault.

LOUISE: You mustn't mention that ever again! Not a syllable. The way you turned up here scared me, I was afraid of unpleasant altercations with my husband.

MANDELSTAM: As if I wouldn't stand by you to my last breath.

LOUISE: Good—perhaps in the course of time we'll become friends.

MANDELSTAM: And Herr Scarron?

LOUISE: But why should that fop concern me?

MANDELSTAM: Fop certainly. But you could be deceiving me. I haven't enough experience with women, even if I'm not altogether a novice. Truly not.

LOUISE: It's not impossible that he has secret intentions here. But you're forgetting me, assuming an understanding which I find outrageous. Do you take me for so blind as not to see that I'd only be another easy victim for that spoiled Don Juan, which he'd abandon just as quickly as it had occurred to him to seize it? I'd sacrifice my reputation and all the advantages of my position for the desires of another man?

MANDELSTAM: His glances at you made me suppose—

LOUISE: Glances can be presumptuous without any encouragement from me.

MANDELSTAM: I will certainly never be presumptuous. Undemanding, satisfied with the least thing, a mere sigh.

LOUISE: Good. Let's leave everything to time.

MANDELSTAM: But don't hope to deceive me.

LOUISE: How lightly dressed you are. You shouldn't. Put something on, it's raining.

MANDELSTAM: The way you say that! It makes me healthy and strong in a trice. I don't notice the weather. I'll take off my scarf.

LOUISE: But no! Better prevention than cure.

MANDELSTAM: The way you say that!

LOUISE: Would you like to take some sandwiches to work?

MANDELSTAM: Fancy you think of that!

LOUISE: I think it would do you good.

MANDELSTAM: I don't need to eat. I have my heavenly dreams. What's earthly misery to me? Would it be all right with you if we sometimes read *The Flying Dutchman* together in the evenings?

LOUISE: Is it a love story?

MANDELSTAM: The most glorious one of all. Listen to what the Dutchman says about Senta: "Will she be my angel? When out of the terrible force of the torments which shroud my head in darkness longing drives me toward salvation, I shall have reached my longed for goal."

LOUISE: Lovely. Go now, or you'll be late.

MANDELSTAM: Then the end: "Alas, without hope as I am, I yet surrender myself to hope." And you should just hear it sung. It moves you to the very marrow.

LOUISE: Till lunchtime.

MANDELSTAM: Soon! Soon! Soon! *(Exit.)*

SCENE 3

DEUTER: *(appears immediately.)* Who is that long-winded creature?

LOUISE: A dangerous nosy parker. Yesterday he too saw what nobody should have seen, and he's wormed his way in under the same pretext as our friend. They're dividing the rooms between them.

DEUTER: Imagine!

LOUISE: Worst of all: he hates Herr Scarron and is making conjectures. What do you think? He's just sworn here that he'll never tolerate—

DEUTER: How stupid!

LOUISE: I think he's capable of running to Theobald with the whole story before the least thing has happened. I'm beside myself. When I came in here a little while ago, my husband said to me: Mandelstam—that's the barber's name—is your lover. It was said laughingly, but the creature must have spoken seriously of such possibilities, must at least have steered his remarks in that direction.

DEUTER: How have you behaved toward him up till now?

LOUISE: I've been flattering him, trying to make him feel confident.

DEUTER: Well done.

LOUISE: But—

DEUTER: I'll watch him closely. You see what a good thing it is to have me on your side.

LOUISE: What's that you're holding?

DEUTER: Guess.

LOUISE: Tell me.

DEUTER: The material.

LOUISE: You darling! How fine!

DEUTER: Do you like it?

LOUISE: Gorgeous! Expensive, I suppose?

DEUTER: It's more fashionable than silk.

LOUISE: How soft it must be on the skin.

DEUTER: Not like your nasty twill. Twill on a figure like yours. I'll just measure the waistband, hold up your skirt. 65, let's say 66 centimeters.

LOUISE: Have you got the ribbon yet?

DEUTER: Here it is.

LOUISE: Heavenly. You're my very best friend. And you're willing to do all this for me and you still young enough yourself?

DEUTER: I've honestly given up all hope. Otherwise it's true I'd not have much time to spare for you.

LOUISE: We'll have to pray for you.

DEUTER: Do you think that'll help?

LOUISE: For an objective as important as that, everything must be tried.

DEUTER: What progress you're making!

LOUISE: My mind is made up. Last night was absolutely decisive for me. A sweet dream already.

DEUTER: Tell me.

LOUISE: You poor thing.

DEUTER: No, don't tell me or I'll burst into tears.

LOUISE: We'll find someone for you yet. How would the barber do?

DEUTER: Ugh! If it comes to that, I'd rather have your husband.

(They laugh exuberantly.)

SCENE 4

SCARRON: *(opens the door from outside and enters.)* What heavenly gaiety. I step from rain into tropical sunshine.

LOUISE: (*softly to* DEUTER.) Stay here!

DEUTER: For a moment, then I must go downstairs.

SCARRON: My doorkey allows me to burst in uninvited on your gaiety and disrupt it. Go on laughing: if I may and can, I'd like to participate. What were you laughing at?

LOUISE: Fräulein Deuter—

(SCARRON *bows.*)

LOUISE: And I were talking about the barber.

SCARRON: Which barber?

LOUISE: Mandelstam, of course.

DEUTER: Frau Maske was saying he was too ugly for her and recommending him to me as a lover.

LOUISE: I said no such thing.

DEUTER: God knows, she recommended him and that was what she meant.

LOUISE: As a joke.

SCARRON: Seriously, it wouldn't do. He's not at all what could be called a man.

DEUTER: All the same, good enough for a spinster who's getting on.

SCARRON: Whom do you mean?

LOUISE: She's fishing for a compliment.

DEUTER: Nothing of the sort, only your verdict on this material, Herr Scarron. What do you say?

SCARRON: Batiste, I suppose, What's it for?

DEUTER: To make some bloomers for this young woman; excuse me: What would you say in your circles—lingerie?

LOUISE: Fräulein Deuter!

DEUTER: You interrupted us while we were taking the measurements.

LOUISE: Fräulein Deuter!

DEUTER: Sixty-six cm, that's what I call slender, eh Herr Doktor.

SCARRON: I oughtn't to have held up such a delicious pastime.

LOUISE: Herr Scarron!

DEUTER: I just need the length still. (*Bends and measures.*) Sixty-three to just below the knee.

LOUISE: That's enough. What are you doing?

SCARRON: Since I blundered into so delicate a situation, may I give some advice? Those ladies interested only in fashion and adornment, who set the tone in all questions of taste, would not perhaps have measured quite as far down as you did, Fräulein Deuter, they would have found the point about two or three centimeters above the knee.

DEUTER: Do help us. I was counting on your being well informed. And does our width of eighteen correspond with the latest cut?

SCARRON: The bloomers are left as wide as possible at the bottom and made tighter fitting further up.

DEUTER: That leaves one question—

LOUISE: *(rushes to bury her head in her bosom.)* Trude, do be quiet; I'll be eternally angry with you!

SCARRON: *(to* DEUTER.) This is extremely important. Are you the person responsible? Do you arrange everything?

DEUTER: You'd not withhold a compliment if you had the opportunity of admiring the finished article in position.

SCARRON: How do I earn your friendship?

DEUTER: Simply by realizing that I'm acting on your behalf!

SCARRON: You seem to wish to be fairy godmother to a happiness that needs a protecting hand even more than any fledgling.

DEUTER: That wants to fly, however—

LOUISE: And doesn't know how?

DEUTER: I'm only half a bird, so to speak, that didn't have the nerve when the time came and was left stranded under the eaves. You can't expect guidance from me.

SCARRON: There's no need.

DEUTER: The nestling, by the way, is bestirring herself. Yesterday I found her already fluttering in intimate contact with the higher regions.

SCARRON: Let us take wing!

DEUTER: A bird of prey is circling on the horizon! Not the fat old owl that's to be feared only by night. A slender hungry cloud that falls on the hiding place with lightning speed.

SCARRON: Who?

DEUTER: A cloud of soapy froth, a froth-beater.

SCARRON: The barber!

LOUISE: He's spying on me! He's watching me, he won't tolerate anything, he told me to my face. I'm very unhappy.

DEUTER: Now that's been said, I'm going. Caution!

SCARRON: Thank you!

DEUTER: I'll do what I can to stop him. *(Exits.)*

SCARRON: Louise!

LOUISE: I'm afraid.

SCARRON: Sit down by the table.

LOUISE: My knees are giving way.

SCARRON: Anyone can come through the door, for I'm not touching you. Opposite you, more than two oceans distant, I am quietly encamped against this mountain slope. Away from life basking in two blue suns. They are sending streams of will toward me, scorching what is near and kindling what is more distant with light, joyous warmth. Your clenched hand has grasped the melting thought and savors it. Your bosom is already seething. I see the muslin heaving. And now you're shedding your leaves from top to root with me, Louise, in one sweet gust, and are felled by fate.

*(*LOUISE *has buried her head in her arms on the table as if asleep.)*

SCARRON: My life began with father and mother. Brothers and sisters moved meaningfully toward me, and from my father there came almost uninterrupted utterance. What became of them? All that I saw was my mother's arm arched like a pleading shadow above me and I stood suddenly alone in a dreadful tumult that tore the ground and cast the heavens down on me. I had a goal but no paths toward it. Stand up, woman, I'm falling into a false passion. Stay! It's something quite different that I have to say to you. There are glorious women living in the world, Louise. Blond women, with pale pink moles when they are uncovered, and dark women with down like young eagles, along whose backs a wave ripples when they are roused. Some in rustling clothes and stones which shimmer like their sinuous places. Others in narrow close-fitting garments, cool as their skins. There are blond ones with down and dark ones with pale pink moles. Submissive brunettes and proud flaxen beauties. The sky is full of stars and the nights full of women. The world is sublimely beautiful—but! *(Grand broken off gesture.)*

*(*LOUISE *has risen.)*

SCARRON: You are the most beautiful woman I have ever set eyes on. I await the moment when you will unleash a storm which will break over me and demolish my mortal remains, and from the refuge of my madness I shall offer up my empty self tenderly at your feet. *(He has stepped up close to her.)* Look at this hand quickly before you clasp it in your own. God may well have chosen it as His instrument to pour out fine new songs in our tormented land's mother tongue. Have you fully realized: I am passionately in love with you, Louise? There must be no doubt of that.

LOUISE: I am yours.

SCARRON: Of what classical simplicity the gesture! A whole destiny clothes itself in three words. What humanity! If I could succeed in catching its living essence in a book—I should certainly count among the greatest.

LOUISE: *(bending toward him.)* Let me be yours.

SCARRON: Table, pen, and ink as close to you as possible: as close as this to such simplicity a masterpiece is inevitable.

LOUISE: Yours!

SCARRON: So be it! To a degree high above both of us. A passion like none ever known spurs me on, happiness can escape me no longer. With the meters vibrating within me I feel my soul take wing. I must capture your image for the whole of mankind before I return to demand the complete reward of your favors. *(Disappears to his room.)*

LOUISE: Why?—*(She goes to* SCARRON's *door and listens. After a few moments she plucks up courage and knocks.)* My God! *(She whispers, listens and approaches the table, from which with a glance at* SCARRON's *door, she picks up* MANDELSTAM's *scarf, which she finally presses to her face. Just then* MANDELSTAM *appears outside the flat door. He can be seen pressing his face against it. Then he opens the door quietly and comes in.)*

SCENE 5

MANDELSTAM: Heavens, my scarf! *(Comes close to* LOUISE.)

LOUISE: What a fright you gave me! Where have you suddenly come from?

MANDELSTAM: Why a fright?

LOUISE: Creeping in like that.

MANDELSTAM: Is that my scarf?

LOUISE: God knows.

MANDELSTAM: *(kisses her.)* Louise!

LOUISE: *(slaps him.)* Impudent fellow!

MANDELSTAM: Forgive me!

(LOUISE *goes to* SCARRON's *door and knocks loudly.*)

SCARRON's *voice:* Five minutes more.

(LOUISE *stands in confusion.*)

MANDELSTAM: I implore you. It was an impulse. Never again. I'll kill myself.

(LOUISE *toward her room.* MANDELSTAM *swoons.*)

LOUISE: God! *(Runs to him.)* What's wrong? Water! *(She fetches water and gives him some.)*

MANDELSTAM: How well I feel.

LOUISE: Your chin is bleeding. What's that pointed thing?

MANDELSTAM: That? A drill.

LOUISE: What's it doing in your pocket? It could have wounded you fatally just now.

MANDELSTAM: Why not, if you would have grieved.

LOUISE: Who wouldn't? Such a promising young man. What madness! Come and lie on the sofa for a minute.

MANDELSTAM: *(lying down.)* It will show me at all times what is going on in Herr Scarron's room.

LOUISE: You're going to—

MANDELSTAM: Bore a hole in the wall. I'm mad with jealousy, Louise, I don't know myself any longer. What drove you to that wretch's door? Don't misjudge me. In spite of my weakness, I'll murder him.

LOUISE: What right—!

MANDELSTAM: I love you, Louise.

SCENE 6

SCARRON: *(quickly from his room.)* Down to the smallest detail tone, color, every nuance held fast, recorded, no longer to be wrested from me. I come, all gratitude and love—*(He notices* MANDELSTAM.*)* Beg pardon!

SCENE 7

THEOBALD: *(comes in quickly.)* Good day, gentlemen. I trust we all have a healthy appetite.

Act 3

SCENE 1

Everyone is sitting round the table covered with the remains of the evening meal.

THEOBALD: *(to* MANDELSTAM.*)* It was hard for your employer to manage this afternoon without you. He said you might have arranged your indisposition for some day other than Saturday.

MANDELSTAM: The first afternoon I've missed in three years.

THEOBALD: He hopes you'll be better by the day after tomorrow at the latest. There's the whole of Sunday between then and now.

MANDELSTAM: Even a dog wants a bit of peace if he doesn't feel *kosher.*

THEOBALD: *Kosher?* Hm. But as you wish. By the way I had a very thorough discussion with a colleague who complains of symptoms similar to yours. He knows the inside of his worn-out body like the salary scale and even operates with Latin names. *(He has got up and goes to the back of the stage.)*

MANDELSTAM: *(follows him eagerly.)* But how, devil take it, could you discuss my case?

SCARRON: *(softly to* LOUISE.*)* I forbid you to stare at that lout all the time.

LOUISE: I'm honestly sorry for him.

SCARRON: He's a cunning scoundrel, a rogue who deliberately spoiled the afternoon for us by his pretence, and you—

THEOBALD: Primarily it's a matter of the nerves, even if the other organs are naturally also infected, some more, some less. If I understood him properly, you have to imagine every nerve as a fine tube, surrounded by a protective second tube. Now in people who've been weakened this other surrounding tube has been partly rubbed away like bark on trees—isn't that so, Herr Scarron?

SCARRON: More or less, as far as I know.

THEOBALD: Yes. And it's surprising how extraordinarily difficult it is to make good the damage once it's been done.

MANDELSTAM: Where in all the world do you get the idea that my nerves are—It's unheard of, without having examined me more closely.

THEOBALD: Do keep calm. I don't want to upset you. But I think many people must have drawn your attention to the state of your nerves already.

MANDELSTAM: Nobody.

THEOBALD: Then I'll ask the completely impartial observer. How does our friend seem to you, Herr Scarron?

SCARRON: Typical neurasthenic.

MANDELSTAM: Ha!

THEOBALD: You see. Other things naturally contribute as well, as I've already said. With the colleague I mentioned it's his stomach, which has been ruined by years of abuse with completely inadequate nourishment, while in your case I'd hazard a guess it's the lungs.

LOUISE: You mustn't frighten Herr Mandelstam, Theobald.

THEOBALD: Quite the contrary. I'm trying to arm him against a catastrophe, to avert it if possible.

LOUISE: But he denies having any serious illness.

MANDELSTAM: Unreservedly.

THEOBALD: All the better. I regard it simply as my duty.

MANDELSTAM: And I regard it as very ill-considered to tell sensitive people such things. Quite naturally one goes on being preoccupied with them inwardly.

THEOBALD: Even when they don't concern one.

MANDELSTAM: Is there a window open?

THEOBALD: A crack.

MANDELSTAM: May I shut it? *(He does so.)*

LOUISE: Put your scarf on.

MANDELSTAM: Many thanks.

SCARRON: *(to* THEOBALD.*)* As far as your sick colleague is concerned—I find incomparable satisfaction in this thought: what is weak and lacking in vitality must give way to what is strong and healthy.

LOUISE: The task of the strong should be to support the weak. Our religion teaches that as well.

SCARRON: The religion of past centuries, not ours.

LOUISE: *(hands* MANDELSTAM *a newspaper.)* Read that!

SCARRON: We're far beyond that. We've introduced a healthy breath of air into the stuffy, musty climate of compassion from past centuries.

MANDELSTAM: Where? It's swimming before my eyes.

THEOBALD: *(shows him.)* Down there. They say the sea-serpent has appeared again in the Indian Ocean.

MANDELSTAM: *(furious.)* What has that to do with me?

THEOBALD: It may divert you.

SCARRON: *(to* THEOBALD.*)* Does the name Nietzsche mean anything to you?

THEOBALD: In what connection?

SCARRON: He teaches the gospel of our time. He shows that it's only through the individual blessed with certain energies that the boundless mass of humanity is given direction. Might is the supreme delight.

THEOBALD: Might is delight I agree. I knew that while I was still at school, when I made others suffer at my hands.

SCARRON: Naturally I don't mean mere brute force. Above all spiritual energies.

THEOBALD: Yes, yes.

MANDELSTAM: I didn't notice till this morning that my room faces northeast.

THEOBALD: One moment. Yes. You're right.

MANDELSTAM: That's naturally extremely disadvantageous, even for the healthiest constitution.

SCARRON: *(to* LOUISE.*)* The spineless dog must be shown who is master. Tonight I'll risk everything to come to you.

LOUISE: Heaven preserve me!

SCARRON: Who do you take me for? Do you think that creep is a match for me when my mind is made up?

LOUISE: Wait a little!

SCARRON: No!

THEOBALD: *(has opened* MANDELSTAM's *door.)* Put the bed against the wall opposite the window, then you'll be sleeping toward the southwest.

MANDELSTAM: I can feel the draught even on the pillows.

SCARRON: *(to* LOUISE.*)* This very night you shall be with me in paradise.

THEOBALD: *(to* MANDELSTAM.*)* Now you're exaggerating.

*(*MANDELSTAM *goes into his room. He can be seen bustling about there.)*

SCARRON: *(to* THEOBALD.*)* Have you never heard these theories discussed? Do you read so little?

THEOBALD: Hardly at all. I work for seven hours. After that I'm tired.

SCARRON: That's regrettable. Where do you find the criteria for your thinking?

THEOBALD: People like us think less than you suppose.

SCARRON: All the same you live according to a certain plan.

THEOBALD: Looking after number one, if you like.

SCARRON: That means you eat, sleep, do your office work? And where will that get you?

THEOBALD: To my pension, God willing.

SCARRON: Deplorable. No interest in politics?

THEOBALD: I used to be interested in what Bismarck was up to.

SCARRON: He's been dead a long time.

THEOBALD: Nothing much has happened since.

SCARRON: Any intellectual pursuits?

THEOBALD: My God! For the likes of us there's not much point in that.

SCARRON: Are you aware that Shakespeare lived, do you know your Goethe?

THEOBALD: Goethe—I know the name.

SCARRON: For God's sake!

THEOBALD: You take it too tragically.

SCARRON: A comfortable theory of living.

THEOBALD: What's wrong with comfort? My life span is seventy years. With the mental attitude I've acquired, I can enjoy lots of things in my own way in that time. If I wanted to adopt a higher way of looking at things, your rules, then with my limited talents, I'd scarcely have learned what to do in a hundred years.

LOUISE: But that there shouldn't be compassion any more?

SCARRON: There simply isn't.

LOUISE: If I really feel it—

THEOBALD: Please don't interrupt when we're talking.

MANDELSTAM: *(comes back.)* I'd like after all to ask Frau Maske for a woollen blanket. I've turned the bed round.

THEOBALD: That was sensible.

LOUISE: You shall have a blanket. *(Goes into her room.)*

SCARRON: I judge every man quite simply according to the degree of his participation in the spiritual development of the human race. The heroes are the great thinkers, poets, painters, and musicians. The layman is significant to the extent that he knows them.

MANDELSTAM: And the great inventors!

SCARRON: Certainly; but only in so far as they make human beings cleverer in communicating the thoughts of the genius more quickly and urgently.

THEOBALD: And what about feeling?

SCARRON: What?

THEOBALD: Didn't I express myself properly? How does the heart fit into all this?

SCARRON: The heart is a muscle, Maske.

(LOUISE *comes back.*)

THEOBALD: Good, but it's a special case. Above all with the women.

LOUISE: *(to* MANDELSTAM.*)* It's big enough for you to wrap up in.

MANDELSTAM: Many thanks.

SCARRON: Where fundamental issues are involved, don't speak to me with such naiveté. Females, let's say women, are, by God, a precious commodity but when a Shakespeare wrestles for Hamlet's soul, Goethe for insight into a Faust, then woman just doesn't come into it.

MANDELSTAM: Schwarz won't have thought of his wife when he invented printing, nor Newton, nor Edison, nor Zeppelin.

LOUISE: Is that certain?

SCARRON: My oath on it.

MANDELSTAM: I'd like to take my oath on it too.

THEOBALD: Leaving Goethe—and as far as I'm concerned Schwarz too—on one side—all the same—if I may put it this way, women do have a heart.

SCARRON: A muscle, Maske.

THEOBALD: I know. But they live by it and are one half of the earth's population.

SCARRON: Well and good. But you're not a woman and ought to be permeated by the dignity of your manhood. Allowing for all the domestic and intimate bonds that unite you with your wife, there are still moments in which you feel that you are a world apart; where the masculine element in you overwhelms you completely and fills you with extravagant pride.

MANDELSTAM: Wonderfully said.

LOUISE: Not all men are like you.

SCARRON: Deep down all of them, madam.

MANDELSTAM: Unquestionably.

THEOBALD: I don't know. There is something in it, certainly but I've really always struggled against it.

SCARRON: There we have it! Struggled against—nature.

MANDELSTAM: The devil!

SCARRON: What else makes a man a giant then, the gigantic obelisk of creation that is unconquerable by woman if not the transcendental will to knowledge which the deepest erotic passion cannot paralyze?

MANDELSTAM: Paralyze—glorious!

LOUISE: My husband happens to be differently constituted.

THEOBALD: Louise, for God's sake, spare me your stupid comments. Speaking from personal experience, I can't convince myself that it would have brought me advantages in my marriage if I had strengthened and expressed this feeling of difference.

SCARRON: Personal advantage—you have to ignore that. Since it's indisputable that all progress for humanity depends on the preservation of the pure masculine principle.

LOUISE: Pah!

MANDELSTAM: Who would have thought ten years ago that we'd be flying?

THEOBALD: Above all I'm glad to see you both so unreservedly of one mind. How pleasant to have two lodgers who don't quarrel with each other.

MANDELSTAM: It's just one man standing by another.

SCARRON: By the way, you still owe us the disclosure of your real opinion. Up till now you've just been rejecting ours.

MANDELSTAM: Is Zeppelin perhaps not a hero?

SCARRON: Can we dispense with Plato and Kant?

MANDELSTAM: What would the world be without railway and telephone?

SCARRON: Without his predecessors Goethe would simply be an impossibility. And even if you deny Pontius and Pilate, I hope you'll admit that Goethe counts?

MANDELSTAM: And Wagner. The most sacred possession of mankind.

THEOBALD: *(slowly.)* That apart, there's so much else as well. Having children and such things—

MANDELSTAM: Always a woman's business!

THEOBALD: Don't attack me so fiercely. Did I for one moment doubt the accuracy of your facts?

MANDELSTAM: Even a God couldn't do that.

THEOBALD: But the two I produce from my experience, that women have a heart and that children are born, make you angry.

SCARRON: Incredible! These are truisms as firmly established as—

THEOBALD: You were saying?

SCARRON: At the moment no comparison occurs to me. An argument with you is pointless.

THEOBALD: Have another glass of beer. Louise, pour some for Herr Scarron.

SCARRON: Thank you.

THEOBALD: We could go to the zoo tomorrow. They've got themselves a giraffe.

MANDELSTAM: *(bursts out laughing.)* Giraffe!!

THEOBALD: What is there to laugh at about that?

MANDELSTAM: I think my thoughts.

THEOBALD: If I'm to be honest: left to myself, I'd never have hit on the idea of looking at such an animal. I'm really averse to such flamboyancies and eccentricities of nature. But since Herr Scarron is pressing me so hard, I want to do something to educate myself.

(MANDELSTAM bursts out laughing.)

THEOBALD: Not so wild, Herr Mandelstam.

SCARRON: My dear fellow, you are pretending to a narrowness of outlook. . . .

MANDELSTAM: Blinkers on!

THEOBALD: *(to MANDELSTAM.)* Don't dissipate your limited resources.

SCARRON: Should not the presence of a noble young woman at your side inspire you to the highest achievements? To raise yourself up out of your ambience?

THEOBALD: My wife's people are tailors, always have been for generations.

LOUISE: Six brothers fell on the field of honor.

MANDELSTAM: Nowadays nobody would be so stupid as to let himself simply be slaughtered.

THEOBALD: Really, isn't that in tune with the times any more? Patriotism out of date?

MANDELSTAM: If you almost made me ill earlier, now you're making me well again. In spite of many physical disadvantages, I feel that I'm different and I know there are legions behind me. No, we don't let rubbish of that sort affect us any more; we know what all that junk is worth. Even the highest born is descended from the ape like me and Herr Scarron, all mankind is fundamentally equal, and everyone can reach the heights.

THEOBALD: I agree. If he wants to. But there are some for whom one place is just as good as the next, and above all they like the one they are in. With what birth bestowed on me I am most favorably situated in my place and certain of it to my dying day, provided I don't differ too much from my colleagues throughout the country. Only special efficiency or extraordinary disgrace could deprive me of the security which it guarantees.

SCARRON: Sir, that's frightful. Slave morality!

THEOBALD: *(grinning.)* Not at all. My freedom is lost if the world pays any particular attention to me. My insignificance is the cloak of invisibility under which I can indulge my inclinations, my innermost nature unhindered.

SCARRON: God forbid that your credo is shared by your colleagues.

THEOBALD: I can't judge how my colleagues think. On the other hand, I can certainly guarantee that progressive ideas aren't popular in higher quarters. One of our heads of department tolerated his wife's affair with another man; as he put it in the document he drew up in his defense, he didn't want to curb the woman's natural tendencies, an expression that used to be popular for horses. Today he's pushing an ice-cream cart round the streets.

SCARRON: A martyr. His wife will look up to him.

LOUISE: His wife despises him thoroughly.

SCARRON: You're quite mistaken.

LOUISE: From the depths of her soul.

MANDELSTAM: I doubt that too.

THEOBALD: Let's leave that to the two of them.

MANDELSTAM: I happen to have proof from my own past. I lived with little Frau Frühling—they have the boarding house in Ahornstrasse—and her husband put up with the liaison.

THEOBALD: That her name was Frühling and she lived in Abornstrasse doesn't give the matter any special weight.

LOUISE: *(stands up.)* Good night!

THEOBALD: You're staying till we all go.

MANDELSTAM: Since then she's venerated the man.

THEOBALD: I must drink a schnaps on that. Is anyone coming to The Golden Basket for a quarter of an hour?

SCARRON: I'm more confused than I can express. It's the first time I've encountered such a view of life held with conviction.

THEOBALD: By a little man.

SCARRON: A man nevertheless. I feel you wouldn't abandon it under any circumstance.

THEOBALD: Under none whatsoever. Because I'd simply go under.

SCARRON: It would be some job. At least the attempt should be made.

THEOBALD: Don't give yourself the trouble.

MANDELSTAM: I regard it as quite useless too.

THEOBALD: I might possibly agree over a glass across the road.

SCARRON: Above all be good enough to treat the matter with the same deadly earnest as I do.

THEOBALD: No! If I did that would be the end of my politeness and many of the things said, that I can put up with at the moment, would find an echo dangerous for all of us. So come along.

SCARRON: Even if you start with a theory of unchangeable values—

THEOBALD: Mandelstam, you too. They've got excellent Munich beer.

MANDELSTAM: No thanks, I'm going to bed.

THEOBALD: Each to his own ways. *(He goes off with* SCARRON.)

SCARRON: *(gesticulating vehemently at* THEOBALD's *side.)* Even if you assume with Kant—

(Both exeunt.)

MANDELSTAM: After that conversation I must view lots of things with different eyes. To live with that pigheaded numb-skull must be hell—I've met confused ideas in other quarters as well, but obstinacy like that—what a swine. And then that gross familiarity, because I mentioned in passing that I wasn't strong. Beside a creature like that Herr Scarron naturally seems like God, if the comparison is adequate. Furthermore it takes devilish brutality to foist a northeast room on a person whose health one assumes to be completely ruined.

LOUISE: You agreed with Herr Scarron that one mustn't feel compassion for anyone.

MANDELSTAM: Who wants compassion? Decency, fineness of feeling is what I demand, such as, I have to acknowledge, Herr Scarron has shown to the highest degree.

LOUISE: How?

MANDELSTAM: In what he said. Didn't he grip you, didn't you feel that the man possesses a great overflowing heart? Isn't it touching that he's still going to try this late in the evening to pour enlightenment into that birdbrain? It's true his only reward will be the same grin that the master of the house had for me when I reproached him about the room.

LOUISE: But we didn't have a third room.

MANDELSTAM: Then it was your duty to warn me against that one.

LOUISE: You asserted to my face that to be near me you had to insist on having the room under any circumstances.

MANDELSTAM: But if it means certain death for me!

LOUISE: You're exaggerating.

MANDELSTAM: *(laughs.)* Exaggerating! Northeast for people with weak chests—there aren't words to express it. And to add to that, naturally my nerves must rebel at the consciousness of such a fact. The bark of a tree! Rubbed off—one can practically see it scaling off. You in your robust health, cheeks red as roses. *(He runs into his room.)* Not even double glazing. Without a woolly night-shirt I'll not last out the night, and my only one is at the laundry. *(He appears again.)* How long do you think it takes to put a weakened organism under the ground? *(Disappears into his room again.)* Didn't he say himself that his colleague would die within three days. The catch of the window doesn't work either. *(Appears again.)* What was that bit about the tube? For God's sake, he spoke about a tube, didn't he? Say something.

LOUISE: You said yourself it's got something to do with the nerves.

MANDELSTAM: I'm completely confused. I've a feeling now he spoke about two tubes and its being impossible to mend them again. *(He disappears again and shouts.)* A hole like this ought to be reported to the police. Policemen stand about at every corner, but when it comes to a poor fellow like me they let him rot in a hole like a mad dog. *(He appears again.)* What was it the doctor always did? Wait. Look at my throat! *(He wrenches his mouth open.)*

LOUISE: But I don't know anything about it.

MANDELSTAM: No, like this! *(He throws himself into a chair and crosses his legs.)* Strike my knee, like this, with the flat of your hand. *(And as* LOUISE *does this and his leg jerks, he screams.)* I'm done for! Naturally, one night facing northeast has ruined me completely.

LOUISE: *(disconcerted.)* But—

MANDELSTAM: *(beside himself.)* And you pretend to feel compassion!

LOUISE: *(near to tears.)* But you wanted to be near me at any cost.

MANDELSTAM: *(bellows.)* Near the grave, monstrous! We'll have to talk about this again!

(He runs into his room, slamming the door shut and locking it from the inside. LOUISE *stands without moving.)*

SCENE 2

DEUTER *appears outside the glass door.* LOUISE *opens it.*

DEUTER: I met both of them arm in arm outside the door?

LOUISE: Where have you been so late?

DEUTER: At the theatre. A splendid play by Sternheim. I'll tell you about it later. You should have seen him, he was literally radiating.

LOUISE: Who?

DEUTER: Not our giant, though he didn't look too bad beside him. Him, our hero! Exuding an aura of power and masculinity!

LOUISE: Ah!

DEUTER: His appearance made Theobald show up well by comparison, he seemed livelier than ever before. You've been able to be together the whole day! Tell me what happened, what went on? I'm burning to know.

LOUISE: Quiet. Mandelstam is in.

DEUTER: Let me look deep into your eyes. Let me clasp you by both hands, by both arms.

LOUISE: Why do you want to do that, Trude?

DEUTER: To drink the breath of your happiness. He sat on this divan, nearer and nearer to your very being every moment. Finally you were pressed against the back and couldn't evade him, even if you had wanted to. Tell me what he did.

LOUISE: I don't remember.

DEUTER: You rascal, you're robbing me. I want a confession with no omissions. Don't be shy, dear Louise, I've read more than you think, and I dream of such things. Even if I haven't experienced it, I know about it all the same. How did it begin? He put his arms round you?

LOUISE: He sat somewhere in the room.

DEUTER: And you?

LOUISE: At the table.

DEUTER: Then he came to you.

LOUISE: He stayed where he was.

DEUTER: And?

LOUISE: Talked.

DEUTER: What? Can you repeat what he said. Glorious things.

LOUISE: I had a roaring in my ears.

DEUTER: He unleashed himself on you like a thunderstorm. It must be like that, I've read it. And your body goes weak in the presence of the male, your feet refuse to function.

LOUISE: That's what happened to me. For a moment all my senses failed me.

DEUTER: Lucky girl! Then?

LOUISE: He came over to me.

DEUTER: Oh Louise! And?

LOUISE: Talked.

DEUTER: And?

LOUISE: Said something.

DEUTER: And then?

LOUISE: What?

DEUTER: When he'd said everything?

LOUISE: He went away.

DEUTER: What?

LOUISE: He went away.

DEUTER: What did he do?

LOUISE: He went away.

DEUTER: Called: I love you!

LOUISE: Yes.

DEUTER: And you?

LOUISE: The same.

DEUTER: I am yours!

LOUISE: Yes.

DEUTER: You did too?

LOUISE: From my heart.

DEUTER: At last. And then?

LOUISE: He went away.

DEUTER: Where?

LOUISE: Into his room.

DEUTER: You followed?

LOUISE: No.

DEUTER: Miserable girl!

LOUISE: When he shut the door, I followed, plucked up courage and knocked.

DEUTER: You knocked?

LOUISE: But he didn't open the door.

DEUTER: What? Shut himself in?—Now I have it, Mandelstam was about!

LOUISE: No.

DEUTER: Are you sure? Not near at hand without your seeing him? But he had already noticed him?

LOUISE: Ha!

DEUTER: Think back.

LOUISE: Mandelstam really did come in just afterward.

DEUTER: Ha!

LOUISE: I'm surprised myself, it has only just occurred to me.

DEUTER: You see, Oh you see! To distort my hero for me! Carried too far in his gestures, he suddenly notices the creeping fox I'd urgently warned him against. At once speech and gesture descend to the everyday, in the fineness of his feeling he departs quickly to spare you, and the greedy eyes of the intriguer see the woman alone as is right and proper. How right I was and how little you're able to understand him. Didn't he use the first opportunity that offered itself later to renew his pledge of love?

LOUISE: Yes, and he showed he was jealous of the barber.

DEUTER: Then the picture I formed of him at a distance was more correct than the one you had when you actually saw him.

LOUISE: But afterward when the men were talking to each other—

DEUTER: What were they talking about?

LOUISE: Then it was quite hopeless. I went out and had to weep.

DEUTER: You were wrong in thinking like that.

LOUISE: Then what I called loathing of my husband and liking for

Herr Scarron was wrong too. If I was misled by the misery that constricted my throat at what he went on to say, then everything in me from the first day of my life has been deception.

DEUTER: You understood him as little in those moments as you understood his earlier consideration. You've not taken in what his intentions are. Listen to me and trust in my deepest conviction: he's preparing the deed that will overwhelm you at one stroke.

LOUISE: I'm plunged in despair, eternally unhappy.

DEUTER: You fainthearted creature, it's not for nothing that he draws your husband away from your side at night, it's not for small stakes that he fascinates him with his vitality and ensnares him deeply in scruples and problems. If you'd been at the theater with me, you'd be counting on happiness to come any minute. There was a man there who climbed walls, burst down doors and started fires to be near his beloved. We poor creatures are engulfed by the conviction of male power. Foolish girl what are we at? The time we're gossiping away is time stolen from the waiting hero. Goodnight, a kiss. I swear by the bones of all the saints, it will come to pass! Quick, go to bed, quickly, put out all the lights. He'll come. *(She flits out.)*

LOUISE: Could it be? *(She sits for a moment without moving and listens. Then she goes to the window and looks out. Sits down again, stands up and goes into the bedroom, where she lights a candle. Coming back, she begins to undress slowly, her face pressed against the glass door. Steps echo on the staircase. She blows out the candle on the stage and stands trembling. But the sound fades again. She says.)* No! *(Her fingers go on unbuttoning mechanically. Now she approaches* MANDELSTAM's *door and touches its knob and goes with dragging steps back to the entrance to her bedroom. She stays there, lit up from behind, in chemise and bloomers, combing her hair slowly and repetitively, while at intervals* MANDELSTAM's *regular snoring shakes the air.)*

Act 4

SCENE 1

THEOBALD: *(calls into the bedroom.)* What a slovenly job you've made of mending my braces again! There's to be no question of my being neglected because of those two.

(LOUISE *enters and pours coffee for him.*)

THEOBALD: Luckily neither of them is here. We won't have to reckon with Scarron at all before midday, praise be. After he'd talked at me like a man in the grip of hallucinations till nearly 2 o'clock in the morning, I had to take him, at his express desire, tired to death as he was, to his other flat because the bed there was better. I drank five pints and three glasses of schnaps, and the result was out and out diarrhea.

LOUISE: He's not coming?

THEOBALD: I don't understand how anyone can sleep as soundly as you with somebody on the trot all the time. Where's the honey?

LOUISE: There isn't any more.

THEOBALD: What a terrible way to keep house! Kindly get some more. Furthermore I don't care to find underclothes of yours on my chair. You don't give me a chance to stop preaching at you.

LOUISE: I had another scene with Mandelstam about his room facing northeast and sank into bed.

THEOBALD: That fellow is completely mad! Where does he get this idea that north and east are inferior parts of the heavens. The sun rises in the east, every painter is extremely keen on rooms facing north, and a miserable barber wants west and south thrown in for five Taler.

LOUISE: South would in fact be better for his weak chest. And you were saying, Herr Scarron isn't coming today: how is that possible?

THEOBALD: Kindly blow your nose, you sound all choked up. What do you mean, how is that possible? He was tipsy and won't be feeling at his best today.

LOUISE: Tipsy?

THEOBALD: All right sozzled. At the finish he was a pitiable sight. The idea that he had to convert me never left him in spite of his condition. By the end of the evening he was rattling on at a tremendous pace.

LOUISE: Good heavens!

THEOBALD: That man is a strange ornamental plant in the garden of our Lord. Furthermore he has bad breath.

LOUISE: Theobald! But he had, doesn't he have something heroic about him sometimes?

THEOBALD: Like someone in a novel, you mean?

LOUISE: Yes, like someone in a novel.

THEOBALD: Oh, God—look Louise: he's not what you might call sound. Wouldn't he have to be a great deal more heroic for your taste—to compensate for the lack?

LOUISE: Yes.

THEOBALD: What he's doing has no real purpose. Deep down I think he's already tired of the fad that drove him to work here. I don't care. He's taken the room for a year—in writing.

LOUISE: Will you let me go to church today. It's almost an emergency.

THEOBALD: Of course, my dove. I think it's a very good idea. Last week held great danger for both of us on account of your fallen bloomers. You're only doing your duty if you thank your Maker. Meanwhile I'll ponder the consequences of something I have in mind.

LOUISE: Tell me what it is.

THEOBALD: You're curious. Rightly so. When you come back, Louise: let me think about it for another hour or so. I have a surprise for you.

LOUISE: Yes?

(She goes into the alcove.)

THEOBALD: What are you doing?

LOUISE: The curtains have to be put up in our bedroom. As it is, anybody can see in.

THEOBALD: Mind you don't fall off the window sill. *(He follows her. He can be heard inside.)* Mmm, my little wife does have a strapping pair of legs.

SCENE 2

MANDELSTAM: *(Comes in, sits down hurriedly at the coffee table, begins to eat greedily. Goes to the alcove to shut the door.)* What! *(As he recognizes THEOBALD.)* I beg your pardon!

THEOBALD: *(embarrassed.)* I didn't hear you coming. We're taking the curtains through to our room.

MANDELSTAM: Had breakfast? *(He sits down.)*

THEOBALD: Yes.

(LOUISE crosses the stage into the bedroom.)

MANDELSTAM: Good morning, Frau Maske.

THEOBALD: You seem to have slept well.

MANDELSTAM: The agitation you plunged me into overwhelmed me with sleep—I slept really splendidly.

THEOBALD: *(laughs.)* In spite of northeast.

MANDELSTAM: Truly. Although—

THEOBALD: An although?

MANDELSTAM: The bed is good.

THEOBALD: Better than the softest bosom.

MANDELSTAM: Although—

THEOBALD: Do you hear noises from the street?

MANDELSTAM: Not a sound, although—

THEOBALD: The morning sun disturbed you?

MANDELSTAM: There's nothing I like more—but of course—

THEOBALD: Five Taler is too cheap a rent for so many advantages. You have my wife to thank for it.

MANDELSTAM: But you're not to raise it the first chance you get.

THEOBALD: Not for the time being.

MANDELSTAM: That's expressed most ambiguously, one doesn't know where one is at all. It's only fair to fix a definite period.

THEOBALD: Why do you want to tie yourself down?

SCENE 3

LOUISE *enters.*

MANDELSTAM: Don't I get any honey today?

LOUISE: Nowhere in the world do people get honey without paying extra.

MANDELSTAM: I thought it was included.

LOUISE: Then you were wrong. Furthermore the sugar is going to run out very shortly. *(to* THEOBALD.*)* Au revoir.

*(*LOUISE *exit.)*

THEOBALD: Why do you want to tie yourself down? If the doctor really finds something really serious and feels that northeast may be harmful for you, you'll be in an embarrassing situation. The bed is certainly good. The mattress is horsehair. You won't find the like on a thoroughbred today.

MANDELSTAM: Indisputably.

THEOBALD: Morning sun and perfect peace and quiet—As it happens, we'd decided shortly before you came to replace the bed with another. Fräulein Deuter, as a matter of fact, a neighbor, had offered us sixty Taler cash for it.

MANDELSTAM: You mustn't ever do that!

THEOBALD: *(has gone into* MANDELSTAM's *room.)* A down quilt like this. And hasn't my wife added a second pillow against my express instructions!

MANDELSTAM: To be brief: for a year. We understand each other, Herr Maske.

THEOBALD: Your ailing condition—

MANDELSTAM: I feel like a giant.

THEOBALD: Prices in this district rise from day to day. After three months the room will easily be worth eight Taler instead of five.

MANDELSTAM: You'll get me so agitated that the benefit of last night will be undone again.

THEOBALD: Six Taler. That's as far as I can go.

MANDELSTAM: I can't.

THEOBALD: You'd better.

MANDELSTAM: Agreed then, to make an end of it, agreed. You with Bismarck and Luther on your lips, I wouldn't have thought this sort of thing of you.

THEOBALD: All settled!

MANDELSTAM: For a year. And let's put it in writing straight away. I'll write: Herr Maske lets Herr Mandelstam a room with breakfast until May 15.

THEOBALD: Without honey.

MANDELSTAM: For six Taler. The bed in the room must not be replaced by another. Sign it.

THEOBALD: Suppose my wife doesn't like it. She finds you revolting.

MANDELSTAM: But good Lord, we have nothing to do with each other.

THEOBALD: Even so. Since she finds your presence in the house uncongenial. Perhaps she'll feel inhibited.

MANDELSTAM: Not by me. I'll swear it to her with a thousand oaths. She doesn't concern me, let her do as she pleases. Don't drive me on to the street. I admit the bed is good. Think of my miserable condition—be merciful.

THEOBALD: Well then—since you press me. I'm not a monster. *(He writes.)* There it is: Theobald Maske.

MANDELSTAM: Would there be an armchair to spare anywhere?

THEOBALD: I'd better tear it up—my wife—

MANDELSTAM: *(wrenches the sheet of paper from him.)* The devil take your wife!

THEOBALD: Here's to an enjoyable life together then!

MANDELSTAM: It won't be my fault if it's not. *(He looks into his room.)* You'd have had to have seen the bed in the lodgings I was in before. A torture rack. And non-stop noise from all sides. In addition, a little menagerie, oh yes, fleas, bugs, my dear fellow; I made a pattern of them on the wallpaper with pins spelling Richard Wagner. *(He laughs.)* I got a bit carried away against you yesterday evening. It wasn't ill-meant.

THEOBALD: I was extraordinarily pleased. Agreement with Herr Scarron comes before all else. He pays well, we owe him some consideration.

MANDELSTAM: *(his hat on.)* I'll do my bit.

THEOBALD: Where are you off to today?

MANDELSTAM: Out to the pleasure gardens.

THEOBALD: Wouldn't it be better if you used your day off to consult a good doctor?

MANDELSTAM: Not as long as I feel as I do today.

THEOBALD: What's her name then?

MANDELSTAM: Nothing at all yet. The last one—Frieda. She's got a technician now.

THEOBALD: Was she buxom?

MANDELSTAM: Extremely. That's what I look for. There'll be others at the fireworks today. *(Exit.)*

THEOBALD: It only occurred to me in passing to charge him more. Thoroughly weak in the head, stupid fellow. Eighteen Taler all told. Eighteen times twelve is one hundred eighty—two hundred sixteen Taler a year. The flat costs one hundred fifteen. That leaves one hundred ten. I earn seven hundred, that makes eight hundred ten, eight hundred eleven Taler, and we'll be living rent free. It'll work, it'll work, it can be done. That's fine, excellent!— Who's that?

SCENE 4

DEUTER *is standing outside the door.*

THEOBALD: *(opening the door to her.)* Do come in, Fräulein Deuter. We were just talking about you.

DEUTER: Who?

THEOBALD: A barber and I.

DEUTER: That nasty fellow.

THEOBALD: And he seemed very interested in you.

DEUTER: Stop joking.

THEOBALD: Raised his eyes tenderly and said Trude.

DEUTER: How does he know my first name?

THEOBALD: Who doesn't know it that has the good fortune to be under one roof with you!

DEUTER: You're making fun of me.

THEOBALD: Heaven forbid.

DEUTER: Is your wife here?

THEOBALD: Gone to church.

DEUTER: And Herr Scarron isn't here?

THEOBALD: He found the flowered dress you had on last night quite "outstanding" and thought up a nice word for you when we got outside.

DEUTER: Which was?

THEOBALD: Give me time. Buttocksome.

DEUTER: What's that mean?

THEOBALD: I can't explain it exactly. But it has something. What are you clasping so warmly to your bosom?

DEUTER: Nothing for you. I find Herr Scarron's word for me rather silly, it doesn't sound at all pleasant.

THEOBALD: I like it and it strikes me as appropriate.

DEUTER: You don't even known what it means—*(She sits down on the sofa.)*

THEOBALD: It is suggestive—

DEUTER: Suggestive—!

THEOBALD: Of a picture. One thinks of a pair of round arms, of all sorts of things.

DEUTER: Quite stupid. A woman is either ugly or pretty.

THEOBALD: Bony or buttocksome.

DEUTER: Bony—God, I *am* an old maid.

THEOBALD: *(who has taken the parcel from her and opened it.)* It's bloomers! And such bloomers. Pink silk bows and peekaboo material. Anyone meaning to wear things like these can only be fishing for compliments if she calls herself an old maid.

DEUTER: Do you think so?

THEOBALD: Old sloops don't hoist silken sails.

DEUTER: To be desirable still.

THEOBALD: In fairy tales. In real life they spare themselves the useless expense. *(He holds the bloomers spread out in the air.)* The things have chic and if they fit as well as I fancy they must be a sight for sore eyes.

DEUTER: Herr Maske! I don't know you like this.

THEOBALD: You don't know me at all. To some extent I was even uncongenial to you till today, and I let that pass because it suited me. But then yesterday you came in that slinky dress, and today these artful bloomers—

DEUTER: I'm carrying them modestly in my arms to show your wife.

THEOBALD: To complete the picture there should be white stockings to go with these.

DEUTER: Fancy you thinking about such things!

THEOBALD: My dear girl, how do you know my thoughts weren't preoccupied with you long since? It seems to me they were. Since you lead me now into talking like this about those delicate little things, those advantages of yours which, Heavens knows, are there for all to see, aren't as new to me as may have seemed.

DEUTER: If your wife were to know about this!

THEOBALD: She knows nothing. I wouldn't tell her such things because it would worry her. I do such things secretly. Not often, but with pleasure.

DEUTER: We're all human—in the end.

THEOBALD: Not in the end at all. In my case from the age of 14.

DEUTER: I'm thirty-two. It's not so easy for a girl.

THEOBALD: Not all that much more difficult.

DEUTER: My parents were indescribably strict. My father struck me if I was a moment late, and he didn't die till I was twenty-nine.

THEOBALD: That's hard.

DEUTER: Then I came to live here; but under the eyes of all the old women in the house—

THEOBALD: Is your flat locked?

DEUTER: I locked it when I came up. Everyone spies in this house.

THEOBALD: Twenty past ten. Now I remember. One evening I happened to look out of our bedroom window just as you—

DEUTER: I'm going. Your wife will be coming back.

THEOBALD: Not for an hour. *(He stands in the open door of the bedroom.)* Look how clearly I can see your room from the place by my bed.

DEUTER: *(goes toward him.)* Really?

(The door closes behind the two of them.)

SCENE 5

SCARRON *enters through the flat door after a moment and looks around in search of something. There is a knock at the door.* SCARRON *opens it.*

SCENE 6

STRANGER: They told me downstairs that there's a room to let here.

SCARRON: The occupier isn't here. Perhaps you'll be good enough to come back some other time. As far as I know there isn't a room vacant at the moment.

STRANGER: The agent says there is.

SCARRON: Of course I can't say anything definite.

STRANGER: Are there many children in the house, anyone play the piano—can you give me any information?

SCARRON: No.

STRANGER: Thank you. When will the landlord be back?

SCARRON: I can't tell you anything about that either.

STRANGER: Good day. *(Exit.)*

(SCARRON goes into his room.)

SCENE 7

THEOBALD: *(looks out of the bedroom.)* Who was that? *(Goes to* SCARRON's *door, listens and runs to the bedroom.)* Come on! Scarron is back.

DEUTER: Do you love me? When shall I see you again? Today again? Tomorrow morning before you go?

THEOBALD: We don't want to overdo things. I'll think over how we'd best manage it. In the end, I think, we'll settle on a fixed day every week, for which I'll make the arrangements.

DEUTER: I'm just to see you one day in seven? What am I to do on the others, since from now on every minute without you will mean an eternity for me?

THEOBALD: Pull yourself together. Otherwise your impatience could be fatal for you. If you're prepared to be contented with a limited number of times, both of us will always be sure of achieving the maximum pleasure.

DEUTER: But—

THEOBALD: Otherwise nothing. And I'd better send my wife down to you if you still want to see her today.

DEUTER: I don't really have anything to see her about.

THEOBALD: All the better. And not a look or a word that might hurt her.

SCARRON: *(comes.)* Good morning to both of you. An elderly gentleman with a beard was here just now wanting to rent a room from you.

THEOBALD: Hallo. So I was right, business is brisk.

DEUTER: I'm just going.

THEOBALD: Should I have sent Mandelstam packing?

DEUTER: Where did I leave my parcel?

SCARRON: *(passes her the bloomers wrapped in paper.)* Voilà.

DEUTER: Thank you, Herr Scarron. Good morning. *(Exit.)*

THEOBALD: Feeling better?

SCARRON: Since you left me for dead outside my door you have a right to that question. But what happened will surprise you very much. For reasons of some insane theory I felt a necessity stronger than the feeblest body to wrench myself to my feet again. And so while you were reeling home—

THEOBALD: I had a stomachache, apart from that I was fine.

SCARRON: The positiveness of your opinion had in fact taken hold of me, and in spite of my tiredness I felt the achievements of years thrown in doubt.

THEOBALD: Surely not, the opinions of a lowly civil servant!

SCARRON: It had in fact become so much of an event for me that it was important to reestablish the truth of my gospel immediately.

THEOBALD: In the middle of the night?

SCARRON: And God was gracious. While I was walking to and fro by a bank of the river with my mind confused and agitated, I noticed that a shadow was following me.

THEOBALD: Ah!

SCARRON: And as I stopped, a woman loomed up close to me.

THEOBALD: How do you mean loomed up?

SCARRON: Don't interrupt! She stared at me with empty eyes.

THEOBALD: The devil she did!

SCARRON: Living incarnation of concern about God and where the next meal was coming from, the first moments were a thrilling exchange with nothing but glances. She entrusted more than a sacrament to me. She opened up and poured body and soul into me and made me the confidant of her thousand shames; and—this was fabulous!—understand this: never, never before in my dealings with children or even the Holy Virgin, was purity so intensely near me as with that whore. And at once I saw: the judgment which you had emphatically pronounced earlier about the immutability of all values—that, of course, is the plain sense of your view of life—

THEOBALD: So?

SCARRON: It was invalidated in the presence of that woman. Year after year, strengthened by my inner beliefs in the human race's capability of development, I have ceaselessly made the most stringent demand on the cultivation of my psychological receptivity. She rewarded me for that.

THEOBALD: So?

SCARRON: I followed her to a wretched home, and what I then wrenched from her locked breast by the light of a smoking lamp was, word for word, confession of such a high, new, and as yet unscaled, human greatness, that I sank to my knees in front of the straw mattress.

THEOBALD: She was lying stretched out in the trap already, was she?

SCARRON: And uttered prayers full of the terrible strength of humility. I would not have raised my head if she had trodden on it with her thorn-torn feet.

THEOBALD: Things like that do happen.

SCARRON: My God, how wretched you all are in the presence of such emotion. At all hours she offered her body to the coarseness of men, and with each day she raised herself through her suffering nearer to God the Omniscient.

THEOBALD: These girls always have a heart of gold.

SCARRON: When the morning sun touched us, she found me less than her equal.

THEOBALD: What did you pay?

SCARRON: I don't resent that question. Too many oceans lie between us. What sort of laughter would you burst into if I said to you: I would not have dared to ask her to be my wife.

THEOBALD: *(worried.)* You haven't slept at all? You look really ill.

SCARRON: There is no sleep for me until I have attained such complete clarity about that soul that I can re-create it in poetic form for mankind. Will you believe me, yesterday I intended for a moment to make you, Herr Maske, the hero of a work of art; but today I feel with incomparably stronger force than ever: only psychological depth determines suitability as an artistic object.

THEOBALD: Foreign words are the devil. What, for instance, is psychology?

SCARRON: *(smiles.)* I forget, you poor fellow; it was difficult for you even to follow me?

THEOBALD: There was a lot I didn't understand. You were with a woman last night.

SCARRON: With an angel!

THEOBALD: A fallen one.

SCARRON: You arch philistine!

THEOBALD: And you won't tell me what psychology is?

SCARRON: Everything is in flux. And thank God, good and evil too.

THEOBALD: My God, that's dangerous!

SCARRON: It is. But I'll live and die thus. Now you mustn't take it amiss if I tell you that I'm leaving you again.

THEOBALD: But you've got a contract for a year.

SCARRON: I don't want to break it. I'll pay you twelve times twelve Taler equals one hundred fifty Taler in advance *(he pays)* and I have no objection to your passing on the pleasant little room. Your personality, however sterling it may be within your own sphere, might have an unfavorable influence on my next artistic task. You understand?

THEOBALD: That's six Taler too many.

SCARRON: Let it pass.

THEOBALD: You're a strange character.

SCARRON: I'm a man of action, that's all. I cannot rest without final elucidation, and so I am irresistibly drawn to that woman, to become the most intimate witness of her way of life; God has made it my duty to measure out the last depths of the human condition, and just as I was elevated for a long time, now I must lower myself into the bottomless pit. Unheard of pleasures may await me.

THEOBALD: You rogue.

SCARRON: Don't misunderstand me! Along with measureless torments.

THEOBALD: I know what you mean. One just has to watch not to take too much out of oneself too soon. A certain regularity above all.

SCARRON: Irregularity, man! Or I'll hang myself.

THEOBALD: But even that with a certain regularity.

SCARRON: I hope very soon to send you a book that will astonish you.

THEOBALD: And if you have a well-to-do friend who needs a room, recommend us. First of all, however, I'd sleep for a few hours at all events.

SCARRON: Herr Maske!

THEOBALD: Quite honestly!

SCARRON: God knows—perhaps that's really not such a bad idea. I am beginning to feel a little tired now—well, good-bye!

THEOBALD: You'll find your way here again sometimes, I'm sure.

SCARRON: Where will I get a cab near here? Damned endless stairs!

THEOBALD: *(laughs.)* Haha, your legs! Have a good sleep!

SCARRON: *(meets the stranger at the entrance as he goes out.)* This is the gentleman who'd like the room. *(Exit.)*

STRANGER: The agent told me you must certainly be at home. You have a room to let? I hear.

THEOBALD: True. Twelve Taler including breakfast.

STRANGER: That's dear.

THEOBALD: A big room. See for yourself.

THEOBALD: No piano nearby, little children, no sewing machine, canaries?

THEOBALD: Nothing of that kind.

STRANGER: Do you keep cats or dogs?

THEOBALD: No.

STRANGER: Have you daughters of marriageable age?

THEOBALD: No.

STRANGER: You're married yourself, is your wife young?

THEOBALD: Yes.

STRANGER: Flighty?

THEOBALD: That would be the devil.

STRANGER: Then you're constantly on guard?

THEOBALD: Certainly. And the convenience on the half-landing.

STRANGER: I will not permit any personal relationship. The maid has to knock three times before coming in. Instead of coffee, I drink tea which I'll provide. I suffer from constipation, but that's my affair.

THEOBALD: Entirely yours.

STRANGER: In these circumstances, I'll try it for a probationary period of a month. I can give notice on the fifteenth. My name is Stengelhöh and I am engaged in academic studies.

THEOBALD: Agreed.

STRANGER: The maid has to enter the room in modest clothing, not ragged and revealing. My things will be here in an hour. Good morning.

THEOBALD: Good morning, Herr Stengelhöh.

(Exit the STRANGER.)

THEOBALD: I'll take out *Joseph before Potiphar*, and hang *Boa Constrictor in Conflict with Lion* in there. *(He carries a picture from his bedroom to SCARRON's old room.)*

SCENE 9

LOUISE *enters.*

THEOBALD: Did you meet Herr Stengelhöh on the stairs, man with a beard?

LOUISE: I think so.

THEOBALD: He's our new lodger. Business is irresistibly on the move. He drinks tea, which he's going to provide and is engaged in academic studies.

LOUISE: Scarron?

THEOBALD: Yes, about Scarron. I've seen through him. He's had enough of us and has disappeared for good after paying a year's rent in advance. He sent you his kind regards. There are other things I could tell you about him, but God protect my wife from such ridiculous ranting. He was a poltroon, a buffoon smelling of violets. Mandelstam, on the other hand, is staying for a year, and I'll train him to shave me for nothing. Has church made you feel any better?

LOUISE: Our great Holy Catholic Church, Theobald!

THEOBALD: Yes, yes,—certainly not an empty illusion.

LOUISE: We're a year married today.

THEOBALD: How time passes!

LOUISE: What do you want me to cook for you?

THEOBALD: I happen to know that you've got a tasty roast of pork up your sleeve.

LOUISE: I'll do it with sauerkraut.

THEOBALD: And put a little onion on it. But now I'll produce my big secret too. Those two people, who erupted into our house, have at last put us in the position to—to what, Louise?

LOUISE: I don't know.

THEOBALD: Can't you guess. *(Softly.)* Now I can take the responsibility of starting a family. What do you say?

(LOUISE begins cooking in silence.)

THEOBALD: Cook it in butter! Stengelhöh is very odd. He doesn't want any personal contact with us. He asked if you were flighty; he suffers from constipation. *(He walks about the room.)* The clock as usual isn't wound up, despite what I keep saying. The flowers need water. *(He waters them.)* The Deuter woman was here about an hour ago, wanted to show you some bloomers she's made herself. Have a look sometime how they use a kind of stud-fastener these days instead of ribbons. With those fasteners that damned business in the street that caused us so much trouble couldn't have happened at all. Given your notorious slovenliness, the outlay of a few coppers will perhaps save us a lot of trouble. *(He sits down at the window and picks up a newspaper.)* There are curious things behind the wallpapers of life, as it were. I still have a stomachache. No more of those departures from routine. Stud-fasteners—sometimes mankind does come up with some really nice and straightforward invention. They say the sea serpent has turned up in Indian waters again; perhaps I read that out to you already.

LOUISE: *(mechanically.)* Good heavens. And what does an animal like that live on?

THEOBALD: The experts can't agree. I find the news of such odd things repulsive. Literally repulsive.

Translated by M. A. McHaffie

Walter Hasenclever

The Son

A Drama in Five Acts

Characters:

The Son	Cherubim
The Tutor	Von Tuchmeyer
The Friend	Prince Scheitel
The Fräulein	Adrienne
The Father	Police Inspector

Time: The present (1914), during three days.

Act 1: The Son's room
Act 2: Same, 24 hours later
Act 3: An anteroom, a few hours later
Act 4: A hotel room, the next morning
Act 5: The Father's consultation room, a few hours later

Act 1

SCENE 1

(THE SON's *room in his parents' house. In the center wall a large window with a view onto a park, in the distance the city's silhouette: houses, a chimney. The room mirrors the moderate elegance of a respectable bourgeois home. Oak furniture, bookcases, a desk, chairs, a large map. Door stage right and left. The hour before sunset.)*

THE SON: I'm twenty now and could be in the theater or build bridges in Johannesburg. Why did I fail with the formula of the truncated cone! All teachers were sympathetic, even the director prompted me. I could have solved the task brilliantly—had I not run away at the last moment. I believe there are things which force us into pain. I could not have endured freedom. Perhaps I will never become a hero.

THE TUTOR: You have failed in your final exam. How often have I been sitting with you at this desk and we have crammed all the formulas. Did I not explain to you that the small cone has to be subtracted from the large! Answer me!

THE SON: Yes, you did tell me. I understand your pain. You are sad because this cone does exist in the world. Believe me, I'm no longer sad! I'm even lacking the fleeting gesture mocking itself under tears. You'll say I'm a weakling or a rascal. But I tell you: I was standing in my black coat in front of the blackboard—and knew very well that I held the chalk in my hand. I even knew that the small cone had to be subtracted from the larger one— yet I did not do it.

THE TUTOR: But why not! I'm asking you: why not?

THE SON: Before me someone else was examined in history: In 1800 or so the Battle of Aspern took place. And while my hand invisibly described circles on the blackboard, I saw archduch- esses and long-winded boulevards. You will understand that math is destroyed in the midst of such loveliness. The dissolution of a single parenthesis would have saved me. But I preferred to despise myself in it.

THE TUTOR: We shouldn't have worked so much in recent days. Your frame of mind is understandable. You are suffering from a mental depression.

THE SON: I believe that man's soul is not quite that simple. This day is an experience. My longing for freedom was too strong. It was stronger than myself; that's why I could not fulfill it. I have felt too much and still be courageous. I have bled to death from my own self. Probably I will never have the strength to do for what I was born. Now you will realize that I could not pass the final exam: I would have perished from something.

THE TUTOR: Calm down. It isn't too bad.

THE SON: Thank you. You are good to me. You will be fired be- cause I am an idiot.

THE TUTOR: I wish I could help you.

THE SON: My father will see to it that this won't happen.

THE TUTOR: How are you going to tell him?

THE SON: Please send him a telegram. You know his address. I am unable to do it myself. I'm not afraid of his anger but I am suffering from every human being and from every street. I am humbled by each existence which diminished my desire for it. I am revolted by the fact that a building is constructed from which the air is ruined by electric waves. How I hate all the communiqués between Emperor and soldier!

THE TUTOR: What should I telegraph to your father?

THE SON: Do not spare him. He hates me. I know he will rage. I am a coward or else I would lie that I was fired from school to make his anger rise even more. Wire him everything you want— except that you love me.

THE TUTOR: I do not understand your father . . .

THE SON: Once you yourself will be a father, you'll become like him. The father—is the son's fate. The fairy tale of the fight for life is no longer valid: it is in the parents' house where the first love and the first hate originate.

THE TUTOR: But aren't you the son?

THE SON: Yes, and therefore I'm right! Nobody can understand that but me. Later on, one loses his own balance. Perhaps we shall not meet again. Listen to one bleeding advice from my heart: Whenever you will have a son, abandon him or die ahead of him. For the day is sure to come when you will be enemies— you and your son. Then God's mercy be with the one who loses.

THE TUTOR: Dear friend, all of us will go astray in this world. Why do you want to be so cruel! Go out into the street and see an animal that is frightened by thunder. Do you know how hungry girls are feeling, and have you ever met a cripple who looks for his bread at 6 o'clock in the morning? Then you will be grateful for having a father. Each one of us is wronged and each one of us does wrong. Who will throw the first stone? I was a poor fellow and my father worked to support me. I've seen how he died. And I have cried. He who has had such an experience, will no longer pass judgment.

THE SON: Who helps me when I'm sad? Do you think I can fall asleep each night when I have to go to bed? Do you think I would not know now the pain of someone not allowed out of the house on Sundays when all the maids go dancing? My father will not tolerate that anyone in the world will become my friend. I have never tasted the sweetness of even the poorest people. And why doesn't he talk with me about God? Why doesn't he talk about women? Why am I forced to read Kant secretly who does not set me on fire? And why all this mockery of everything that is worldly and beautiful? Do you think it is enough when, sometimes in the evening, he shows me the Great Bear in the sky? Smoking his cigar, he sits on the balcony below when the last car has long stopped running in the city. But I stand upstairs, fighting with all the gods and die before a woman I do not yet know. How often have I walked the stairs at night in my night-gown filled with longings like a ghost finding no rest!

THE TUTOR: If you still had a mother, you would feel well.

THE SON: My mother died at my birth. I know nothing about her. All sleep at night when I am unhappy. My mother has never appeared to me in the golden sky. She has never consoled me when I became feverish. I believe she is too young to understand this. My mother married when she was eighteen. How distant, how childish are the times into which I was born!

THE TUTOR: I do not know what to tell you. I do not want this hour to fall into the well without a drop of goodness coming over you. Perhaps your father means well! Later on you will learn how difficult it is to love someone else. Today you only know yourself. I had to go through a lot of evil in life but I do not want to make others pay for it. And because I recognize this, I will enjoy my gray hair. Dear boy, there is still so much time for hate. I feel miserable because I cannot help you. You move me so much . . . Pardon me . . . *(He cries.)*

THE SON: A year ago I would have cried with you, out of fright. Today I can only laugh. I am disgusted with these feelings. Do you want a glass of water?

THE TUTOR: Thank you, it's all over. I could not convince you even if I were the Prophet Isaiah. I must think about it for many days in order to believe in God again. Why is there enmity in the world?

THE SON: This smells after Salvation Army.

THE TUTOR: Goodbye. You are young. You should know that you are alive. Therefore everything you do will be good—how could it be otherwise? Now you laugh about me because I speak of love. Someday it will overcome you too and you will cry. Then think of me! Now I will send a telegram to your father. *(Exits.)*

SCENE 2

THE SON: *(Alone. Goes to the window, opens it. The evening sun shines.)*

> Down under, beautiful to see
> Wonder nights, out of reach for me
> In the black room where my youth I spent,
> My bookshelves and my notebooks here:
> Rise up, my magical sphere
> When first to Golgotha I went.
> The sun goes down. The world of all my dreams,
> Where in my tennis suit I darkly stand.
> I call you, roads and trees and beams
> And you, the ball, held in my little hand!
> In my old room I now go on my knee
> And all my life tumbles into this hall:
> Table, chairs and wall—oh, do not flee
> And world, now take me with you on this fall!
> *(He kneels with spread-out arms.)*
> In vain I knock at the bronzed door,
> Separating my prison from the lust.
> Music and dance I am waiting for,
> A poor body, still burning in the dust.
> And yet I lived, lived a life so vast
> On this soil which could never last
> Boundless longing was my fate—
> Without the power it ever to attain.
> Into the void I fling myself in pain
> From which I have landed now afraid.
> Up then, silken cord, let's make an end!
> Never have I loved, and I am alone.
> The last circle of immortal faces bend
> To give me wings to a new home!

(He pulls a green cord from his pocket and fastens it at the window.)

Green creature, by strange hands you're made
Why am I overwhelmed by your sight?
I am a human being too, now at the gate.
Oh, evening sun, no longer do I want to fight.
Do you have to find me at this spot!
Hand does not loosen, Earth will dwindle not.
An unknown fire makes me shiver,
In this hour around my heart an aching ring:
I am with all of you—with you I want to live!
Where, oh Death, where is thy sting—

(He tumbles, overwhelmed by excitement, backward into the room.)

Thou secret, which from me has sprung!
I do sense women, beautiful and tall,
I feel arms around to which I clung
And a sweet face my name will call.
In the threatening evening wind I hear
Unfortunate and poor ones to me so dear;
In the coffin a little child I do see sway
I have learned of so much pain and also joy.
Perhaps on this vast world there is
Still comfort and a bridge to bliss.
With twenty years I do not want to go.
I have to live. Learning is slow.

(He comes back to the window. The sun is setting.)

Infinite feeling! Thou gave me a sign
The miracle to see now is my foremost task.
Concert and town—soon you will be mine!
My car approaches in the dusk.
I sit in boxes, I shall dine
With actors and the best of wine.
With a duchess in London I shall be
And a diamond pin will be given me.
A new system discover I will
How to jump by parachute from the house—
The audience should get their fill:

I shall live! Oh, gold! Oh, applause!
Thus break thou cord, instead of me thus fade—
But you, tall figures in the evening light
Make me purer and free of every hate
To be eternally alive, and with delight!

(He tears up the cord and throws the pieces out of the window.)

SCENE 3

*(*THE FRIEND *enters.)*

THE FRIEND: You speak to yourself, you are very courageous.

THE SON: Today I see you for the first time.

THE FRIEND: We haven't met in a long time. I am coming from the railroad station. You are astonished?

THE SON: That I'm still here—this astonishes me much more.

THE FRIEND: I heard you failed in school. Did you want to kill yourself?

THE SON: To say it simply: yes.

THE FRIEND: Why didn't you do it?

THE SON: I stayed alive.

THE FRIEND: You owe your life to a plagiarism from *Faust.* Are you still not allowed to read Goethe? Does your father let you go to the theater?

THE SON: No.

THE FRIEND: Why does Death meet with us so often? Today, on the train, a child was run over.

THE SON: I've seen the child. When I wanted to kill myself, I saw her. A girl, with black, curly hair, in a white dress.

THE FRIEND: It was a girl. How did you know?

THE SON: I know more than you suspect. But don't be afraid. I am not yet speaking from the beyond. I had a revelation, right here. I believe that throughout the world there exists a profound community. This I didn't know until today. I've stayed alive because once again I'm happy! When God has mercy on me, some day I shall experience love and pain. How can I explain it? There is a long road from school graduation to the supernatural.

THE FRIEND: I've rushed over to see you. I felt you would do something.

THE SON: Thus we have met in the evening en route with the express train.

THE FRIEND: Wait a moment. Let us talk about reality. My heart beats strongly. Yesterday I dreamed of you: both of us loved one woman. I had a feeling we did not know each other. We plodded along far-away snow fields before a childlike horizon. Now that I'm here, you're so close to me!

THE SON: You enter this room at the right time. It is not for nothing that you have first seen this incredible world two years earlier than me. A voice called you to help me, poor creature. Everything in me is so tense today that the sounds of the trolley cars before our house, which I detest, remind me of eternity.

THE FRIEND: Can I help you?

THE SON: Already this life has begun for me. Help me to retrieve the world to come! You saw a child die who has rescued me from death. From her little hands the power of existence has dropped on me like golden rain on the shepherd's seeds. Now that I'm alive, I want to learn much because I shall be loved. In the past I could not stand to see a street because my brain burst from all that I saw. Now I would like to go with the metal workers into their pits in order to feel there too that I am a human being.

THE FRIEND: You are drunk from being, but you do not know its poison. I perceive with terror how you have changed. Today that you begin to live, your dying begins.

THE SON: I believe in everything I saw. Why do you doubt me?

THE FRIEND: The child on the tracks is your downfall. You've tasted the blessedness of the world on your firmament. But I hate these stars, and love disgusts me for too deeply have I felt its weaknesses. All that tempted me, I have enjoyed. It was not too much that killed me but too little. I came to see you because I thought you were still pure and untouched. I wanted to warn you, listen to me! I'm spoiled in paradise and now that I am fleeing, I am alone. Why wasn't I born a cripple, then I would never have had a woman or a friend, and I would not now be here.

THE SON: We are standing across from each other, each one on his pole. But there is still a zenith to which we shall rise, you and me. Is there something I can do for you?

THE FRIEND: Return to me the fragrance of a flower in summertime while it was still forbidden to pick it for the beloved one. Return to me the longing for that trick in the circus which people love. Let me travel again, in childlike fantasy, on a rainbow from Argentina to Venice. How was I moved by the first smile of a girl sitting next to me on a church bench! And how did the little suburb carry me off to Berlin when the evening sky rose with a red tinge on the horizon! Now I walk the same boulevards where once immortality grew in me and weep that I do no longer experience anything nor can sacrifice anything.

THE SON: I look through you—you speak the truth. You have not yet reached your highest curve, due to weakness and imperfection. But only he lives who knows strongly what he is! I want to say to you: "Rise and follow me." When the world's gates will open up for me, it can only happen from beauty and greatness. Perhaps you, with your experiences, can point out to me the keys. I ask you to do it because I am so helpless.

SCENE 4

(THE FRÄULEIN enters.)

THE FRÄULEIN: It's getting dark. Should I bring the lamp?
THE SON: Yes, Fräulein. When shall we have dinner?
THE FRÄULEIN: In ten minutes it will be nine o'clock.
THE SON: Then bring the lamp. *(THE FRÄULEIN exits.)*

SCENE 5

THE FRIEND: A beautiful girl!
THE SON: Don't you know her? She is the third governess. I have to have dinner with her every night at nine. My father wants it that way.
THE FRIEND: Did you see how she entered the room? Can you imagine a woman coming to you while the world is full of other men? Aren't you a human being and don't you feel her divine steps in the dusk? You should bless your father that he lets you live with her every night—every night, oh, man! Do you know how long you will be living? Aren't you happy that so much is happening to you? She shares the dishes with you and drinks

from the same pitcher. What harmony, what earthshaking word that she has to sleep like the rest of us, prepares tea and dusts rooms while she is a godlike creature living on islands.

THE SON: I never knew what you said. How can something so beautiful be alive?

THE FRIEND: Think of Penelope!

THE SON: Since I have seen these words on cabaret programs, I no longer get dizzy in Homer's palace.

THE FRIEND: Someday you will learn why God made all women alike—for better or worse.

THE SON: Continue to talk of this woman. I am afraid.

THE FRIEND: A wave of her hair is still lingering in this room. Why don't you love her?

THE SON: How can I?

THE FRIEND: She will open your eyes, you fool, at the closed gate. Through her the bolts will be blasted open and you might experience some of the drama of the world. Don't be afraid, she is kind. Your mother was a woman like her too. You will be her child!

THE SON: Deep sorrow fills me for what I will never be able to see or say. I only think of Siberian steppes even though sometimes I find an old man in a ditch and know that many in the snow die of hunger. I'm seized with fear that nowhere do I understand creation! I think of the moment when I walk in the spring and yet am no more than a warning sign on the sky bearing down on me. All that happens to me, happens eternally! What remains of me in this life's restless chain?

THE FRIEND: The needs of your heart, the tear in the night and the resurrection in the morning!

THE SON: Come back soon, then I will be closer to you. I want to learn of the miracle before the shadows of my solitary room will envelop me once again. I want to enter this enchanted garden even at the sacrifice of my sight. Half an hour ago I swore that I belong to joy which I do not yet know. Some time, my life will answer me, perhaps today, perhaps in a hundred days. I feel the time is not too distant.

THE FRIEND: I am confident: a good star guides you. I'll be back when you need me. Thus fly away!

THE SON: You too, my friend, in infinite emotion!

THE FRIEND: The wave still carries you forth. It has called me back. Good-bye. *(He exits.)*

SCENE 6

(The room gets darker. THE FRÄULEIN *enters with the lamp. She sets the table and serves dinner.)*

THE SON: Fräulein, I see you have blond hair. You are standing between the lamp and dusk.

THE FRÄULEIN: *(At the window.)* The clouds are still light. In our village the cows are now coming home. How beautiful is this evening!

THE SON: *(Softly.)* And how beautiful you are!

THE FRÄULEIN: *(Watching him attentively.)* Are you sad?

THE SON: Sad? Why? Because I've failed in school? No, not at all. I'm happy.

THE FRÄULEIN: Then we will have dinner. *(They sit down.)*

THE SON: *(Not touching anything.)* We have been sitting so often at this table, like strangers. And we've gotten used to it.

THE FRÄULEIN: Have I always been so strange to you?

THE SON: Fräulein, I've been told that you are alive and in this world. I must learn to understand much. That you have a voice and that you walk on silvery feet through the room.

THE FRÄULEIN: *(Smiling.)* My, who has told you all that? You don't believe it, do you?

THE SON: *(With extreme seriousness.)* I believe everything and even more.

THE FRÄULEIN: Should I prepare a sandwich for you?

THE SON: I cannot eat anything.

THE FRÄULEIN: Often I have been thinking of you and feeling pity for you because you are treated so harshly. I would like to, but I'm not allowed.

THE SON: You're right. It's dark in here.

THE FRÄULEIN: Don't think of it. Good times will return.

THE SON: If I were to ask you for something, would you do it?

THE FRÄULEIN: What should I do for you?

THE SON: I must make love to a woman. Let me go out tonight.

THE FRÄULEIN: Little boy! When did this come over you?

THE SON: Today, Fräulein. Today.

THE FRÄULEIN: Hasn't your father issued strict orders not to let you go out at night?

THE SON: Fräulein, when I was seven, my father took me on a trip. How I was frightened in the tunnel—I thought of it as hell. We took a boat downstream and for a moment stood in the boiler room. Then for the first time I saw the giant fires and the black men sweating. Do you know what my father did? He gave to each of the stokers one Mark. I was so happy for the poor devils.

THE FRÄULEIN: You have a good heart.

THE SON: When I grew up, I often wished my father would give me one Mark for I wanted to buy sweets. But he never did it. I don't know why. He said I would get sick from them.

THE FRÄULEIN: If I had one Mark now, I would give it to you.

THE SON: What good is one Mark to me now! With it I cannot even pay the cab I want to take.

THE FRÄULEIN: There are bad women. Perhaps you will return sad.

THE SON: Could I become still sadder than in the twenty years I have been waiting for the star so close by? When will I finally hear the trumpets? Oh, Fräulein, there are hours when we leave our sphere, dreamlike, when in the summer we sit in concerts with pink ladies at the banks of the eternal river. Give me the house key!

THE FRÄULEIN: *(Hands it over.)* Here, have it.

THE SON: *(Snatches it.)* So I am holding this treasured possession. *(He jumps up and staggers.)* Oh, I'm like a blind man. My eyes are not used to the light. I'm afraid I might lose it. Take it back! *(He returns the key.)*

THE FRÄULEIN: You will not go out?

THE SON: *(Attentively.)* Wasn't this a sacrifice, a gift from you? If my father knew it, wouldn't you lose your job?

THE FRÄULEIN: *(Smiling.)* Then help me write a letter to your father. He wants to hear each day how things are going. I don't know what to write to him. *(She takes pen and ink.)*

THE SON: By the way, I want to talk to my father. Write him to come back.

THE FRÄULEIN: *(Near the lamp, writing.)* What date is today, the twentieth?

THE SON: Yes, I want to talk to him. He should know it. Soon I must do something real big. I have stopped learning in that school. How much will I tell him?

THE FRÄULEIN: *(Looking at him.)* Should I write all this?

THE SON: I will go to Hamburg and see the transatlantic boats. I will also keep some women. Don't you believe it, Fräulein?

THE FRÄULEIN: But I cannot write this to your father!

THE SON: *(Standing behind her, pointing to the writing paper.)* Then write to him that he should come back. *(THE FRÄULEIN writes. THE SON puts his hands on her shoulder, trembling.)*

THE FRÄULEIN: *(Without turning around.)* What are you doing? I cannot write this way. *(THE SON opens her blouse, touching her.)*

THE FRÄULEIN: Oh, no—now there is a blot on the paper. *(THE SON bends down lower to her.)*

THE FRÄULEIN: *(Withdrawing, almost above the paper.)* No, no, if your father—

THE SON: I love you. *(She turns around; he kisses her with ardent, anxious force.)*

THE FRÄULEIN: *(She gets up, turns away, then puts her hair in order. After a while)* What's going to happen now?

THE SON: *(In great confusion.)* Something has happened. Don't be angry with me.

THE FRÄULEIN: *(In a soft, kind voice.)* You were never a stranger to me. *(She takes the lamp.)* Good night! *(Exits fast.)*

SCENE 7

THE SON: *(Alone. Night. August sky.)*

> Since infinite stars are shining,
> How differently am I devoted to each star!
> They created me for living and for whining.
> I'm closer to the eternal, at the bar.
> Not to wild ecstasy nor painful recognition
> But lead to the highest rapture me today.
> So that in the most horrendous combustion
> I learn in this world what I have to say.
> Already do I hear the nights revealing
> To the unknown spirit bliss and sorrow;
> My life will overflow with feeling
> Like ev'ry human, I can wait for the morrow.
> For a creature in love, himself renewing,

Becomes greater in the fullness of the day.
This greatest does inspire me into doing
And thus into my life will fall a ray!
A thousand times closer let me be
That life's miracles won't me lull.
That in every birth and death I see
God is with me. This woman sure is beautiful!

Act 2

SCENE 1

(The next day. The same room. The same hour.)

THE SON: A beautiful woman in our city has taken her own life. Lake Lucerne is being combed but her body is not found. Some maintain she has not died and is still alive. I shudder hearing this. Is she going to be resurrected from the dead? How unimportant whether her husband had a mistress! I could not fall asleep last night. I went to the park and lay down in the bushes under the sulphur-colored sky. What storm has carried this woman away into unrestrained space from her seat in the box of the theater where she could be seen twice a week! In what darkness has she disappeared? Who has helped her in her need? Does anyone know about her tears before her rippled face submerged in the lake?

THE FRÄULEIN: She has two children, a little girl.

THE SON: Therefore she cannot vanish in dust or vapor. The guardian angel lives on—you children! She will assist you during the painful hours of the day. How much of the immortal is in us! When I got up, a bird screamed over the pond: there I saw your breasts, white in the shadow of the room.

THE FRÄULEIN: It was so muggy. I couldn't sleep either. For a long time I stood at the window.

THE SON: And I felt you to be sweet too and thought I was under your protection.

THE FRÄULEIN: We are bad. We are sinking deeper and deeper. And your father's confidence rests in me.

THE SON: What pleasure to betray him! When yesterday I kissed you in his room—how did I enjoy this happiness. And the couch where we embraced has felt my revenge. And the dead, sheering pieces of furniture in front of which my father used to beat me, have all seen the miracle. No longer am I the despised, I'm becoming a human being.

THE FRÄULEIN: Your father has helped many people in need. We must be grateful to him. Often when the nightbell rang, your father got up, fetched wine from the cellar and hurried to a dying patient. He radiates consolation in the darkness of death and poverty. He has done more good than we have.

THE SON: Yes, Fräulein, and that's why I want to talk to him. He must listen to me, he must help me—he, a doctor, who stands at the bedside of thousands of people. Will he desert his own son in his hour of despair? I will tell him everything that is in my soul. I trust that my strength is greater than his distrust has been all these years. Thus I want to stand before him: it is necessary for us to hold close together, one with the other. Let me feel your warmth before the frost of this meeting chokes my heart. If I could only overcome him! Through your mouth I heard the voices of the living and of mercy. But I will try to find my father in nobility, as the God of Happiness has announced to me last night. Achilles's horses will be harnessed fiercely before my carriage! Now I have the courage to do everything for I believe in myself.

THE FRÄULEIN:* Your eyes are shining—how beautiful is this fire! You're still with me, I still possess you. Yet I know that for you I am only a small footprint in the garden of high feelings. Come on, perhaps you'll have forgotten me in the morning. And today I am so much in love with you.

THE SON: Dear Fräulein, let me be with you tonight. I want to make love to you! Fulfill what innocent reverence has still shyly veiled for me. This day of waiting fate must end in purple happiness. You fires at the sky of my homeland! You blast furnaces and poplars! Let me become a man in azure light! This too I must possess in order to learn what kind of a person I am.

THE FRÄULEIN: My little boy, come to me when it makes you happy. I want to be close to you! I caress your hands, and when this happens it cannot get lost. In the future you should think of

---

*From the Fräulein's speech to the end of this scene the two use the more intimate "Du" instead of "Sie."

me in gratitude. Don't go to any other woman. I will take care of you. And you're allowed to do with me whatever you like.

THE SON: Tell me that you love me, then I don't have to be afraid of anything. For you I could win a battle. I will do it when I face my father.

THE FRÄULEIN: *(Caressing him.)* And yet how little of what you will do tonight will happen out of love. What do you know of love and sacrificial death! In you there is manliness: you will fight. I wish you would return with torn clothing and a bleeding face—then you would learn what a woman is like! But no—you should be victor! You do not love me because you love me. You must possess me. And you do not know what I do for you.

THE SON: I will not touch you if you don't want it.

THE FRÄULEIN: I'm with you, nonetheless. Could I love you, yet not bring you a sacrifice? I know that I am condemned to shed many tears. But it has to be that way. What painful blessedness on the swaying bridge of pleasure!

THE SON: I will kill everybody who hurts you, even if he were my father.

THE FRÄULEIN: How ignorant you are and how sweet! You are standing before me so strong, so bold. I must kiss you, my little, sweet hero. Thanks to God that he created such youths! Think of me whenever another woman holds you in her arms as I do. And do not kill yourself—you will soon hurt me very much. Now your star is turned towards me at its highest point—now that you have not yet loved anything and soon will have enjoyed everything. This hour will not return. Heavens may protect you from sadness.

THE SON: Tonight—swear to me that you are coming!

THE FRÄULEIN: Yes, I come! There must be a human being in this world through whom your soul will pour itself out for the first time. A being who protects you and will accompany you toward the light.

THE SON: Fräulein, everything in me is heavy and dark. I see both of us standing in the clouds, midway between expectation and pain. Aren't we in my father's house which surrounds us with old age and enmity? And you speak to me in beautiful and strange words as never before. Is the riddle returning in the dark power of the dreamer? Is Aladdin's magic lamp on the nurse's knee? Oh, for that miracle which God has promised me! How can I understand it—today there is a night and tomorrow a day—shall I see the sun which sends his rays to all of us?

THE FRÄULEIN: *(After a while, softly and slightly bitter.)* There are many suns and you will see them.

THE SON: What can I do for you? Should I tell my father that I'm in love with you?

THE FRÄULEIN: And what is going to happen when he believes it? Will you take me with you to Hamburg?

THE SON: Yes, Fräulein.

THE FRÄULEIN: I feel it, you are courageous. But who will pay for the ticket?

THE SON: Can't we walk there? Somebody will help us on the way. There must still be people, just as in the golden times, who give bread to one another, from sea to sea—I don't need my father. Just as I could die without him, I will live twice as well without him. A rustle of your dress and I won't enter this house anymore.

THE FRÄULEIN: Yes, you would abduct me on shooting stars. You glow. How embarrassed you will be when the first reception clerk will ask for our name. How clumsy will you be when you shop for bread and butter in the evening. In what kind of dreamland did you live! You speak of Hamburg, and you think of Babylon and the waters of the Red Sea . . . No, don't tell your father anything. You will be going soon, but let me stay. Here I will always have something, power from you, something firm in space. If I now had to leave, how subterranean would be my steps! I want to see the day which brings you back as triumphant victor over your childhood. The lawns and the trees before your father's house—perhaps you will drive by and not enter it—will reveal to you what you have suffered. You will be happy.

THE SON: Why don't you want to come with me?

THE FRÄULEIN: Because I have lost you even before you are suspecting it. Because you must leave me. Because you will live and fight.

THE SON: Then help me!

THE FRÄULEIN: Today I am still able to do it. Tomorrow someone else will do it.

THE SON: Will I see you sometimes on my way? Will you appear to me, spiritually at the edge of the great boulevards?

THE FRÄULEIN: The many of us who are blessed cannot get lost in someone else's heart. Remember this word when your emotions are highest! Who can say that life's vicissitudes are at an end, and where does the star rise?

THE SON: A childlike face appears before me. I brought tulips to my father at one of his birthdays. He took me to his chest—then I knew that I was alive, that I existed. A governess, one of your predecessors, once beat me up because I was singing softly in bed. Now I feel it again. Birth and existence—oh, blessedness! I shall be eternal, eternal—*(He kneels before her.)*

THE FRÄULEIN: *(Holding him.)* Everything is fleeting. There is only one thing that remains: your happiness. And when I'm still holding you now in my arms firmly and when you look up to me, then I know: a message of life has been revealed to you; that's why I am here.

THE SON: I shall never leave you.

THE FRÄULEIN: And when the angel will get me with his sword?

THE SON: I'm holding you. I will see you again. I will conjure you from the violets of the Acheron. Beloved woman, I would find you, tomorrow night at the cinema as unattainable queen and imaginary cocotte in a Montmartre bistro. Oh, that I have been allowed to experience this! The world becomes ever more beautiful before me! *(A car rolls by, he jumps up.)* This is my father. Come to me tonight . . . I expect you here. *(He rushes toward the window.)* A car stopping in front of the house. It's him. I recognize his step. Now may it start! With this fullness in my heart I will confront him. *(THE FRÄULEIN exits to the right. THE SON returns.)*

SCENE 2

(THE FATHER *enters.*)

THE SON: *(Taking a step toward him.)* Good evening, Father!

THE FATHER: *(Looks at him, without reaching out for the hand, after a while.)* What do you have to tell me?

THE SON: I have not passed my exam. This worry is over.

THE FATHER: That's all you know? Did I have to return for that?

THE SON: I asked you to—because I want to talk to you, Father.

THE FATHER: Then speak up.

THE SON: I detect in your eyes the features of a scaffold. I'm afraid you will not understand me.

THE FATHER: Do you expect a gift from me because you had to pay the price for your laziness?

THE SON: I was not lazy, Father.

THE FATHER: *(Goes to the bookshelf and derisively throws some of the books down.)* Instead of reading this nonsense, it would be better to learn your vocabulary. But I know—you were never lacking excuses. It's always the fault of others. What do you do all day? You sing and recite—even in the garden and at night in bed. How long do you expect to stay in school? All of your friends are long gone. Only you are the loafer in my house.

THE SON: *(Goes to the bookshelf, puts the books back in order.)* Your anger was directed at Heinrich von Kleist. *(He touches the book fondly.)* He has done nothing to you.—What standards do you apply?

THE FATHER: Are you already a Schiller or Matkowski? Do you think I don't hear you? But these books and pictures will disappear. I shall also keep an eye on your friends. Things can't go on like this. I have not spared any money to help you. I have kept tutors to work with you. You are a disgrace to me!

THE SON: What have I done? Have I forged notes?

THE FATHER: Stop such talk. You will become aware of my harshness because you do not listen to my kindness.

THE SON: Father, I thought to stand differently before you today. Away from severity and kindness on a scale with men where the difference in age no longer counts. Please take me seriously for I know quite well what I'm saying! You have determined my future. My prospect is an honorable chair in the court building. I have to keep for you a list of my expenses—I know. And the eternal disk at this horizon will turn me until some day I will have gone to my fathers. I admit not having thought of that until today, for the period until the end of school seemed longer to me than my whole life. Now that I've failed—I began to see. I saw more than you, Father, excuse me.

THE FATHER: What language!

THE SON: Before you beat me up, please listen to me until I have finished. I remember well the time when you taught me Greek grammar with the whip. Before falling asleep in my nightgown, my body was covered with weals. I still know how in the morning you made me repeat my lessons, shortly before going to school; in fear and despair I still had to learn at home after school had already started. How often did I vomit my breakfast while running the long way to school! Even the teachers sympathized with me and no longer punished me—I've had my share of shame and worry. And now not. Am I not younger and more courageous than you? Then let me live! I want to be rich and blessed!

THE FATHER: *(Scornfully.)* From what book is this coming? From what journalistic brain?

THE SON: I'm the heir, Father. Your money is my money, it is no longer yours. You've worked for it, but you have also lived. It's up to you now to find out what comes after this life—enjoy your generation! What you have, belongs to me, I'm born to possess it for myself. And I'm here.

THE FATHER: Hm. And what do you intend to do with my money?

THE SON: I will enter into the enormity of the world. Who knows when I must die. Just for one brief thundershower I want to hold in my fingers the potential of my life—I shall no more attain this happiness. The greatest, yes, the noblest lightning I will use to look beyond the borders for only when I have completely exhausted reality, I shall meet with all the wonders of the spirit. That's how I want to be. That's how I want to breathe. A good star will be with me. I will not perish from any half measures.

THE FATHER: You have come a long way, indeed! You let me see all your meanness. Give thanks to God that I am your father. With what effrontery have you spoken of me and my money! How shamelessly have you spoken of my death. I have been mistaken about you—you are bad—you are not of my kind. But I'm still your friend and not your enemy, therefore I punish you for this word as you deserve it. *(Comes close to him and slaps him briefly in the face.)*

THE SON: *(After a while.)* In this room, where the heaven of my childhood still is standing, you have not spared me of the most cruel things. You have slapped me in the face before this table and these books—and yet I am more than you! Prouder do I lift my face above your house and do not blush before your weakness. You hate in me only the one you are not. I triumph! Just continue to beat me up. Clarity comes over me, no tear, no rage. How different am I now and so much bigger than you! What happened to love, what to the bonds of our blood? Even enmity no longer exists. I see before me a man who has wounded my body. Yet from his body there once came a crystal determining my life. This is the inconceivable, the dark. Fate stepped in between us. Alright. I live longer than you. *(He staggers.)*

THE FATHER: You are trembling. Sit down. Don't you feel well? Do you want something?

THE SON: *(For a moment somewhat weak in his arms.)* Oh, I have such a big load on my heart.

THE FATHER: *(In a changed voice.)* I punished you because I had to. That's past now. Come. You don't feel well.

THE SON: When once I fell from a ladder and broke an arm, you took care of me. When my childish conscience beat because I had cheated a conductor you made him gifts and thus stopped my tears. Today I came to you in greater need and you beat me. It might be better if you release me from your arms. *(He gets up.)*

THE FATHER: You did not come in need, you came in disobedience. That's why I slapped you. You know me and you know what I am asking of my son.

THE SON: How can you move a word on your lips and say: That's how it is! Don't you see constantly death in the hospital, not knowing that all is different in the world!

THE FATHER: I am a man and I have gained experience which you have not. You are still a child.

THE SON: When God allows me to live, I can start anything. Why do you want to repudiate me for that? Haven't you also played on the flowering earth and had dreams which did not come true?

THE FATHER: I have done my duty; that to me was the important thing. And you make a monster out of me without giving a thought to the fact that I was standing at your cradle. You were loved. Believe me that even now I spend many a sleepless night on your account. What will become of you? What happened to the words of your childhood, to your pure and unaffected soul? You have become stubborn and you deride advice and help. And now I should help you while you come to me bleary-eyed and evil. Am I now supposed to trust you?

THE SON: You have become a stranger to me. I have nothing more in common with you. The good which you think is so easily attained, has not reached me in your rooms. You have brought me up within the limitations of your mentality. This was your choice. But now set me free!

THE FATHER: How much has the rottenness of our times already destroyed you in that you feel so troubled. Was I not right in keeping you away from everything ugly and mean? As I see with horror, you are fired by desires. What has spoiled your heart? As a physician I have protected you from the poisons of our time because I know of their dangers. In later life you will be grateful to me for just that. But how did it happen—why did they reach you nonetheless? From what canal did this rat break into your youth? My poor boy, you're so confused. Let us forget that. *(Puts a hand on his shoulder.)*

THE SON: *(Wiggling out.)* No, Father. I love my time and do not want your sympathy. There's only one thing I ask of you: justice! Don't make me doubt you in this respect too. My life is about to come over me. The time is here to say good-bye; therefore we stand before each other. No, I'm not ashamed of longing for all that is actual and beautiful. Out into the oceans of impatience, into the liberating light! No longer the dreariness of your house and the dailiness of your person. I feel it. I'm going forward toward a happy world. I will become its prophet.

THE FATHER: Are these your last words in the house which has fed and protected you for so many years? Who are you, smashing wantonly the noblest barrier between father and mother? Do you know what you leave behind and where you will be going? Fool that you are, who will give you food tomorrow? Who will help you in sorrow and ignorance? Am I already dead that you dare to speak to me in such a way?

THE SON: Yes, Father, for me you are dead. Your name has melted away. I do not know you any longer; you only live in the commandment. You've lost me in the snowfields of the breast. I tried to find you in the wind, in the cloud. I went on my knees before you, I loved you. You slapped my flaming face—then you tumbled into the abyss. I don't hold you. Soon you will be my only terrible enemy. I must gird for this fight: now both of us have only the will to power over our blood! One of us will be victorious!

THE FATHER: This is enough. For once, listen to me! Isn't there a breath of gratitude, some respect on your foaming lips? Don't you know who I am?

THE SON: Life has called on me to overcome you! I must accomplish it. A heaven that you do not know will help me.

THE FATHER: You are blasphemous!

THE SON: *(In a trembling voice.)* I will rather eat stones than your bread.

THE FATHER: Aren't you frightened by what you're saying?

THE SON: I'm not afraid of you. You are old, you will no longer walk all over me in jealous selfishness. Woe thee when you call your curse into the fields of this happiness—it would fall on you and your house! And when you drive me away with a thrashing—how did I once tremble before you in poor and homeless fright—I shall no longer see you, your tyrant's hand and your graying hair: only the powerfully falling light above me. Try to understand that I have floated away into the heights of another spirit. And let us part in peace.

THE FATHER: My son, there is no blessing over you. . . . What will happen if I were to let you go in your blindness? Let me warn you of the sweet worms of this melody. Don't you want to accompany me on my rounds in the hospital *(scornful):* there the ruddiness of your youth bows depravedly in foam and tumor, and what rose from your mouth gaily into the air, becomes madness in the sorrowful countryside of the decaying. Thus God breaks the wings of him who ran away in spite and pride. Do not in this hour repudiate my hand; who'll know whether ever again I'll offer it to you as cordially.

THE SON: In your hands people have died whose nearness has surrounded us. But what are all these dead against me, who lives in despair?! Had I been afflicted by cancer, you would have fulfilled my every wish. For a patient who is beyond help is still allowed to use a wheelchair to ride to the coast of the blue oceans. You the living—who saves you? You call up the horror from the graves; but only he on whose head the trumpet of death has sounded, may distrust beautiful happiness! I am rising from twenty years, from twenty caskets and breathe the first golden beam—you have committed the sin against life by teaching me to recognize the worm while I stood at the highest point. Crumble to dust in the catacombs, old time, rotting world! I do not follow you. In me there is a being to whom hope has become stronger than doubt. Where shall we be? In what direction shall we go?

THE FATHER: *(To the left, locking the door.)* In this.

THE SON: What does this mean?

THE FATHER: You will not leave this room. You are sick.

THE SON: Father!

THE FATHER: Not in vain have you called on the physician in me. Your case belongs to the medical magazines, you talk feverishly. I must keep you locked up long enough until I can return you in good conscience to my house. Food and drink will be brought to you. Now go to bed.

THE SON: And what's going to happen with me later on?

THE FATHER: Here my will still dominates. You will pass your school exam. I have fired your tutor. From now on I shall determine everything. In my last will I shall provide for a guardian to carry out my intentions should I die earlier . . .

THE SON: Thus hate until the grave!

THE FATHER: You finish your studies and then take up a profession. That's the way it will be for the future. If you acquiesce in my will, it'll be to your advantage. But if you act against me, then I'll repudiate you and you'll not be my son anymore. I would rather destroy my inheritance by my own hand than give it to one who brings shame on my name. Now you are informed. And now let's go to bed.

THE SON: Goodnight, Father.

THE FATHER: *(Walks toward the door, but returns once more.)* Turn over all the money you have with you.

THE SON: *(Does it.)* Here.

THE FATHER: *(Overcome by emotion.)* I'll come tomorrow to look after you. Sleep well! *(He leaves, locking the door from the outside. THE SON rests, immobile.)*

SCENE 3

THE SON: *(Alone. A bell rings in the house. He rushes toward the door. He rattles it. It does not yield. The bell rings again. Voices are heard, a visitor is being sent away. He staggers toward a chair, sits in the middle of the room. In the window the disk of the yellow moon.)* The moon is here, just as yesterday. I live too much. Send me your angel, God! Imprisoned, in bitter need—me, a slave in the rising light. *(Looking upward.)* You are lighted for me, tree full of candles. May I again listen to you at the room's edge, oh, what gift, oh, what gift! Why don't you come, you, my car? Do I have to suffer pain being so close to happiness? Could I only cry! Could I be born! *(In the window, in the light of the moon, the face of* THE FRIEND *becomes visible.)*

THE FRIEND: Don't lose heart.

THE SON: Who are you, face of light?

THE FRIEND: The doors are locked, a servant sent me away. The route is unusual.

THE SON: It's you! You love me! Oh, God, oh God!

THE FRIEND: *(Rises in the window to half his height.)* Am I coming at the right hour?

THE SON: Can any man still be my friend, now that I'm so deserted?

THE FRIEND: Have you forgotten that Beethoven is still alive? Don't you know anymore that we have sung the chorus from the Ninth Symphony? Didn't you want to embrace all people? On, my boy, it dawns. Fulfill your heart right to the moon's crust—let us stroll under the melody of joy as we once did when the lights in the concert hall went out and we were united into the night. The hour has come.

THE SON: What shall I do?

THE FRIEND: Flee!

THE SON: I am too poor, I have no money.

THE FRIEND: But in the closet there you have a tailcoat. Put it on. I will take you to a celebration. The train leaves in half an hour. Here take this mask. I'll expect you at the exit of the park. *(Gives him a black mask.)*

THE SON: It's a matter of life and death. When I'm discovered, I'm lost—my father will kill me. Is there a car available?

THE FRIEND: Many friends whom you do not know stand ready tonight to help you. They are waiting with guns behind the trees in the park.

THE SON: And whither shall we go into the night?

THE FRIEND: To life!

THE SON: How do I get out?

THE FRIEND: Leave silently through the window. We take you in our midst. Don't be afraid. *(He disappears.)*

SCENE 4

*(*THE SON *rushes to the closet and, from among his clothes, takes out the tailcoat. He takes off his jacket and begins to dress.*

Through the window the lights of the city become visible in the distance. Lilting, almost like waltz music in coffee houses, we hear from afar and softly in the wind, the Finale from the Ninth Symphony. Allegro assai vivace—alla marcia. Tenor solo and men's chorus):

> *Froh wie seine Sonnen fliegen*
> *Durch des Himmels praecht'gen Plan,*
> *Laufet, Brüder, eure Bahn,*
> *Freudig, wie ein Held zum Siegen.*

SCENE 5

(A key is turned in the lock. The door opens. THE FRÄULEIN *stands on the threshold, in her hands a candle and a tablet.* THE SON *and* THE FRÄULEIN *have returned to the formal "Sie.")*

THE FRÄULEIN: I bring the dinner.

THE SON: Oh, it's you, Fräulein. I have completely forgotten you.

THE FRÄULEIN: Your father went to bed.

THE SON: So much the better for him.

THE FRÄULEIN: *(Coming closer.)* What has happened?

THE SON: You see me in a black coat so that I can step in dignity out of this house. Yonder the lanterns are already lighted! Do you see the lights on the horizon? Do you hear music, waltz, and clarinet? The smell of exultant houses surrounds me. Tonight all the trains will take me into the immensely singing night.

THE FRÄULEIN: Has he slapped you?

THE SON: How can you still talk of him who faint-heartedly is decaying on his bed! Look into his face tomorrow—it will pale from helpless anger and rage. This hero in the family circle: a stroke of lightning from the ether has touched him. His power was great over waifs and waiters—now it is broken. The health insurance people adore him, I laugh at him. Farewell to him!

THE FRÄULEIN: Perhaps there is still light in his room. He can see you in the garden.

THE SON: His whip no longer reaches me. Below my crowd is awaiting me. Some are armed. Perhaps they share my feelings, then I will call upon them to liberate the young and noble in the world. Death to the fathers who despise us! *(For a few seconds* THE FRIEND'S *face reappears in the window, then vanishes again.)*

THE FRÄULEIN: Don't you want to eat something? The road is long.

THE SON: No, Fräulein, in this house I will not touch anything anymore. Soon I shall enjoy nectar and ambrosia in the laps of beloved women!

THE FRÄULEIN: *(In a trembling voice.)* Oh, dark and dangerous night!

THE SON: Don't be afraid. I march towards my star; I follow the law. Because the blood of the defiled slaves burns in my veins, I shall rise forcefully to a fight against all the prisons on earth. Like a criminal in the darkness, without any possessions, I leave through the fence. My house! This fire I carry away from you to pour it over people and cities. The chains are falling, I'm free! One step only, among the trees . . . Portal, how I love thee, and thee, the road, shimmering silvery to the awakening look! I'm no longer faint in heart. I know for whom I live. *(He has finished dressing himself. Stands before her.)*

THE FRÄULEIN: You have forgotten the tie. I will bind it for you. *(She comes close fastening the tie.)*

THE SON: *(Bends down to her hand, formally.)* Thank you, Fräulein. Good-bye! *(He jumps through the window, disappears. The lights are stronger. Music is heard. A train rolls by.)*

SCENE 6

THE FRÄULEIN: *(Alone at the window, bending down after him. She presses a small pillow close to herself.)*

He rushes to the park as if in flight
Toward the God who has his head adorned,
For him day and night live unmourned
And twelve white eagles follow his might!
Dawn will not bring him back,
As long as the world is in his bosom mounting,
As long as women and stars
Sweet friend, may happiness never lack!
Heaven's rich hour has transported me
From the small room away to the big sea.
The wave, the night heavily on me weigh:
Where's rest, where solace, where hope's ray?

Oh, could I be somebody, and something for him do
Instead, only this little pillow I will sew
On which rest will be given him each night:
May he be guarded, without me at his side.
But when his eye in golden air will roll,
Then I wish to be close to the one so dear,
Will watch eternally for the call
In darkness and unallayed tear.

(She bends over the pillow and begins to sew, wrapped up in tears.)

Act 3

SCENE 1

(A few hours later. Toward midnight. The anteroom to an auditorium. In the center a curtain is stretched, behind it, invisible to the onlooker, a lectern and the auditorium perspective. In the anteroom there are only a few pieces of furniture: easy chairs and a small table with glasses. On one wall hooks for clothing. Stage left and right small doors. The room leaves the impression as if a closed party were held before a meeting.)

CHERUBIM: *(In tailcoat, the text of a speech in his hand, strolling through the room. Von Tuchmeyer enters, also in tails.)* Is everything ready?

TUCHMEYER: Everything. How's your speech coming along?

CHERUBIM: I'm holding it in my hands. Are the lights on in the hall? Is a glass of water on my table?

TUCHMEYER: *(Lifting the curtain a little.)* You can convince yourself: everything has been taken care of. Within twenty minutes, exactly at midnight, the chairs will be occupied. I understand many students will be coming. The hour has been well chosen. Those we want to reach will appear in large numbers. They expect the utmost from you! And who, in the middle of the night, is not burning with the desire to get revelations?

CHERUBIM: And the police?

TUCHMEYER: We are among ourselves. I have announced that we are celebrating the anniversary of our club "For the Survival of Joy." I was told if guests were to come, it is up to them. You need not be concerned.

CHERUBIM: I shall become very political and rabble rousing. Friend, my breast is full of new ideas which I will announce for the first time. I do not doubt my success! If ever, then tonight I will establish with you my "League for the Reorganization of Life." I tell you, things will be moving in an anarchistic way. That's why there should be continuous music while I talk. People should drink champagne, and those who want to dance should do so. Are we all assembled?

TUCHMEYER: *(Pulling a telegram from his pocket.)* Just now The Friend wired me that he'll be here within a few minutes. An important matter led him back. Thus we shall hear from him before the festivities get underway.

CHERUBIM: Since when do you have this news?

TUCHMEYER: For about two hours. It came from his home town. Yesterday he left here without saying good-bye. Perhaps he will bring new friends with him.

CHERUBIM: Between you and me, Tuchmeyer, haven't you noticed something in him?

TUCHMEYER: What do you mean?

CHERUBIM: I'm afraid of his shifty ways. He is not one of those who is willing to sacrifice everything for an idea.

TUCHMEYER: I have never noticed any doubts in him. On the contrary, he belongs to us wholeheartedly. How did you get that notion?

CHERUBIM: His sudden departure worries me. What may have motivated him? Did he want to pass over our celebration? Doesn't he know how important it is?

TUCHMEYER: He is one of those critical temperaments who always strive for the very opposite of themselves. He is his own contradiction, but therein lies the affirmation of his nature. Just like you I value in him something spiritual which is hidden. That's why I subordinate him unconditionally to you for you have the courage to be an exhibitionist. You are the representative ideal for our ideas, he is their counterpoint. You need each other if something is to be accomplished.

CHERUBIM: His departure is on my mind. He knows what's at stake.

TUCHMEYER: You forget his inhibitions. Before doing something, he needs to argue with himself. You live upon inspirations, he hates them. And he does not care for loud celebrations. But he is indispensable to us—the way we have grown together. Perhaps he is the strongest—the greatest he certainly is not.

CHERUBIM: Sometimes I have openly trembled before him as if he were a rival. I say that openly. But tonight, for the first time, I am totally superior to him. Whether he comes or not—I do not feel any anxiety anymore. My will is firm.

TUCHMEYER: Soon you will be standing in the hall!

CHERUBIM: Let us make good use of the time until then. I think I must talk to you. For you, the son of a privy counselor, you have lavished your inheritance on us. With you we rise and fall. My dear Tuchmeyer: to the devil with your father had he acquired something which in the long run would have benefited his son less than a good factory or mine. Therefore I keep you informed about all fluctuations to which our capital is subjected. Tonight I believe that I have achieved a satisfactory balance.

TUCHMEYER: Dear Cherubim, as long as my father lived, I sat in his office as a little clerk day after day and to me his death was a cheerful matter. Only since we became acquainted, do I know that one can live in spite of his money: that's why my belief in you is boundless. My father let me work for him and he cheated me as any little merchant in Poland. Had he not died at the right time when I detected this dirty slavery, I think I would have . . . well, etcetera. Even today I still think squeamishly of this paternal instrument with the double entry bookkeeping, of this Jewish jobber, who has spoiled my most beautiful years. Therefore I ask you: don't speak to me about balances; else I get mad!

CHERUBIM: I feel the responsibility—more than you realize. I know you are unable to redeem a note, and if you had to certify bliss with your signature, you'd rather oversleep. You are wonderful but you're unmindful of values. I don't want you to be poor some day. Your fortune finances our idea. Where would we be without you? Poor wretches without even a place to hold discussions. I have seduced you to a generosity which some day you may come to rue. No, don't blush—that's how it is. By the way, soon I will speak quite differently in the hall. Here we are only concerned with ourselves, therefore we speak under four eyes.

TUCHMEYER: To all that you tell me, I shall always answer. I would be quite unhappy if I were unable to return the dumb money, which my father has scraped together, to an idea common to people. It is only just that something which has been acquired without joy and to which so much misfortune clings, makes joy again! I'm literally burning for unsuspected sensations which, in spite of all the idiots, will materialize in this world! And if we have to accept the Ten Commandments, then one of them would be for me to extinguish the memory of my father among the living. Besides, I'm quite an egotist and would have fun doing so.

CHERUBIM: Well, then, listen to me. Just a year ago, we met accidentally—You, The Friend, the Prince, and me, in a plain bar. With a few libertines, who made us pass the intervals between nights of discussion with pleasantries, we got together in a club, naming it "For the Survival of Joy." Since then we met frequently and celebrated some orgies. But I ask you now: what has happened? No dogma was proclaimed, but a couple of youths with small allowances and a few unsatisfied women have joined us—interrupt me if I am wrong. It is unnecessary for us to compete with the stars, to wage revolution in China or to make a discovery in the nervous system of frogs—all of this we are unable to do. We have the ambition not to do it. But it is important to enthuse those, who will soon be sitting in the hall, in something. It should be made clear to them that during the last twelve months none of us died. And that is much! Think of what life is like!

TUCHMEYER: Is that a contradiction to this year?

CHERUBIM: It is a contradiction. Listen to me to the end: we may have lived during those twelve months—but we do not know for what purpose. Life in itself is not enough. This question I intend to answer tonight: we live for us! And I shall raise this part of my speech to an immense pathos; we want to make a sacrifice to death which has spared us!

TUCHMEYER: Not out of fear of the audience but out of curiosity: what is the sacrifice going to be?

CHERUBIM: By toppling the god of the weak and the deserted from his throne. In his place we raise the trombone of friendship: our heart. For we, people of today, live for the untold new! We are destined for each other. Thus let us correct the small laws of creation. Fight, deprivation and the limits of imperfect nature— let us have the courage to brutalize our ego in the world!

SCENE 2

(The curtain opens in the center. PRINCE SCHEITEL, in overcoat and tails, enters.)

SCHEITEL: Good evening, gentlemen! Never mind. *(He takes off the overcoat.)*

CHERUBIM: *(Toward him.)* Prince Scheitel, it's you! You are coming at the right moment. We're discussing the possibilities for a new religion. Tonight I'll attempt a coup d'etat.

TUCHMEYER: Prince, we admire your faithfulness. You bring us the ultimate sacrifice, for you the most dangerous. How did you succeed in getting away from your father, the sovereign, for tonight? We did not expect you anymore.

SCHEITEL: Gentlemen, why all this balderdash? One learns here too. The other day I saw a play about a villain, the disguised story of my cousin the Duke. You know he had an affair with a singer, and this story was adapted for a Paris theater. I did exactly what he did: I mixed a sleeping potion into my aide-de-camp's glass and disappeared behind a curtain. Notice that aide-de-camps always have to drink! Now I feel quite under the spell of a bad novel. Too bad that there is no woman around here. But you talk of something else. Please go on.

CHERUBIM: *(Cordially.)* Dear Prince! Right now we keep busy listing all our profits at the stock market. You could not be missing. I admit that sometimes I distrusted you slightly because of your well-cared appearance. Now I realize how right you were. Your quiet charm often threw us into the sphere of elegance. From you we received the fame of the monocle in the eye and the crown of silent salute when once you drove by, unrecognized as the prince, in a roll of drums. Your friendship was the greatest because it was indeed the most difficult.

SCHEITEL: But gentlemen, you make me blush! You are much more important and you have better chances than I have in my position. Unfortunately, luxury on the thrones has not reached as far as the mind, or else I would be the first one to come out for a republic. I have come to you because I joyfully anticipate this evening—and because I am a member of your Club for the Survival of Joy! Gentlemen, I still feel that this is a good club. Besides, I would not want to be absent on such an important occasion—even though I am only backstage.

TUCHMEYER: How did you get here?

SCHEITEL: In accordance with my rank, but on foot. When I climbed up the stairs, a couple of cars arrived and some persons already used the checkroom. These people are so nice—we shall have a great audience. Von Tuchmeyer, you must keep me company behind the curtain where we want to watch the success. I would love to sing the National Anthem; may God keep my father alive so that I may remain your friend for a long time. When he dies, I must ascend to the throne, if only on account of the newspapers. There is nothing I can do about it. In principle, I shall not take part in any coup since I have to be considerate of the brains of my descendants. You, gentlemen, are able to change the world at any time. Out of greater wisdom I have to leave it the way it is.

CHERUBIM: And we will make use of this right, Prince! Having reconciled ourselves to the idea that we are less important in this world, we want to achieve at least the highest possible development. I have the means for it and I shall apply them. Have trust in me. (*They sit down, smoking cigarettes. With oratorical emotion.*) Down in the hall I shall call everyone by his name. He may take his glass of champagne and stand next to me, and I shall say to him, you live—feel that you are happy. And then I shall assemble around me at the lectern, surrounded by women like Apollo in the Valley of Edymion, cheerfulness. You know Adrienne, with her sweet face? Think of that woman with her radiating shoulders! I will bend over her and pronounce that all men are born to happiness. And I wonder whether they will not cheer me, despite fear and confusion, and whether amongst us there is a traitor.

SCHEITEL: Bravo! Most certainly a farce in the view of statistics, but very amusing. Besides your lectern you'll find a basket with flowers. I had them placed there for you. Perhaps at that point you will throw the roses to the audience!

CHERUBIM: Yes, I am in favor of such an effect. You may hear it now: A League for Life Propaganda—therefore I must preach unscrupulous joy. Enjoy the smell of the rose without thorns. Put up tables at which one only wins and never loses! Bring women who love all of us! Long live our beautifully worldly feeling!

SCENE 3

(Through the door suddenly enters:)

THE FRIEND: You are lying, Cherubim. (*All turn around, terrified. He pulls off his mask, standing before them in tails.*)

CHERUBIM: Oh, it's you!

THE FRIEND: Yes, I confess my guilt: I listened at the door. No repetition is necessary. I heard everything. And I declare war on you!

CHERUBIM: What does this mean?

THE FRIEND: This means: in ten minutes the hall will be crowded but you will not give a speech tonight.

CHERUBIM: Are you mad? I must talk. Whence this tone?

THE FRIEND: You will find out. Of course, I cannot prevent you from talking, but then I will speak after you.

CHERUBIM: *(Pale.)* What are you going to talk about?

THE FRIEND: About truth, my dear. You have been very diligent, one must say. Except, I'm afraid, this time your tricks will fail you.

CHERUBIM: My tricks . . . ?

THE FRIEND: And the roses, my friend. Watch out they are not transformed into rotten eggs which are going to land on your head. *(They all surround him.)*

CHERUBIM: Say, what has brought about your change within twenty-four hours?

THE FRIEND: It seems you're all tense. The hour needs brevity. Cherubim! This beautiful name you have given to yourself. Until now I did not think much to pronounce this name in its full sound. Now I am revolted. I cannot look into your eyes anymore. How did you dare to use this name of the angel! And indeed: do you intend to continue preaching to these infatuated people intoxication and drunkenness? Doesn't anything in you revolt against the lie? Deceived admiration which we paid to your curly head! You who proclaim God on earth—how shallow is your empire!

CHERUBIM: *(Jumping back with all signs of horror.)* A leper is among us!

THE FRIEND: *(In great seriousness.)* No, but one who has begun to recognize the thorns. What are you enjoying? What have you accomplished? Have you done in abundance something good or bad which has opened your eyes? Did you cry when, after a wasted night, news of a catastrophe appeared in the newspaper? Have you killed one of your enemies? And even when you felt the impotence of all that is earthly—was that of any help to you? What good is this gesture, this loud-mouthed baroque? I am revolted. You intended to fly off in cheerfulness and you are only deeper in morass. And you call this a new program?

TUCHMEYER: Don't listen to him. He is mad!

THE FRIEND: Herr von Tuchmeyer! It's true: you have sacrificed your inheritance to the idea of joy—but what if that idea was a fallacy? Who proves to you the correctness of an action? Your money and your soul are in this club—what would you say if you live for only a ridiculous thing? Yes, you childish minds: this proof is not difficult to produce in view of such heroes! If one has reached the end of his wisdom, the antithesis usually sets in. With one word: why are you still alive? Your aim has been achieved. Why don't you disappear? *(Nobody answers him.)* Your silence speaks loudly. Why didn't those questions cross your minds? What have you really pondered? Defend yourself! Is there an error in my presentation? Now, you monuments of nothing, go into your house of cards.

CHERUBIM: I only want to say one thing against you, dearest friend: how painful it would be if you too were away from us, in the fields beyond this laughing world!

THE FRIEND: Does that say anything against me? Is it at all necessary to live? And does it justify your masquerade? I am here to prevent that others, who feel bad, share your joy. To possess joy is to kill. I will eradicate that bacillus! Therefore don't be cheerful about me. It is still too early.

TUCHMEYER: What madness to talk against the world because you are alive! A trap for your mind which we have so much admired. You have stumbled miserably. A penitent always seems funny. Go into a monastery or, if the part of a clown is more appropriate to you, join an American circus.

THE FRIEND: Dear sir, for a year now I have, together with you, become frail—that's why I do neither the one nor the other. But as you will understand, I have the desire to liberate myself from you—you would do the same thing if you were in my place. Therefore let me speak!

CHERUBIM: In short: what do you want?

THE FRIEND: To convince those over there that there is no use.

CHERUBIM: *(Rushing toward him.)* You will not do that!

THE FRIEND: Step back! Is this your face? Now you reveal yourself to me: I thought your will is so firm! Why, then, don't you dare to fight? Let both of us talk, one after the other—or did you secretly already give in? Then have the courage to confess it and leave quietly. Why all this noise?

CHERUBIM: Traitor! Out with you! *(He and* TUCHMEYER *push him against the door.)*

SCHEITEL: *(Seizing them by the arm.)* Gentlemen, stop this! Let me say a word too. Are we here in parliament? Let everybody do what he wants. I have nothing at all against rebels and anti-monarchists. And I say it openly: I put myself on the side of the rebels—I feel they are right! He asked: why? His questioning impresses me. Can you give him an answer?

CHERUBIM: *(Drying his front.)* My God, yes—but not today! This paradoxical fluff—where everything is at stake.

SCHEITEL: Forget about the stakes. He who is stronger will be victorious. I don't believe in either of you. You want something—then battle for it! I can't help it, but there he is right. I consider it irrelevant to actions of any kind. But when it happens, it should be done honestly. You, Cherubim, don't impress me any longer as a man certain of himself.

CHERUBIM: Prince, I haven't worked for nothing. I cannot fight because I am conditioned to all registers of enthusiasm. If something goes wrong now, everything will tumble . . .

SCHEITEL: Let it tumble! One thing tumbles after the other! You do not have to husband your mental gifts: be glad about that. Nothing is yet lost—or did you seriously believe in yourself? Just before you have talked of your relevance. Then you have lied! You have subjected yourself to the eternally new—do it now!

CHERUBIM: *(In despair.)* No, I don't. And I don't want to. I cannot.

THE FRIEND: *(Coming closer.)* Cherubim, for the last time this blasphemous name and then into the nameless tent. Something bigger than you has entered here—fall into line. You've had your share of the pink star, do not any longer attach a false glitter to the urn. You have wasted all your heart and for that we loved you. That you erred was unimportant: you have lived, you have not achieved the heights. Nonetheless *(tries to grasp his hand)* thank you!

CHERUBIM: *(Pushes him away.)* I don't want your gratitude. I still live! I take up the fight. *(He straightens up.)* Where are my friends? Let's see whether they all desert me. *(He looks around.)*

TUCHMEYER: *(Walking towards him.)* I stay with you.

THE FRIEND: Fine. You want me to pull the mask off your face in front of all. I shall not spare you. Fight to the end. If you fall, you will be trampled upon—and fall you will. *(The musicians in the hall begin to tune their instruments. Light and the noise of those who have already arrived.)* Do you hear the music? Say—are you not afraid? Watch out—I'll talk against everything—and against you. Your women and your curl will be of no avail. I know the purposes of roses and champagne! When I talk, there'll be no fooling around. I shall prove the emptiness of your arguments—I know all your ins and outs! I will bring the howitzers of doubt into play: just watch out that not all of your joys will burst like air bubbles in view of such salute. My son, the hour of judgment approaches; I too am armed with fire. *(Rousing audience in the hall.)* Are you listening! Are you listening! Already you are pale. Not an earthquake, just a little word will destroy your heaven. I'll search out the demons from all corners and let them waltz around. I'll make a death's head out of your face. I'll uncover you just as an accountant uncovers graft. They'll stone you, my friend!

(Cherubim, trembling, grabs a bottle of champagne and drinks.)

THE FRIEND: You drink? Courage! You might stammer. You don't want to be spared—fine, I'm wicked enough to call the police. I'll have you arrested for incitement to lewdness! Then you may ponder for a while all your nonsense. Why should you not bear the consequences of what you are teaching? Better people than you have died on the cross.

SCHEITEL: Gracious goodness, one does not talk like that of my state. Please, that's no fun. If the police are really coming, I could not help you, I'm not yet of age. What are your thoughts?

THE FRIEND: In that case you disappear through the emergency exit.

TUCHMEYER: *(With cold composure.)* As long as I am here, nothing is going to happen.

THE FRIEND: Herr von Tuchmeyer, I know you have money. Others have it too. That does not make you worse than others—but beware of blunders. By the way, you will always come out alright; just don't make others comrades of your subaltern feelings. You may waste your money without qualms, some day it will roll again on your shoulders. But what good is this world of Monte Carlos and operettas to us? Aren't we older at every well and does not a new darkness surround us? Are we alive only to use this word continuously in barracks? To hell with such jokes! I hate all people who while dying still see the green in the mirrors of the trees. All those who have not felt aversion, despair, and the penetrating risk in running away quietly, should be hanged. It must be recognized that we approach eternity through danger. What can we make of the cock's crow of luck! Learn to despise yourself! God punishes him who has too much enjoyment.

TUCHMEYER: Haven't you exchanged with us enthusiastically vows of friendship? Why do you leave us? You commit perjury. I am ashamed of you.

THE FRIEND: Dear Tuchmeyer, forget about the crusade. You may still be blessed with champagne and embraces. We cannot do so any longer. Permit us to think about it. We do not always stay at the age of twenty, and there are hardly any geniuses here *(he turns toward the* PRINCE*)* with the exception of you, Majesty. I say it for the last time: I am rotten and I have the courage to admit it publicly today. Whoever may talk before or after me: I shall prove the opposite. And if you don't believe me, come closer: my heart does not beat, I have barely more than eighty beats of the pulse per minute. *(He opens his jacket slightly. Renewed applause from the hall, then quiet. The overture begins.)* I hear the overture already. A good arrangement. *(To* CHERUBIM.*)* Prepare your wrists. Things get started.

CHERUBIM: *(Breathing heavily across the table.)* Let's agree on a compromise. I will not speak. But you won't speak either.

THE FRIEND: Nothing. No compromise. One of us will speak.

CHERUBIM: That means you want a scandal . . .

THE FRIEND: I leave you a way out: a third person will speak.

CHERUBIM: Who is this third one?

THE FRIEND: You agree? Decide for yourself!

CHERUBIM: My beautiful, my brilliant work. . . .

TUCHMEYER: Don't do it. I'll stand by you.

CHERUBIM: *(As if awakened by this voice, stares at him.)* I yield. I save your money!

THE FRIEND: Now I get to the bottom, old chap! You secure for yourself the capital. Good luck! We don't need it. You have not

spared yourself this final effect. You a fighter in God's hand!
Now, Iscariot and Company, speak up again: may God grant
you faithfulness, and comfort your widow.

TUCHMEYER: Stop it; I am still here! Who is the traitor around
here? You, Cherubim, have cowardly deserted your greatness.
And you, who have you become all of a sudden? Now the
threads have been torn—I hesitate too—in whom should I believe? Was my money and, worse, was my belief in vain? Does
my dead father thus avenge himself? Is this a way to bankruptcy?
*(The overture ends. Loud applause. The noise from the hall in-
creases.)* The first number is over. Fast now! Things must go on.
I start to become my own stage director. We cannot very well
stop in the middle of the program . . . after the first number. *(In
despair to the* PRINCE) Prince, say something! Now comes the
main thing. When nothing happens, the people will kill us . . .
You are silent too? There is no emergency exit here. Doesn't
anybody give a sign???

THE FRIEND: *(Raising one arm.)* Now all of you be quiet—not a
single word. Not one word, do you understand me? I give you
the sign. *(Goes to a door, opens it, calling.)* Come on, now!

SCENE 4

(THE SON, wearing a black mask and tails, enters.)

THE FRIEND: *(Guides THE SON, who does not see, hypnotically,
without even touching him with his fingers.)* Breathe! There are
human beings here! The ride is over. No more the fearful confinement on the train. Nobody pursues you. Here you will live.
*(He lifts THE SON's mask for a moment, looking into his vision-
ary face.)* Raise your face! Earth rises—here there are no guards
to beat you up. *(He leads him in front of the curtain, close to
the hall.)* Do you hear them there? They wait for you. Talk to
them. Evoke the pains of your childhood! Tell them what you
have suffered! Call for their help, call on them for a fight! *(Soft
music from the hall, as at the end of act 2 from the Ninth Symphony.)* What do you see?

THE SON: *(Under the spell, remote and lost.)* What brilliance!
What brilliance! Eye, you're shining! Here it is beautiful. Here
the star is greeting me.

THE FRIEND: Whom do you see?

THE SON: *(With groping arms.)* When we had a celebration, I was allowed as a child to appear before the ladies during the dessert. Now I stand anew among ice cream and fruits, under the brilliant chandelier. Ladies and gentlemen—I know you—an awkward boy says hello to you. *(He bows slowly.)* I have seen their traces at night! Oh, that I am allowed to be with them. I come from the lightless ether, one of the poorest, yet I am here. That I can partake of such a miracle!

THE FRIEND: *(Pulls open the curtain and pushes THE SON onto the lectern in the hall.)* Now talk to them. No longer a dead man—you are free!

SCENE 5

(Roaring noise in the hall, the music stops. Briefly, the lighted hall with many people is seen. A long sound of expectation, surprise and astonishment is heard, then quiet.)

THE FRIEND: *(Muted.)* Stand next to the curtain, Tuchmeyer, and listen! *(He rushes forward as if he were directing invisibly, and from behind the curtain, a choir.)* Let us all take part in this act. Now everything depends on ... *(The voice of the speaker is heard but the word cannot be made out. In the anteroom there is an air of great excitability.)* There stands a man who in twenty years has suffered more than we have enjoyed in one year. That's why God has sent him ... *(Unrest in the hall.)* What's the matter?

TUCHMEYER: He pulls off his mask. His eyes cannot see anything yet. He speaks of his childhood. Many cannot understand him ... Now he talks louder. A few get up and come closer.

THE FRIEND: *(Clenching his hands.)* Does he move his hands?

TUCHMEYER: No—yes—now.

THE FRIEND: *(Opening his arms.)* ... does he stretch them out like this?

TUCHMEYER: He is mad. He says that he takes upon himself the torment of the childhood of all of us.

THE FRIEND: He speaks the truth! Go on, what does he say?

TUCHMEYER: Now he has jumped down from the lectern. He stands among the people. He says: we all have suffered from our fathers—in basements and attics—he speaks about despair and suicide.

THE FRIEND: *(Bending forward, all his muscles tense.)* May the spirit assist him! *(He moves his hands and the features of his face with magic force.)* Do you listen! Tell it to them! *(A terrible will works within him to force the speaker under his thoughts.)*

TUCHMEYER: There will be a disaster. He says: the fathers who torture us should all be brought to justice! The audience is delirious . . . *(Tremendous tumult in the hall.)*

CHERUBIM AND SCHEITEL: *(Left and right at the curtain.)* All in revolt! They close in on him. The chairs are moving, the tables . . .

CHERUBIM: *(Screaming hysterically.)* Bravo! Marvelous!

THE FRIEND: *(In front.)* Quiet! *(He draws a gun from his pocket.)* I'll kill him if he loses!

TUCHMEYER: *(At the curtain.)* There—now—

THE FRIEND: *(His back toward the hall, without turning.)* What?

TUCHMEYER: He tears off his clothing. He bares his chest. He shows the weals from his father's beatings—the scars! Now he is surrounded by so many that no longer can he be seen. Now—they grasp his hands—they hail him—

THE FRIEND: *(Triumphant.)* Now he is victor! Now he has achieved it! *(He puts his gun in a pocket, turning around. In the hall roaring applause and cheering.)*

TUCHMEYER: They carry him on their shoulders. The students carry him!

THE FRIEND: What does he say?

TUCHMEYER: He calls for a fight against all fathers—he preaches liberty—"We must help ourselves, for nobody helps us." They kiss his hands—what a tumult! They carry him on their shoulders out of the hall! *(More cheering.)*

THE FRIEND: He has established The League of the Young against the World! Everybody should add his name to the list!

TUCHMEYER: *(Tearing his notebook in two.)* All should register. My father does not live anymore. Today he died a second time. *(He throws pages on the table.)*

CHERUBIM: Death to the dead! My father does not send me money anymore. *(In a loud voice.)* I sign up!

THE FRIEND: *(To SCHEITEL.)* And what does Your Majesty think? *(He holds a list close to him.)*

SCHEITEL: Give it to me!

THE FRIEND: This is called revolution, Brother Prince!

SCHEITEL: *(Ecstatically jumps on a table, putting up his arms similar to the beacon of the Statue of Liberty.)* Gentlemen, we are a generation. We will never be as young as we are now. There are many idiots—but, oh hell, we live longer! *(Standing on the table he intones the Marseillaise. The others join in, also some voices from the hall.)*

ALL:

> *Aux armes, citoyens!*
> *Formez vos bataillons!*
> *Marchons! Marchons!*

Act 4

SCENE 1

(The next morning. A hotel room in the style of a chambre garnie, *but without bed. Breakfast is served on the table.* ADRIENNE *makes her hair in front of a mirror.* THE SON, *slack in his tailcoat.)*

THE SON: Now that you comb your hair, it occurs to me that you must have made love to many men before me.

ADRIENNE: Why?

THE SON: I am tortured by a strange vanity.

ADRIENNE: *(Continues combing.)* I love you.

THE SON: But you have taken money from me!

ADRIENNE: And you? Are you living off the air? Haven't you also taken money for your speech last night? We all must eat.

THE SON: That's true. I took the money. I have performed for it an act from my childhood.

ADRIENNE: It's no one's concern with whom I will sleep tomorrow. I am a woman and cannot do anything else.

THE SON: I have been lifted unto shoulders. I must reflect about it, then it becomes clear to me. I am in another world.

ADRIENNE: You have made revolution yesterday? Don't you remember? Perhaps there are already reports in the paper.

THE SON: What happened eight hours ago is already history for me. Yesterday I still crammed history.

ADRIENNE: *(Wistfully.)* There you can see how revolutions come about!

THE SON: *(Smiling.)* No, you are wrong. I am not that clever. I am not an actor. I was genuine.

ADRIENNE: You don't know anymore what you did?

THE SON: I remember, we took a car driving toward the outskirts. I saw you only fleetingly. You seemed very beautiful to me. My God, I have completely forgotten to thank the students. They carried me around in the rain for about half an hour. Somebody pressed money into my hand.

ADRIENNE: Is it much?

THE SON: It'll be enough.

ADRIENNE: You come from a distinguished family. It is obvious from your underwear.

THE SON: How does this occur to you?

ADRIENNE: My boy. You are inexperienced in love and don't know anything about the most beautiful games. You still need an education. A man of your station must have it.

THE SON: I thought this comes by itself.

ADRIENNE: Men are not that intelligent. Some day you will want to marry. You might be taken in badly, your wife will deceive you because you do not know anything.

THE SON: I did not know that. What is to be done?

ADRIENNE: Do you want to learn from me? I'll teach you everything there is to know. And you'll become very clever.

THE SON: My father did not even teach me what to do after making love. This at least would have been his duty.

ADRIENNE: Fathers are ashamed before their sons. It's always been like that. Why aren't the sons sent to us? They are sent to universities.

THE SON: How much disgust and misfortune could be prevented if only a father were moral!

ADRIENNE: Instead we are being pursued by the moral squad!

THE SON: I understand. You begin to play a part. One has to demand from one's father to lead us with a free heart to the whore. . . . A new goal for our League. I will mention it in my next speech. *(He runs around excitedly.)*

ADRIENNE: *(Finishing her hair.)* In the meantime, let's have breakfast. *(They sit down.)* Have you never before had breakfast with a lady after the first night?

THE SON: Never. Why?

ADRIENNE: You are awkward. All have buttoned my blouse. You don't know the simplest rule of etiquette.

THE SON: I am a beginner in love: this I realize fearfully. But the art is great, and a young man must know about it before doing advanced math. I accept your proposal. Teach me! I admire you: you know so much more than I do. When last night we went up the stairs, passing by the rude waiters—I was so anxious. We have been wandering through the miracles of life—from all the rooms of this ill-reputed hotel streams poured forth, dark and subconscious ones. . . .

ADRIENNE: Pass me the butter!

THE SON: Yes, and how you took the overcoat and threw it on the bed—I shall not forget it. So naturally, so clearly. Now I know how to ask for a candle which is missing.

ADRIENNE: Next time you shouldn't be so uneasy.

THE SON: For the first time I saw somebody disrobe. And to savor this slowly! How beautiful is a money deal. We are all among ourselves.

ADRIENNE: Did you like me?

THE SON: First blue, then pink; the black of the stockings? I liked the laces very much.

ADRIENNE: And me?

THE SON: I do not remember how you looked.

ADRIENNE: (*With great composure, taking another slice of bread.*) You don't love me yet.

THE SON: Seriously—don't be mad at me. I was disappointed. How prosaic is a body and quite different from what one imagines. Adrienne, you lived for me when you left the car and entered the corridor. How you know everything in a strange house! You are a heroine! Without you I would have crushed to the earth in shame! In faded velvet at the bannister—I think it is just as charming to walk across gold fields and into Malaysian joints. I have not noticed any longer something terrestrial in your feet!

ADRIENNE: Some men love my feet only. I have to dance naked for them on the carpet!

THE SON: Whither does this word lead to? What a magic circle! In the panopticum there once was a lady with blue tattoes— there are many things one knows nevertheless.

ADRIENNE: Why haven't you slept?

THE SON: I was not tired. I loved you so much in the dawn, resting on the same bed with you when you no longer felt anything for me. I believe that only then did I love you completely.

ADRIENNE: *(With quiet superiority.)* You can't do it yet. But you will learn it.

THE SON: I am eager to learn this art. What fears are rising to take what is being offered to you! One has to overcome them.

ADRIENNE: I have lost my gloves. Give me a new pair!

THE SON: *(Putting a gold coin on the table.)* I don't know the price of gloves.

ADRIENNE: That's too much. I'll bring you some of it back. *(Putting on her hat.)*

THE SON: Where are you going?

ADRIENNE: Home, to change.

THE SON: When will you be coming back?

ADRIENNE: Should I fetch you?

THE SON: I shall be waiting for you.

ADRIENNE: Do you have some small change for the trolley?

THE SON: *(Gives it to her.)* Do you have any siblings?

ADRIENNE: Let's not talk about this. My sisters are decent girls.

THE SON: It's strange to think of that.

ADRIENNE: Why do you want to know?

THE SON: I am looking for someone equivalent to my weakness. You are too superior to me.

ADRIENNE: I'm not losing my balance that fast!

THE SON: I hate everybody who knows about my condition. I can understand a man killing a woman who sees through him.

ADRIENNE: But Bubi! Who talks about such things at your age!

THE SON: You are awakening my slumbering talents. Since I know you, I see certain things in myself clearer. The delight at your sex stimulates thinking. You always find a way to yourself.

ADRIENNE: *(Confidently.)* Tonight there is dancing at the Piccadilly. I'll introduce you! Afterward we go to a bar. *(She now wears hat and overcoat.)*

THE SON: *(Watching her slim figure.)* "Toréador, en garde. . . ."

ADRIENNE: Good-bye, Bubi!

THE SON: *(Kisses her hand gentlemanlike.)* Good-bye, Madame! *(She exits, waving to him.)*

SCENE 2

(Lighting a cigarette, THE SON walks with long steps through the room. He deposits the ashes on a plate. THE FRIEND enters.)

THE FRIEND: Good morning.

THE SON: You are here already?

THE FRIEND: You don't seem happy to see me?

THE SON: *(Embarrassed.)* Oh, yes—what's the time?

THE FRIEND: It's eleven o'clock. You have just had breakfast? At home you usually do not get up at such a late hour.

THE SON: I need a new suit. How do I get one?

THE FRIEND: Listen, I just saw sweet Adrienne leave.

THE SON: I love her.

THE FRIEND: No, you're wrong.

THE SON: She will teach me.

THE FRIEND: I didn't mean that. What will she teach you? You may just as well jump that grade—you are preparing for better things. To take seriously a woman of her kind is not quite worthy of you. You will get into a conflict with the doctors. I advise against it.

THE SON: It tickles me to experience a new danger. I'm really mad about her.

THE FRIEND: Soon you'll have enough of her.

THE SON: In what area?

THE FRIEND: Do you forget that your father may pick you up any moment now. You are not yet of age, my son.

THE SON: Now that I enjoy life for the first time, back into slavery? Never.

THE FRIEND: Don't call that trivial situation life. A dull night with a woman—and you are not even disappointed? You were never as shallow as with this woman. Each one of your mad words last night was greater. I have come to meet a prophet and find a little fugitive who is in love. You play a satire on yourself! Your Fräulein in your father's house was tremendous. But this whore, what a stupid dummy!

THE SON: In my life she is at least as important as you are.

THE FRIEND: Let's be serious. If you could see your little feelings under a magnifying glass, you would be astonished to find how it's crawling with lice.

THE SON: But I don't want to see it. I tell you, she will pick me up here and that's it.

THE FRIEND: Then be happy. *(He takes his hat.)*

THE SON: Where to?

THE FRIEND: I leave you to the whore. I feel sorry for you.

THE SON: Are you mad? Is that a way to leave the room?

THE FRIEND: No, my boy. It's either—or. Pimps are born every day.

THE SON: After so many stations I finally want to do something completely.

THE FRIEND: You have this opportunity.

THE SON: And how?

THE FRIEND: When is the rendezvous?

THE SON: In half an hour.

THE FRIEND: Then we can talk for twenty minutes. Let's sit down. (*They sit across from each other.*) You admire that girl? She may be trained and quite efficient in her field, I admit. That's much. But haven't you done something a few hours ago? Man, you were standing in a European hall—think of that! What fame rests upon your shoulders? Do you think it is that easy to shake off responsibility? Then you deserve to be hanged. He who tosses an idea into the world and does not see it through, should die in the fires of hell. There is only one thing I recognize unconditionally as having a right to exist—the action. And how do you now stand here? They saw you from out front, Prometheus, and now they see your behind—nightingale and simple-minded fellow! Somebody should hold up your trousers.

THE SON: What are we talking about? Of your action, not of mine. You bear the responsibility for me—I was under your spell, I know. Why didn't you say all this yourself? Above all, answer this!

THE FRIEND: They know me, unfortunately. Too often have I shared their need. I'm no orator. The flame is denied to me; in the end I would only talk against myself. But you own their souls. I don't know why, but you do. It's the greatest power—and you don't use it. That's enough to drive me mad. First I get you out of your cage and for two hours you are the embodiment of the force of my ideas. But already you betray me and hide behind the instincts of the mob.

THE SON: When today in the dawn I made peace with myself, I also recognized this strange stage play. I had to ask myself who I am. The suspicion grew that your help was not quite so impartial. I don't complain about my role, but—

THE FRIEND: I will admit that my will dominated you. I abused you from the very beginning. Even during the speech I dictated to you, without your knowledge, words and gestures. Your hatred of me is quite understandable.

THE SON: *(Getting up.)* Hm.

THE FRIEND: *(Pushing him down.)* Just a moment. Now the talking is up to me. When I saw you then, in the hour of suicide, bleeding from your fight, it suddenly became quite clear to me: here was the man whom I needed. For I saw with the greatest excitement that you possessed what we all were lacking—youth and the glow of hatred. Only people like this can become reformers. You were the only one, then, the vital one, the caller: it is God's will. Thus I resolved to put you on a pedestal from which you cannot fall down.

THE SON: Are you certain of this?

THE FRIEND: Yes. An indestructible, unspent force drives you to the front. Perhaps it should not have happened. But since it did happen, you can no longer back out.

THE SON: And what shall I do?

THE FRIEND: Destroy the tyranny of the family, this medieval furuncle, this witches' Sabbath and torture chamber filled with sulphur! Do away with the laws, restore freedom, man's greatest treasure.

THE SON: At this point of the axis of the earth I am glowing again.

THE FRIEND: Then ponder that the fight against the father is the same as the revenge against the princes one hundred years ago. Today we are right! Then crowned heads oppressed and enslaved their subjects, stole their money and imprisoned their spirits. Today we are singing the Marseillaise! Every father may still let his son go hungry and enslaved without being punished, and prevent him from doing great things. It is only the same old song against injustice and cruelty. They stand on the privileges of the state and of nature. Away with both of them! For one hundred years now tyranny has disappeared—let us help a new nature to grow! They still have the power which those once had. They can still call the police against the disobedient son.

THE SON: An army be summoned! We too have to conquer the castles of the robber knights.

THE FRIEND: And to destroy until the last generation. We will preach against the fourth commandment. And the theses against idolatry must be nailed once more at the Castle Church in Wittenberg! We need a constitution and protection from beatings which force us to respect our torturers. I will formulate the program for I can prove its correctness. You'll lead the army.

THE SON: But who is going to help us? Until we have reached the twenty-first year we are subject to the whip and the madness of the paternal ghost.

THE FRIEND: Is it the first time that something is being done for freedom? Long live the flags and scaffolds of the revolution! When the old is dead, new laws are made. We will shout until we are heard in parliament under the golden dome. We risk our blood for something great. And this idea, this fire, powerful on each day in the world, will not be extinguished by superior power or deceit. We must be victorious because we are stronger.

THE SON: Aren't we alone—the two of us in this room? From what places will there be an echo?

THE FRIEND: From all where there are young people. Haven't you spoken last night? Didn't you hear the voice of the one a thousandfold? Be convinced: the hour has struck! And it demands the sacrifice.

THE SON: What can I do? I am only a poor devil who has been banished.

THE FRIEND: You have made a beginning—finish the work. Now do the utmost. Take up the holy duty!

THE SON: What great thing have I accomplished that you put all your cards on me?

THE FRIEND: The fate of millions lies in your hands. What you saw last night is only a small part of the powerful nation of sons ready for your action. The spark is ignited—toss it into the powder keg! Now a tremendous, unprecedented fall must occur which will make the whole world revolt. Yesterday your speech went out—today you must do it!

THE SON: Then tell me, as once before at a turn of my life, what I should do.

THE FRIEND: *(Taking a gun from his pocket.)* Do you know this black instrument? It harbors death. A quick clutch—and life is snuffed out. Look carefully: with this piece of metal I would have destroyed you last night, but you were victorious. You have overcome death: that makes you immortal in life. Look at it, it is loaded. I give it to you. Take it.

THE SON: Against whom?

THE FRIEND: Soon you'll be a captive.

THE SON: No!

THE FRIEND: Yes, the bloodhounds are on your tracks.

THE SON: No!! No!!

THE FRIEND: Your father knows where you are. He called the police.

THE SON: Who—has done this?

THE FRIEND: You want to know: me.

THE SON: You . . . !

THE FRIEND: *(With great composure.)* I told your father where you are.

THE SON: *(Grasps the gun and aims.)* Betrayal! Pay with your life! *(He fires, the gun fails to go off.)*

THE FRIEND: *(Unchanged.)* You didn't wind it up. I knew you would shoot at me. But it's still too early. I am not the right target. You must pull the gun apart—this way —now the bullet is in the barrel. *(He does it and gives the gun back to* THE SON.*)* Now you may shoot.

THE SON: *(Dropping the gun.)* Forgive me. *(He puts the gun in his pocket.)* I'll keep your gift.

THE FRIEND: And now that the last cliff has been navigated—how useless would a murder be at this very moment—I will tell you why I did it. I know of the temptation to go to bed with fame and women. But I need not be afraid—I see you're still burning. That is good. But everybody has to put himself to the test, if only on account of the weakhearted and ignorant. In a campaign both have to be considered. *(He looks at his watch.)* In not more than ten minutes, figuring the speed of the police, you'll be led off in chains before your father. You stand before him, the chains off, eye to eye. And he will pronounce your verdict: forced labor. What will you be doing then? *(He stands quite close in front of him.)*

THE SON: *(Stepping back.)* What end of the world have we reached? . . . Can thinking still go on? . . . I feel dizzy. . . .

THE FRIEND: *(Following him.)* What will you do? Where are you going?

THE SON: *(Pressed toward the wall.)* You are terrible. There is nothing left here. *(Screaming.)* Patricide!

THE FRIEND: *(Stepping back.)* God be with you.

THE SON: *(Plunging forward, grasping his arm.)* I can't do it! I can't do it! *(In unspeakable fright.)* Let go of me! *(He falls down before him.)* I beg you!

THE FRIEND: *(Unyielding.)* Man! Once the grandiose idea has taken hold of you, you can no longer escape it. You are in its grip, for better or worse. You have no more rest. Go forward and carry it out!

THE SON: *(After quite a while.)* How can I end a life—me who hardly was born. Superhuman courage is necessary even to destroy the smallest animal. Once I choked a dog to death and was unable to sleep for a few nights. I am too weak. Don't make a murderer of me! The Erinnyes are already within me now.

THE FRIEND: Is cowardice victorious? And you wanted to go into battle!

THE SON: Save me from a terrible nightmare.

THE FRIEND: And yet just before you have aimed the gun at me in cold blood! How can this be reconciled? Why does not my shadow pursue you? Did I do more to you than your father? Answer, why could you do it in my case?

THE SON: How well was this effect achieved! I understand—behind me the trap was closed. Woe upon you for you won't save me. I hate you boundlessly . . . Now I feel: I could do it.

THE FRIEND: Who cares about us and a dead man. Hundreds of thousands will live!

THE SON: There are noble fathers!

THE FRIEND: We do not fight for the exception—we fight for the deed!

THE SON: Why do I have to achieve it in horror?

THE FRIEND: Because no one but you is given the power.

THE SON: *(Rising proudly.)* Whatever I'm doing, I will not do it for power's sake. What do I care! I want to suffer to the end for my own poor generation. I alone had to suffer the great injustice. I shall do it! With you I have nothing any longer in common.

THE FRIEND: You gave your word. *(Quiet sets in.)* A few more minutes and you'll be freed from my presence. Shall we meet again? Perhaps not. One of us could make the great jump— perhaps it won't be you. I mean the full distance. *(*THE SON *does not answer.)* I could appear to you in a seance. But I don't care for that. Rather would I decay monistically. While on shifting grounds still next to each other, we should make things clear to ourselves.

THE SON: *(Absentminded.)* To disappear from the golden star . . . once again into the night . . . who will now help me in my need?

THE FRIEND: *(In a firm voice.)* For the first, the most important time: you will help yourself. Here in death your life begins. You stand in midst of the greatest fate. What you have lived for so far were confinement and night chapels or so it seemed to you. One does not live with his signboards. Prove, my boy, that you are not lost!

THE SON: *(Quietly and meekly.)* I am so much afraid of death.

THE FRIEND: Haven't you died before? How come I surprised you at it?

THE SON: Then I didn't know the world. Then I was rich. Then I could die.

THE FRIEND: Be courageous. Today you are better.

THE SON: And when I stood in the hall—you forget?

THE FRIEND: Only now will you totally become yourself. I take my leave. You have overtaken me. There is nothing anymore I could give you.

THE SON: I'm going to my death. Do you know what that means?

THE FRIEND: Him or you. He must die who has not achieved his life. . . . He who hates life in another person should not be afraid of his own death. No dog is defeated without a fight! With us it is best that we are seeking out dangers, that we are not born without them. Thus save your generation—our whole generation: the best we possess. Even though bad and transient, we must get there some day.

THE SON: And the one against all! Is there space in the old world?

THE FRIEND: Down with all profiteers! Give no quarters—none was given to you! Don't shudder: it is God's will that laws change.

THE SON: Let's wait for the police. These few seconds are a trial by ordeal. I am ready to go. The hangmen will find me courageous. No, I shall not submit. If no one enters here to chain me, I shall flee, and no harm will come to him. But if it happens *(raising a finger)* I swear! And I will provoke the most awful duel. But I want to see the crime that a father hands over his son to the police. When that occurs, nature has been dehumanized. Then someone else may guide my hand!

THE FRIEND: Think of that oath!

THE SON: The cloud is billowing in the sky. I could pray: keep the evil away from me!

THE FRIEND: You need no Christ on the cross. Kill what has killed you!

THE SON: *(In tears.)* I am weak like the small sacrificial animal. Yet I have strength.

THE FRIEND: *(In profound emotion.)* Doubt and temptation are given to us just as the infinite to make us time and again founder on our own will, yet attain the highest. Believe me for I know all the pitfalls, and I say it trembling: we only live in order to be even more glorious. Happiness and torture and madness are not in vain—so let us go to work, Brother, between the shadows, so that Death will not reach us until the very end. There is only little space left between us—the bridge of the common stream is already arching. Hither you now go. I'll call your name with respect; soon many will do so.

THE SON: Is there absolution for what I am doing?

THE FRIEND: It is in the belief of people whose savior you will become.

THE SON: And if it fails? When I am fooled by ghosts? When hope will founder?

THE FRIEND: Then we would not be standing here. Our little being is the grain of great fulfillment. You only live out the fate of your birth. What once moved your soul—today you'll finish it.

THE SON: I feel as I had lived a long time ago.

THE FRIEND: Then live anew! Live in order to understand your being's endless chain! Don't have doubts any longer. A beacon illuminates our poor fate. Brother before death: once more we are allowed to be together.

THE SON: *(In great emotion.)* Give me your hand!

THE FRIEND: Is there anything I can do for you?

THE SON: Here, take the money. I received it yesterday. *(He hands it over.)* I left my father's house poor and I intend to return that way. Believe in me! *(They stand opposite each other, highly determined.)*

SCENE 3

(A knock at the door.)

THE SON: *(In a clear voice.)* Come in!

INSPECTOR: Who of you gentlemen is the son of the doctor?

THE SON: It's me.

INSPECTOR: *(Approaches him.)* Please follow me.

THE SON: Your identification?

INSPECTOR: *(Showing his badge.)* Here.

THE SON: *(Polite.)* Thank you. May I ask you one question to clarify things for me: has my father sent you?

INSPECTOR: We have been asked to take you to him.

THE SON: Alright. *(*THE SON *and* THE FRIEND *look at each other.)*

INSPECTOR: *(One step closer.)* Since you are under suspicion that you might flee, I have to tie your hands.

THE SON: Then you take away a criminal?

INSPECTOR: *(With a shrug of his shoulders, apologizing.)* I'm sorry. . . .

THE SON: *(Stretching out his hands.)* I do not object. *(He is tied,* THE SON *and the* INSPECTOR *exit.)*

SCENE 4

THE FRIEND: *(Alone, opens the window.)* They push him into the wagon. In chains! Now, on to the guillotine, hangmen! It's your heads which will roll! *(He steps forward.)* He will do it. Triumph! Here my strength is at an end. *(He sinks into a chair.)* I think it's now my turn. *(He looks at himself as a photographer would.)* Is this the correct posture? Please smile! Who photographs the moment of disintegration? *(He pulls out a flask.)* Nothing more than this sensation on earth—that's little. One should not think of one's end. *(He opens the flask, smelling.)* Damn it! Curiosity is great. Is it true that one dies out of interest? Would it be possible to write down the memoirs of this second? But fame is sad and art no longer attractive. No, rather this way. And even when he commits the deed, what will have happened? He lives and will hate me even more. What have I talked him into? I will disappear and give the lie to myself. To say yes to life is permitted only to a scoundrel who knows already in advance how he will end. It's time now. Monologues before death are frequent. I lived to my own satisfaction. I swear: the madness will not reach me here! I am faster than the ghosts. *(He pours the liquid in a glass and reflects.)* Beautiful things occur to me. Ghost manufacturers could enrich themselves from my death. Devil, why am I still talking? I am afraid to trot all by myself into the yonder!!! *(He jumps up, trembling, and listens.)* What's that: steps on the stairway? That's most certainly sweet Adrienne! Heaven gave her a job: she should serve me destruction in a drop of champagne . . . *(He leaves to meet her.)*

Act 5

SCENE 1

(A few hours later. THE FATHER's *consultation room. A long room: in the central wall a door left and right, on the side walls one door each. To the left* THE FATHER's *desk with books and telephone, in front of an easy chair. Before the center wall glass cabinets with medical instruments, to the right an examining table. On the right side wall a bookcase, a smaller table with chairs. On one wall a reproduction of Rembrandt's* Anatomy.*)*

THE FATHER: Thank you, Inspector. Did my son resist?

INSPECTOR: The young man was rather quiet. We had expected to find a madman. Instead we encountered two gentlemen talking. There was no reason to use force. Nevertheless, according to your wishes, we tied his hands. The trip over here was also absolutely without incident. Perhaps, sir, the measures taken were a little too harsh. Often called to judge men, I have always used coercion only with regret. Perhaps it will be possible to lead the young man on the right path with kindness. I am convinced he is not a bad man. There are much worse ones around!

THE FATHER: Inspector, I have watched him for twenty years. I am his father; furthermore, I am a physician. I ought to know.

INSPECTOR: Sorry, sir, I did not want in any way . . .

THE FATHER: Quite the contrary: I am asking you for your opinion. You are certainly an experienced man but you look at things from your perspective. I believe I am not mistaken. I have pondered long before making a decision. Kindness is no longer possible! Only the utmost severity can change him to the better. This boy is depraved to the very bottom of his character. He wants to evade my will—that cannot be allowed to happen under any circumstances. You haven't heard his speeches! Today's youth is battling all authority and decency. Be glad you don't have a son like him.

INSPECTOR: Sir, I do have sons. And I love them! I could not call a curse on their heads. I know the terrible tragedy only too well! We have to deal with criminals and animals. Before pushing my own blood into this abyss, I rather would not want to live anymore. Even in the case of youthful criminals reprimands and probation are possible under the law. What terrible things has your son committed? Did he rob, forge, murder? These are the creatures we deal with: this is the company you will drive him to. May I ask your advance forgiveness for a candid word: you stigmatize him for the rest of his life. You stamp him with the mark of the court. He has undertaken a little fling against your will. . . .

THE FATHER: *(Laughs scornfully.)* A little fling!!

INSPECTOR: You have the right on your side and you will punish him. But does that justify humiliation? I'm afraid the use of chains cannot be undone—a misfortune may happen!

THE FATHER: He has refused to obey: it is not for the first time. If he—who is my son—leaves my house disgracefully, what else can I do but make him feel my power! Otherwise I am the dishonored one. What will people think of me? How will I be looked at? If no other means will help, I must use this ultimate one. I owe this to my sense of duty—toward myself as well as toward himself. I still believe I can change him to the better. He is young—this may serve as a warning for his life. Inspector, to me you are a stranger. Nevertheless, I have told you more than anybody else. Please have confidence in me. In this hour I feel heavily burdened. I only want the best, according to my conscience. But this I cannot let pass! You are a father yourself. What would you do in my place?

INSPECTOR: A being whom I have fathered cannot be depraved. That to me is the ultimate law! We are aging. Why should our sons not be young?

THE FATHER: Inspector, I have been a member of a students' club. I have fought for my honor with the sword. I am still bearing the traces. *(He points to a scar on his face.)* I have to keep my house pure. I cannot allow insults from a child to go unpunished. Besides, to me the responsibility of an educator weighs too heavily to be compared to that of a twenty-year-old boy.

INSPECTOR: I am afraid we talk at cross-purposes. I too have fought in my youth. But the number of semesters and student duels doesn't seem to me to be a valid yardstick. Our sons require that we help them. Sir, we have got to do that. Whether they are better or worse than we are is a matter of time, not a matter of the heart.

THE FATHER: I am shaken—I also apologize for an open word in a serious hour. How can a father, an official talk like that! Our young people get worse and more depraved from day to day. That is a well-known fact! And we should not check such decay in adolescents? I consider it my holiest duty to fight aberrations and I shall do it as long as I breathe. In what kind of world are we living! Here, read in the paper how far we have come! *(He takes the paper, points out a story.)* Yesterday a stranger preached against fathers in a secret meeting. That can only be a madman!! But thousands listen to such poison and suck it up voraciously. Why doesn't the police take action? These bums are a danger to the state. All seducers belong under lock and key; they are the scum of the earth.

INSPECTOR: *(With a look at the paper.)* This meeting was known to the police. It is a club of young people. It stands under the protection of a highly placed personality.

THE FATHER: Well, well, then we shall soon have anarchy!

INSPECTOR: I can set your mind to rest about this lecture. It was directed only against immoral fathers.

THE FATHER: *(Scornfully.)* Against the immoral! And the government supports such activities? All the more it is our duty to protect ourselves against betrayal in our own families. No, Inspector, the utmost harshness, the utmost harshness!

INSPECTOR: We are the people of the courts. How much perdition do we see! Believe me, I don't want to hang an innocent, least of all my own son. And if he does me wrong a thousand times, I am still his father. We fathers have to win our sons first before knowing what they are.

THE FATHER: You seem to see a son as something quite peculiar.

INSPECTOR: *(Modestly.)* I look at him as a creature given to me and whom I have to serve.

THE FATHER: *(Getting up.)* Inspector, I thank you. I too know my duty as a father, but in a different sense. I do not wish any disappointments on you! Even in this case I shall try to talk kindly to my son—as long as this is possible. I cannot say anything more. Please bring him in now!

INSPECTOR: I shall untie your son. He will find his way to you by himself. *(He bows and leaves.* THE FATHER *sits down on the chair at the left.)*

SCENE 2

*(*THE SON *enters slowly through the center door. He is still in the tailcoat and remains at the door, in a watchful posture.)*

THE FATHER: *(Gets up and walks toward him.)* Here you are. *(He stretches out his hand.)* Don't you want to give me your hand?

THE SON: No, Father.

THE FATHER: We have to talk to each other. Sit down. *(He walks to his desk, looking at him.)* You don't look well—do you want anything to eat?

THE SON: I am not hungry.

THE FATHER: Do you first want to change clothes and go to your room?

THE SON: No, thank you.

THE FATHER: *(Sits in easy chair, back of the desk.)* Well, then sit down. Let us talk. *(*THE SON *sits down, opposite him, at smaller table.)*

THE FATHER: Last night you secretly left your room: you have been forbidden to do so.

THE SON: You have called the police. You had me brought here in chains.

THE FATHER: I wish to get an answer to my question: where have you been during the night?

THE SON: Under the guise of education you have committed a crime against me. This will be revenged.

THE FATHER: *(Jumps up, but controls himself.)* I warn you!

THE SON: I am not here to beg you for something in yesterday's tone. I have found you to be small-minded and inferior, I am here to demand an explanation, and also atonement: an eye for an eye. You will not hear from me a single superfluous word. Today I shall play the sober part in which you did not succeed yesterday. Keep all your little emotions aside. Do you want to examine me about my mental state—you are welcome to do so. I am not indulging in fantasies. Should I lie down on this table? *(He turns toward the examining table.)*

THE FATHER: *(Pulls from behind the desk a whip and bends it over his knees as if he wanted to examine it.)* Go on!

THE SON: *(Upon the gesture with the whip dips his hand in his pocket and leaves it there.)* You may have your merits in auscultating lesser individuals. But beware of touching the whip! *(He lifts, without* THE FATHER *noticing it, the gun halfway from his pocket.)* I have my own certificate. I am completely sane and know exactly what I am doing.

THE FATHER: *(Subconsciously intimidated, lets the whip drop momentarily; at the same time the gun disappears in* THE SON'S *pocket.)* You were found in a hotel of ill repute this morning—what do you have to say?

THE SON: It's the truth. I was there.

THE FATHER: *(Astonished.)* You don't deny it?

THE SON: Not at all. Why should I?

THE FATHER: *(Taking notes on a sheet of paper, as in an examination.)* What did you do there?

THE SON: I slept there with a woman.

THE FATHER: *(Rising rigidly.)* You have ... enough ... get out of here!

THE SON: *(Without moving.)* Our talk is not yet finished. As I told you already: it concerns you.

THE FATHER: I tell you: get out of here!

THE SON: *(Also rising.)* You allow that I absent myself?

THE FATHER: Everything else you'll hear in your room.

THE SON: *(Walks to the center door, locks it.)* Then I must compel you to listen to me. *(He takes the key, stretches out his arm in a threatening gesture.)* Sit down or there will be a catastrophe. You don't want it any other way—you'll get it. *(He walks toward* THE FATHER *who raises the whip as if he wanted to use it, but in a sudden spell of dizziness he falls backward into the easy chair.)* For the last and bloodiest time I am asking you here and now: will you let me leave your house peacefully? You have tortured me long enough. But your power over the defenseless child is now at an end. Before you there stands someone determined to go all the way. Choose! *(He waits for an answer. It does not come. He goes back to his table, sits down again.)* Let's go on talking.

THE FATHER: *(Comes to from his absentmindedness.)* My hair has turned white.

THE SON: What do I care about your hair—think of yesterday's words you have spoken. We are men. At least I consider myself one.

THE FATHER: What is it that you still want here?

THE SON: My right. And this time I intend to succeed to the very end.

THE FATHER: Give thanks to your creator that in this hour I am too old. Otherwise. . . . But the last word has not yet been said. Speak up! I will not bear the reproach on my deathbed that I was the first one. . . . Finish speaking! I want to get a clear picture of you before tearing up the bond which still ties me to you.

THE SON: Father, you won't have to tear up anything. Whichever way you may be on your deathbed—you don't move me any longer. Just leave me to the furies and take care that you can die peacefully! Therefore listen and believe me what I say to you: set me free! I stand before you in terrible seriousness.

THE FATHER: I laugh at your seriousness. An insane man stands before me.

THE SON: Father, let us forget all this. But end this posture. Your life is at stake!! Everything be undone, torture and revenge and deceit. Cross me out in your heart as a son. And now, let me go. . . .

THE FATHER: (*Scornfully.*) Not yet, my son.

THE SON: Well, then—when I fled from your power many, who were hidden in the garden, went with me, armed with guns.

THE FATHER: (*Attentively.*) What does that mean?

THE SON: And in the same night, one hour later, I have talked to them, against you, the tyrants, the fathers—you, who have contempt for everything that's great—yes, turn pale. I am no longer given unto your hands. Your intellect is too small for an idea, thus yield to the deed! We are not insane, we are people and we are alive. We live doubly because you want to kill us. You will not take one step out of this room without being beaten, spit upon and crushed by the thousands I have called. Thus we take our revenge on you and your power, and none of the gods will desert us. (*As* THE FATHER *wants to answer:*) Yes, I have begun the revolution in the midst of the torture chamber in which I stand—and soon my name will be in the headlines. Now a nation of sons is fighting when you will long be decayed to

dust. Here, read in your newspaper. *(He throws a paper at him.)*
Are you trembling? Is this your true face? Yes, it was me! I
have spoken!

THE FATHER: You are lying! You are lying!

THE SON: Here is the mask of the unknown. *(He pulls it out and
swings it through the air.)* Do you still have doubts? It is me!!!
Now I want to see your end—in your own room. . . .

THE FATHER: *(Shaking over the table.)* Say that you are lying, or
else I forget myself.

THE SON: *(Erect.)* Will you set me free? I don't want your money.
I'll give it to the poor. You can disinherit me. The only thing I
want is my life! I still have much to do in the world. I will not
bleed to death from these few seconds.

THE FATHER: I am your father no longer.

THE SON: You never were. Father—who knows it today? Where
was I born? I was a stepchild only. Should I ever have a son, I
will make amends for the evils I suffered. Oh, wonderful, great
light, could I experience to be a sweet child's protector!

THE FATHER: *(In all his harshness before him.)* Your wish will be
granted. You don't have a father anymore. I have offered you
his hand—you have turned it down with contempt. The curse
may come over you. I repudiate you. But because you have
brought shame over me last night, I also extinguish you. In my
hour of death I will think of my word: I have forgotten that you
are my son. Today you see me for the last time. Don't dare to
ever enter my house again. I will have you driven out by dogs.
Here I take the whip and throw it at your feet. You don't deserve
that my hand still touches you. *(He throws it down.)* Now you
may go.

THE SON: Father . . .

THE FATHER: Do not pronounce this word!

THE SON: Will you set me free?

THE FATHER: Free? *(He laughs shrilly.)* One more year you are still
under my power. At least one more year I can protect humanity
from you. There are institutions existing for such a purpose.
Now leave my room and don't ever return!

THE SON: *(With iron calm.)* The room is locked. No one is leaving.
*(THE FATHER gets up, walks slowly, awkwardly to the side door
on the left. THE SON speaks in a frightful voice.)* Stop! Not

another step! (THE FATHER *for a moment almost paralyzed by the voice, sits down at the desk.* THE SON *pulls unnoticed the gun from his pocket.*)

THE FATHER: Help against madness ... (*He grabs the telephone receiver.* THE SON *lifts the gun high up.*) Please police headquarters.

THE SON: Look here. (*He aims at him and says in a clear voice.*) One more word and you are no longer alive!

(THE FATHER *makes an involuntary motion to protect himself. He raises his arm. The telephone receiver falls down. The raised arm sinks down. They look each other in the eye. The gun remains aimed at* THE FATHER's *chest. Then* THE FATHER's *body begins to twitch, the eyes roll and become rigid. He is briefly convulsed, then he slowly slumps over the chair to the floor. A stroke has ended his life.* THE SON *with unchanged face notices* THE FATHER's *fall. His arm sinks down, the gun comes down with a thud. Then he himself sinks automatically, as if his consciousness were interrupted, into a chair near the table.*)

SCENE 3

(*Through the right side door* THE FRÄULEIN *enters. She sees* THE FATHER, *rushes toward him but realizes he is dead. Then she recognizes* THE SON *in the chair and slowly moves toward him.*)

THE FRÄULEIN:
Now you are here again—and at your feet
The home is blended with the wonderland.
Is there no voice near you to greet!
Now be welcome by a mother's hand!
And your brow, after such heavy fight,
I will carefully dry to the last bead.
I do not ask, I know the suffering knight.
He will no longer hate you: he is dead.
THE SON:
Do you still know the boy who left you here?
Don't ever believe that to you I've return'd.
Where is the man to overcome such fear?
THE FRÄULEIN:
Poor friend, all your bridges are now burn'd.

THE SON:

No, Fräulein, wherever this may lead,
From the horizon no longer comes the pull.
I know that only sacrifice precedes deed;
My heart is bleak, once it was all too full,
Much have I done, but I'm no more of use,
Gone is the passion once so great.
Much is fulfilled—yet far I'm from profuse:
The cloud moved on. The force remained.
When over the dead I step once more here
Into life—then I am away and far.
In ecstasy I cannot disappear,
Thus I may vanish toward a new star.
What in my mind now seems quite sore,
Soon I'll see quite bright and clear.
If I shall kindle fires more and more,
I will not be there: I shall be here!

(THE FRÄULEIN *kneels before him, as he did, before her, in act 2.*)

I see the heaven over you now shine
The one I have seen in my very first night.
Could I now on your bosom whine
My tear would appear in a diff'rent light.
And could today the words I say—
Birth and existence—in your lap once both—
Your love would no longer make us sway.
I am too poor. The Earth has let me go.

(*Slowly both get up.*)

Into pain and lovelessness, into the fate
Of what I recognize, my body drives away.
If I'm surrounded by emptiness and hate:
My mind is fully creative on this day.
With me for what is vital to unite
I have not shunned Death's eternal might.
Now man's greatest power to proclaim
Toward freedom, is my heart's new aim!

(They clasp their hands together, then exit toward different sides. THE FATHER's body, in the center of the room, remains.)

Translated by Henry Marx

Georg Kaiser

From Morning to Midnight

A Play in Two Parts

Characters

Cashier	Waiter in Hotel
Mother	Jewish Racing Stewards
Wife	One Two Three Four Female
First and Second Daughter	Masks
Manager	Gentlemen in Evening Dress
Assistant	Waiter
Commissionaire	Salvation Army Soldiers and
First and Second Gentleman	Officers
(Fat Man, Other Man)	Public at a Salvation Army
Messenger Boy	Meeting (Clerks, Prostitutes)
Maid Servant	Workers, etc.
Lady	Policeman
Son	

The little town of W. and the big city of B.

Part 1

Interior of small bank. Left, cashier's counter and door marked
Manager. *In the center, door marked* To the Strong Room. *Exit
(right), behind the barrier. Beside it a cane sofa and table with
water jug and glass. Behind the grille, cashier and at the desk,
assistant, writing. The* FAT GENTLEMAN *seated on the cane sofa*

snorts. Somebody goes off right. MESSENGER BOY *at the counter stares after him.*

CASHIER *raps on the counter.* MESSENGER BOY *quickly places his chit in the* CASHIER'S *waiting hand.* CASHIER *writes, takes money from under the counter counts it out into his hand, then onto the counter.* MESSENGER BOY *moves to one side with money and sweeps it into a linen bag.*

FAT MAN: *(stands up.)* Now it's the turn of us heavyweights. *(Pulls a bulging leather wallet out of his inside coat pocket.)*

(Enter a LADY. *Expensive fur. Rustle of silk.* FAT MAN *stops short.)*

LADY: *(has difficulty opening the barrier, smiles involuntarily in the* FAT MAN'S *direction.)* At last!

*(*FAT MAN *pulls a face.* CASHIER *raps impatiently.* LADY *makes a questioning gesture to the* FAT MAN.*)*

FAT MAN: *(stepping back.)* Always last, we heavyweights.

*(*LADY *with a slight bow steps up to the counter.* CASHIER *raps.)*

LADY: *(opens her handbag, takes out an envelope and places it in the* CASHIER'S *hand.)* Three thousand, please.

　　　*(*CASHIER *looks at it from all sides, pushes it back.)*

LADY: *(understands.)* Sorry. *(She extracts the folded letter and pushes it across.)*

　　　　　*(*CASHIER *as before.)*

LADY: *(unfolds the letter.)* Three thousand, please.

*(*CASHIER *skims over the paper and places it in front of the* CLERK. CLERK *stands up and goes through the door marked* Manager.*)*

FAT MAN: *(getting down in the cane sofa again.)* I'll take longer. We heavyweights always take longer.

　　　　　*(*CASHIER *busy counting money.)*

LADY: In notes, please.

　　　　　*(*CASHIER *does not look up.)*

MANAGER: *(youngish, rotund—comes out left with the letter.)* Who is—*(Struck dumb at the sight of the* LADY.)

*(*ASSISTANT *writing again at his desk.)*

FAT MAN: *(loudly.)* Good morning.

MANAGER: *(with a brief glance in his direction.)* Everything all right?

FAT MAN: *(patting his paunch.)* Rolling along nicely, thanks.

MANAGER: *(laughs briefly. To the* LADY.) You wish to draw some money?

LADY: Three thousand.

MANAGER: Yes, three—three thousand. I should be delighted to let you have it—

LADY: Is there something wrong with the letter?

MANAGER: *(saccharine-sweet, self-important.)* Nothing wrong with the letter. Up to twelve thousand. *(Spelling it out.)* B-A-N-C-O.

LADY: My bank in Florence assured me—

MANAGER: Your bank in Florence has written a perfectly valid letter.

LADY: Then I fail to under—

MANAGER: You had this letter made out in Florence—

LADY: I did.

MANAGER: Twelve thousand and payable at the towns—

LADY: —at which I break my journey.

MANAGER: You had to give the bank in Florence several specimen signatures—

LADY: —which have been sent to the banks listed in the letter, to identify me.

MANAGER: We have not received any letter of advice with your signature.

*(*FAT MAN *coughs, winks at the* MANAGER.)

LADY: Does that mean I have to wait till—

MANAGER: We have to have something to go on.

*(*MAN *wrapped up in winter coat with fur hat and woollen scarf comes in, takes up position at the counter. He darts furious looks at the* LADY.)

LADY: I wasn't prepared for this—

MANAGER: *(with a brash laugh.)* We were even less prepared, in fact not at all!

LADY: I do need the money urgently!

(FAT MAN *on the sofa laughs loudly.*)

MANAGER: Which of us doesn't?

(FAT MAN *on the sofa neighs with laughter.*)

MANAGER: *(as if addressing an audience.)* Me, for instance. *(To the* MAN *at the counter.)* You've probably more time than I have. You can see I'm still talking to this lady. Now come, madam, what did you imagine? Did you expect me to pay out—on your—

(FAT MAN *on the sofa titters.*)

LADY: *(quickly.)* I'm at the "Elephant."

(FAT MAN *on the sofa hoots.*)

MANAGER: Delighted to have your address, madam. I'm a regular at the "Elephant."

LADY: Can't the hotel manager vouch for me?

(FAT MAN *on the sofa having a wonderful time.*)

LADY: My luggage is at the hotel.

MANAGER: Do you want me to inspect the contents of your trunks and cases?

LADY: I'm in a most unfortunate position!

MANAGER: Then we're in the same boat. You can't—I can't. That's the position. *(He gives her back her letter.)*

LADY: What do you advise?

MANAGER: Our little township is a pleasant place—the "Elephant" a famous hotel—there are nice surroundings—there are nice people—and time soon passes—a day here, a night there—take it as it comes.

LADY: A few days here wouldn't matter.

MANAGER: The company at the "Elephant" will be delighted to help make your stay pleasant.

LADY: But I simply must have the three thousand today!

MANAGER: *(to the* FAT MAN *on the sofa.)* Anybody here prepared to put up three thousand for a lady from abroad?

LADY: I couldn't possibly accept that. I shall be in my room at the "Elephant." May I ask you to inform me by telephone as soon as the verification comes through from Florence?

MANAGER: I shall telephone personally if madam wishes!

LADY: Whichever way is quickest. *(She pushes the letter into the envelope and puts it in her bag.)* I shall call in again this afternoon.

MANAGER: At your service.

*(*LADY *departs with curt good-bye.)*

*(*MAN *at the counter moves up and bangs a crumpled paper onto the counter.)*

*(*MANAGER *ignoring this, looks at the* FAT MAN *on the sofa in merriment.)*

*(*FAT MAN *on the sofa sniffs.)*

MANAGER: All the fragrance of Italy—out of a perfume bottle.

*(*FAT MAN *on the sofa fans himself with his hand.)*

MANAGER: Brings on the heat, doesn't it?

FAT MAN: *(pours himself a glass of water.)* Three thousand is a bit steep. *(Drinks.)* Three hundred is more like it.

MANAGER: Perhaps you could bring the price down—at the "Elephant," in her room?

FAT MAN: That's not for heavyweights like us.

MANAGER: Our waistlines protect our morality—they keep us out of trouble.

*(*MAN *at the counter bangs his fist on the counter for the second time.)*

MANAGER: *(unperturbed.)* What's the matter with you? *(Smooths out the paper and hands it to the* CASHIER.*)*

*(*MESSENGER BOY *has been staring at the* LADY, *then the speakers— misses the barrier and collides with the* FAT MAN *on the sofa.)*

FAT MAN: *(takes his money bag away from him.)* Yes, my lad, making eyes at pretty girls can be a costly business—now you've lost your money bag.

(MESSENGER BOY *gives an embarrassed laugh.*)

FAT MAN: Now what are you going to do when you get home?

(MESSENGER BOY *laughs.*)

FAT MAN: *(returns his bag.)* Let that be a lesson to you. All your life. You are not the first whose eyes ran away with him—and then all the rest of him.

(MESSENGER BOY *exits.*)

(CASHIER *has been counting out coins.*)

MANAGER: And to think people entrust money to a young rascal like that.

FAT MAN: Stupidity brings its own punishment.

MANAGER: A wonder his boss can't see it. Chap like that absconds the first chance he gets. Born embezzler. *(To the* MAN *at the counter.)* Is there something wrong?

(MAN *examines every coin.*)

MANAGER: That's a twenty-five pfennig piece—forty-five pfennig all in all. All you had coming, wasn't it?

(MAN *pocketing it with great care.*)

FAT MAN: You want to be careful and keep such a vast amount in the strong room.—Now it's time for the heavyweights to unload.

(MAN *at counter off right.*)

MANAGER: Well, what have you brought us?

FAT MAN: *(places the leather bag on the counter and brings out his wallet.)* You with your chic clientele. Can I still trust you? *(Shakes hands.)*

MANAGER: Anyway, pretty faces can't influence us where business is concerned.

FAT MAN: *(counting out his money.)* How old was she? What's your guess?

MANAGER: Haven't seen her without make-up. Yet.

FAT MAN: What's she after here?

MANAGER: We'll find out tonight at the "Elephant."

FAT MAN: Who might be interested?

MANAGER: Any of us in the long run.

FAT MAN: Whatever does she need the three thousand for here?

MANAGER: She must need it pretty badly.

FAT MAN: I wish her the best of luck.

MANAGER: In what?

FAT MAN: In getting hold of her three thousand.

MANAGER: From me?

FAT MAN: Who from is beside the point.

MANAGER: I wonder when the notification from the bank in Florence will come.

FAT MAN: If at all!

MANAGER: If at all—that has me even more intrigued!

FAT MAN: We could whip the hat round to help her out of her difficulties.

MANAGER: Something like that is probably what she has in mind.

FAT MAN: You're telling me.

MANAGER: *(laughs.)* Have you won the lottery?

FAT MAN: *(to* CASHIER.) Take this off me. *(To* MANAGER.) What does it matter whether we invest our money outside or let it accumulate interest with you—open an account for the Building Society.

MANAGER: *(sharply to the* ASSISTANT.) Account for the Building Society.

FAT MAN: There's more to come.

MANAGER: Keep it rolling in, gentlemen. We can use it, just now.

FAT MAN: Fifty-sixty thousand-fifty thou. in notes—ten thou. in gold.

*(*CASHIER *counts it.)*

MANAGER: *(after a pause.)* Everything all right otherwise?

FAT MAN: *(to* CASHIER.) Yes; that note is patched.

MANAGER: We'll accept it, of course. Soon get rid of it. Reserve it for our customer from Florence. She had beauty patches herself.

FAT MAN: But there's a thousand in this one.

MANAGER: Collector's piece.

FAT MAN: *(uncontrollable laughter.)* Collector's piece—that's good!

MANAGER: *(in tears.)* Collector's piece—*(Gives him the* CASHIER'S *receipt.)* Your receipt. *(Choking.)* Sixty—thou.—

FAT MAN: *(takes it and reads it: ditto.)* Sixty-thou.—

MANAGER: Collector—

FAT MAN: Coll—*(They shake hands.)*

MANAGER: See you tonight.

FAT MAN: *(nods.)* Collector—*(Buttons up his coat, departs shaking his head.)*

(MANAGER stands there, wipes away tears from behind pince-nez. Exits left into his room.)

(CASHIER bundles up the notes he has just received, stacks the coins in rolls.)

MANAGER: *(comes back in.)* That lady from Florence—supposedly from Florence—ever had a vision like that appear at your counter before? Furs—perfume. Still linger on, romance fills the air!—That is the full treatment. Italy, the very word has a dazzling effect—fabulous. Riviera. Mentone. Bordighera. Nice. Monte Carlo! But, where oranges grow, crooks thrive too. There is not a square yard of ground free of fraud down there. That's where the raids are planned. The gang scatters in all directions. Slip away to the smaller towns—off the main highways. Then visions in silks and fur. Women! They are the modern sirens, singing their song of the blue south—*o bella Napoli!* One captivating glance and they'll take the very suit off your back, you're stripped naked, stripped to your bare skin! *(He drums on the CASHIER's back with his pencil.)* I don't doubt for an instant that the Bank in Florence which issued the letter knows as much about it—as the man in the moon. The whole thing is a swindle, long prepared. And the perpetrators are not in Florence at all, but in Monte Carlo! That's the place that immediately springs to mind. Can count on it. We have seen before us one of those beings who thrive in the jungle of the gambling den. And I wager we never see her again. The first attempt was a failure. She won't risk a second one! I maybe like a joke—but I still keep my eyes peeled. We bankers!—I should really have tipped off our Police Chief—But what happens now is not my business. After all the bank is expected to observe a discreet silence. *(At his door.)* Watch the out-of-town papers: when you read that a woman swindler has been arrested you'll see what I'm talking about. Then you'll have to admit that I was right. That's the last we'll ever see of our lady friend from Florence. *(Exit.)*

(CASHIER seals rolls.)

PORTER: *(enters from right with letters, gives them to the* CLERK.*)* One registered letter. I keep the receipt.

(CLERK *stamps the chit, gives it to the* PORTER.*)*

(PORTER *re-arranges glass and water carafe. Exit.)*

(CLERK *carries letters into* MANAGER'S *office—comes back.)*

LADY: *(returns; walks up to the counter quickly.)* Oh. Excuse me.

(CASHIER *sticks out his hand, palm up.)*

LADY: *(louder.)* Excuse me.

(CASHIER *raps on counter.)*

LADY: I don't want to trouble the MANAGER again.

(CASHIER *raps.)*

LADY: *(smiling in despair.)* Listen, please, wouldn't it be possible if we did it this way—I leave the bank the letter for the whole amount and you advance me three thousand? *(*CASHIER *raps impatiently.)* I should even be prepared to deposit my diamonds as security. Any jeweler in the town will give a valuation on them. *(She pulls off a glove and fumbles with the bracelet.)*

· (MAID SERVANT *enters quickly from right, sits down on the cane sofa, turns everything out of her shopping basket, looking for something.)*

(LADY *has turned round slightly startled: her hand comes to rest on the hand of the* CASHIER *for support.)*

(CASHIER *bends over the hand he holds in his. Slowly his bespectacled eyes travel up her wrist.)*

(MAID SERVANT *finds the check with a sigh of relief.)*

(LADY *nods in her direction.)*

(MAID SERVANT *puts things back in basket.)*

(LADY *turning to the* CASHIER *suddenly meets his gaze.)*

(CASHIER *smiles.)*

LADY: *(rescues her hand.)* I wouldn't want to make the bank do anything irregular. *(She puts on the bracelet, has difficulty with the catch. Holding her arm out to the CASHIER.)* Would you be so kind—I can't manage with just one hand.

(CASHIER bushy beard bristles; eyeglasses sink into glowing caverns of wide-open eyes)

LADY: *(to MAID SERVANT.)* Will you help me?

(MAID SERVANT does so.)

LADY: Now the safety catch. *(Utters a faint cry.)* Oh, you are sticking it into my bare flesh. That's it. Many thanks. *(Waves to the CASHIER. Exit.)*

(MAID SERVANT at the counter, lays her check down.)

(CASHIER seizes it in fluttering hands. Gropes around under the counter for a long time. Then pays out.)

MAID SERVANT: *(looks at all the money; then at the CASHIER.)* I don't have all that coming.

(CASHIER writing.)

(ASSISTANT beginning to take notice.)

MAID SERVANT: *(to ASSISTANT.)* That's too much!

(ASSISTANT looks at CASHIER.)

(CASHIER takes back some.)

MAID SERVANT: Still too much!

(CASHIER writes.)

(MAID SERVANT shakes her head, puts money in her basket. Off.)

CASHIER: *(his voice struggling through hoarse croaking.)* Fetch—glass—water!

(ASSISTANT goes from the counter to the table.)

CASHIER: That's stale. Fresh—from the tap.

(ASSISTANT goes with glass into the Strong Room.)

(CASHIER quickly to electric bell—presses.)

(COMMISSIONAIRE *enters.*)

CASHIER: Fetch fresh water.
COMMISSIONAIRE: I'm not allowed to leave the outside door.
CASHIER: For me. That's slime. I want fresh drinking water.

(COMMISSIONAIRE *into the Strong Room with the water carafe.*)

(CASHIER *with quick movements stuffs the notes and coins he has just sorted into his pockets. Then he takes his coat from the hook, throws it over his arm. Then his hat. He comes round the counter— and exits right.*)

MANAGER: (*enters left, deeply engrossed in a letter.*) The confirmation from Florence has come!

(ASSISTANT *with the glass of water from the Strong Room.*)

(COMMISSIONAIRE *with the carafe of water from the Strong Room.*)

MANAGER: What the devil does this mean?

Writing room in a hotel. Glass door at the back. Writing table and telephone left. Sofa right, with table and journals, etc.

(LADY *writing.*)

(SON *enters with coat and hat on—under his arm large flat object wrapped in a dust-sheet.*)

LADY: (*surprised.*) You've got it?
SON: The wine merchant is sitting in the lounge downstairs. The funny old codger suspects me of wanting to run off with it.
LADY: Why, this morning he was glad to get rid of it.
SON: Now he smells something fishy.
LADY: You must have aroused his suspicion in some way.
SON: I did show I was rather pleased.
LADY: That would open a blind man's eyes.
SON: And believe me, they *shall* open their eyes. But keep calm, Mama, the price is the same as this morning.
LADY: Is the wine merchant waiting?
SON: Let him wait.
LADY: I'm afraid I must tell you—

SON: *(kisses her.)* Silence. Solemn silence. Don't look till I tell you to. *(Flings off hat and coat, sets the picture up on a chair and lifts the dust sheet.)*

LADY: Not yet?

SON: *(very quietly.)* Mama.

(LADY turns round in her chair.)

SON: *(comes to her, puts his arm round her shoulders.)* Well?

LADY: It certainly does not belong in a wine bar.

SON: Well, it was turned face to the wall. The wine merchant had stuck his own photograph on the back.

LADY: Did you buy that too?

SON: *(laughs.)* What do you think of it?

LADY: I find it—very naive.

SON: Marvelous, isn't it? Fantastic for a Cranach.

LADY: Do you really rate it so highly—as a picture?

SON: As a picture? Of course! But also for the remarkable presentation. Unique for Cranach—and for the treatment of the subject unique in the whole history of art. Where will you find the like? In the Palazzo—the Uffizi—the Vatican? Even the Louvre can't match this. Without a doubt we have here the first and only erotic presentation of the first human couple. The apple is still there lying on the grass—out of the indescribably green foliage leers the serpent—we see that the scene takes place in Paradise itself and not after the banishment. This is the Fall itself!— Unique! Cranach painted dozens of Adam and Eves—stiff—with the branch of the tree in the middle—and always the two separate. It is written: they knew each other. Here for the first time the glorious proclamation of the birth of true humanity trumpets forth: they *loved* each other. Here a German and Northerner reveals himself as a master of the erotic of truly southern, completely southern vigor! *(Gazing at the picture.)* And yet, at the same time how great the discipline in such ecstasy. This line of the male arm cutting across the female hip, the horizontal line of her thighs underneath and the diagonal line of his. It never wearies the eye for a moment. It creates love in the beholder—the flesh tone naturally helps a great deal. Don't you find the same?

LADY: You are naive, like your picture.

SON: What do you mean?

LADY: I beg of you hide the picture in your hotel room.

SON: It will really only take effect on me once I have it at home. Florence and this Cranach. I shall have to postpone finishing my book for a long time. This kind of thing has to be digested, and then re-created out of one's own flesh and blood, otherwise the art historian betrays his trust. At the moment I feel completely overwhelmed—fancy finding this picture on the first stage of the trip.

LADY: You were pretty sure it was here.

SON: But one is still blinded by the reality. Isn't it enough to drive one out of one's mind? Mama, I must be born lucky.

LADY: You are reaping the benefits of your intensive research.

SON: And what about your help? Your kindness?

LADY: My happiness lies in yours.

SON: You are infinitely patient with me. I drag you from your lovely, quiet life in Fiesole. You are Italian, I drag you through Germany in the middle of winter. You sleep in trains—second and third-class hotels—get involved with all sorts of people—

LADY: I've certainly had my fill of that today.

SON: I promise to hurry. I am impatient myself to get my treasure to safety. We leave at three. Will you give me the three thousand?

LADY: I have not got it.

SON: The man who owns the picture is here now.

LADY: The bank could not let me have it. The notification from Florence must have been delayed.

SON: I agreed to pay cash.

LADY: Then you must give him back the picture until the bank can let me have the money.

SON: Can't that be speeded up?

LADY: I have just made out a telegram. I'll have it sent off. We left so quickly—

(WAITER knocks.)

LADY: Yes.

WAITER: A gentleman from the bank wishes to speak to madam.

LADY: *(to SON.)* They've sent the money straight to the hotel *(To WAITER.)* Ask him to come right up.

(WAITER exits.)

SON: Call me when you have the money, will you? I don't want to let our man out of the hotel.

LADY: I'll phone you immediately.
SON: I'll be in the lounge downstairs. *(Exit.)*

(LADY closes her writing case.)

(WAITER and CASHIER appear behind the glass door. CASHIER passes the WAITER and opens the door; WAITER turns and goes.)

(CASHIER still with coat over arm, enters.)

(LADY points to a chair and sits on the sofa.)

(CASHIER his coat beside him on the chair.)

LADY: Has the bank—?

(CASHIER sees picture.)

LADY: This picture is closely connected with my visit to the bank.
CASHIER: Is it you?
LADY: Do you see a likeness?
CASHIER: *(smiling.)* Yes, in the wrist!
LADY: Are you a connoisseur?
CASHIER: I'd like to—become more of one!
LADY: Are you interested in pictures like these?
CASHIER: I'm in the picture!
LADY: Do you know of the existence of more such pictures in this town? You would be doing me a great favor. Why, that is even more important to me—well, as important as the money!
CASHIER: I've got money.
LADY: In the end the sum I had my letter of credit made out for won't be enough.
CASHIER: *(pulls out the notes and rolls of coin.)* This is enough.
LADY: I can only draw up to twelve thousand.
CASHIER: Sixty thousand.
LADY: How is that possible?
CASHIER: That's my business.
LADY: What do I have to do?
CASHIER: We have to take a trip.
LADY: Where to?
CASHIER: Across the border. Pack your case—if you have one. You leave from the Central Station—I walk to the next stop and board the train there. We'll spend the first night at—timetable? *(He finds it on the table.)*

LADY: Have you brought more than three thousand from the bank?

CASHIER: *(busy.)* Put sixty thousand in my pocket. Fifty thousand in notes—ten thousand in gold.

LADY: Of that, I'm entitled to—?

CASHIER: *(breaks open a roll, counts them professionally into his hand and then onto the table.)* Take it. Put it away immediately. We may be observed. The door has glass panels. Five hundred in gold.

LADY: Five hundred?

CASHIER: More later. When we're safe. Here we mustn't let anybody see. Let's go. Put it away. This is not the moment for tenderness. The wheel of time turns, crushing any arm stuck in the spokes to stop it. *(He leaps up.)*

LADY: I need three thousand.

CASHIER: If the police find it on you, you'll be put behind bars!

LADY: What have the police got to do with it?

CASHIER: Your presence was observed by the whole bank today. Suspicion attaches to you, the link between us is clear.

LADY: I entered the bank—

CASHIER: Coolly.

LADY: I asked for—

CASHIER: You attempted—

LADY: I tried—

CASHIER: —to defraud the bank by presenting a forged letter.

LADY: *(taking the letter from her handbag.)* This letter isn't genuine?

CASHIER: As genuine as your diamonds.

LADY: I offered my valuables as security. Why should my precious stones be imitations?

CASHIER: Women of your type only dazzle.

LADY: What type am I then? Dark hair-dark complexion. A Southerner, from Tuscany.

CASHIER: From Monte Carlo!

LADY: *(smiles.)* No, from Florence!

CASHIER: *(suddenly his eye falls on coat and hat of the* SON.*)* Am I too late?

LADY: Too late?

CASHIER: Where is he? I'll make a deal with him. He'll listen. I have the wherewithal. How much should I offer him? How high do you reckon the compensation? How much should I stuff into his pocket? I'll go as high as fifteen thousand—is he asleep? Still sprawling in bed? Where's your room? Twenty thousand—five thousand extra for immediate withdrawal. *(He seizes hat and coat from the chair.)* I'll take him his things.

LADY: *(baffled.)* The gentleman is sitting in the lounge.

CASHIER: That is too dangerous. Too many people downstairs. Ask him up. I'll checkmate him. Ring the bell. Tell the waiter to hurry. Twenty thousand—in notes! *(He counts them out.)*

LADY: Can my son vouch for me?

CASHIER: *(staggers back stunned.)* Your—son?

LADY: I'm traveling with him. I'm accompanying him on a study-trip from Florence to Germany. My son is collecting material for his book on art history.

CASHIER: *(stares at her.)* Son?

LADY: Is that so appalling?

CASHIER: *(confused.)* This—picture.

LADY: Is his great find. Three thousand is enough to buy it. That's the three thousand I need so badly. A big wine-merchant—whom you are sure to know when you hear his name—is prepared to part with it at that price.

CASHIER: —furs—silk—shimmered and rustled—the air was heavy with exotic perfumes!

LADY: It's winter. I don't dress out of the ordinary, by my standards.

CASHIER: The forged letter.

LADY: I've just been making out a telegram to my bank.

CASHIER: Your wrist—all naked—I was supposed to put the bracelet on.

LADY: Everyone is clumsy with the left hand.

CASHIER: *(dully.)* I have—embezzled—

LADY: *(amused.)* Are you and the police satisfied now? My son is well known in academic circles.

CASHIER: Now—right at this moment, they'll be missing me. I asked for a drink of water, once to get rid of the assistant—and again to remove the porter from the door. The notes and coins have disappeared. I have embezzled!—I mustn't be seen on the streets—in the marketplace. Must not go to the railway station. The police are on the alert. Sixty thousand!—I must go across country—through the snow, before the general alarm is given.

.

LADY: *(horrified.)* Be quiet!

CASHIER: I pocketed all the money—you pervaded the bank—you shimmered and rustled—you rested your bare hand in mine—I felt the warmth of your body—the caress of your breath—

LADY: I am a lady!

CASHIER: *(doggedly.)* Now you simply must—!!

LADY: *(controlling herself.)* Are you married? *(He makes a sweeping gesture.)* I think that matters a great deal. If indeed I'm not to take the whole business as a joke. You have let yourself be carried away. Committed an ill-considered act. You must repair the damage. Go back to your counter and intimate that suddenly you weren't feeling quite yourself. You still have all the money on you?

CASHIER: I took money from the—

LADY: *(abruptly.)* Then I can take no further interest.

CASHIER: I robbed the bank—

LADY: You are becoming a nuisance, sir.

CASHIER: Now you must—

LADY: What I must do is—

CASHIER: Don't you see, now you must do it!!

LADY: Ridiculous.

CASHIER: I have robbed, stolen. I have sacrificed my life—I have destroyed my existence—I have burned my boats—I am a thief—a criminal—*(Flinging the words across the table at her.)* Now you must. You simply must!!!

LADY: I'll call my son, perhaps—

CASHIER: *(suddenly changed, alert.)* Call somebody? Sound the alarm? Splendid!—Stupid. Clumsy. They won't catch me. I won't walk into the trap. I've got my wits about me, ladies and gentlemen. Your wits are always a long way behind—I'm invariably miles ahead of you. Don't move. Sit still till I—*(Stuffs the money in his pockets, pulls the hat over his face, clutches the coat to his chest.)* Till I—*(Alertly and silently off through glass door.)*

(LADY remains standing, somewhat bewildered.)

SON: *(enters.)* The man from the bank just left the hotel. You are all tense, Mama. Is the money—

LADY: The interview was rather a strain. Money matters, my boy. You know they always tend to upset me.

SON: Have difficulties arisen which might delay payment?

LADY: Perhaps I'd better tell you—

SON: Do I have to return the picture?

LADY: It's not the picture I'm thinking about.

SON: But that's all we're really interested in.

LADY: I think I ought to notify the police immediately.

SON: About what?

LADY: Send the telegram. At all costs I must have a confirmation from my bank.

SON: Is your letter of credit not enough?

LADY: No, not quite. Go to the Post Office yourself. I don't want to send the porter with an unsealed telegram form.

SON: And when will the money get here? *(The telephone bell rings shrilly.)*

LADY: They're ringing me already. *(Speaking into the phone.)* Who? Oh, the Bank Manager? It has arrived! I'm to call for it myself. Gladly. Don't mention it. I am not angry at all. Florence is a long way away. Yes, the Italian Postal Services. What? Why? Why? Yes, why? Oh, I see, via Berlin—that is a long way round.—Not in the least. Thank you. In ten minutes. Good-bye. *(To* SON.*)* Everything's fixed; my telegram is no longer needed. *(She tears up the telegram form.)* You have your picture. Your wine merchant can come along with us and be paid his money at the bank. Pack up your treasure. From the bank we drive straight to the station. *(Telephones, while son drapes picture.)* The bill, please. Rooms 14 and 16. Immediately. Please.

Snow-covered field, tree with maze of low-hanging branches. Sun casting blue shadows.

CASHIER: *(comes in backward. With his hands he is shoveling snow over his tracks. Standing up.)* What a wonderful piece of work a man is. How smoothly the mechanism works. Suddenly potentials are uncovered and briskly activated. How do these hands of mine know what to do? Where did they ever shovel snow before? Now they displace such masses of snow that the flakes fly. Moreover, my tracks across the snowfield are effectively obliterated. An impenetrable incognito is achieved! *(Peels off his soaked cuffs.)* Dampness and frost are conducive to chills. In no time, fever breaks out and influences decisions. Control over actions is lost, land in bed, and you're finished! *(He takes*

cuff links out, flings the cuffs away.) Retired from active service.
Lie there. You'll be missed in the wash. The lamentations will
wail through the kitchen: a pair of cuffs is missing. A calamity
in the washtubs. End of the world! *(He picks up the cuffs again
and stuffs them into his coat pockets.)* Amazing, my wits are
working again. With infallible precision. I take infinite pains to
cover my footsteps in the snow and betray myself with two bits
of laundry flung away foolishly. Mostly it's a mere trifle—a
slip—a piece of carelessness, which betrays the criminal. Hopla!
(He hunts out a comfortable seat in the fork of a tree.) I'm really
curious. A tremendous feeling of tenseness is building up in me. I
have reason to think I'm on the brink of momentous discoveries.
Experiences gained in flight will be invaluable. This morning,
still a faithful employee. Considerable fortunes were entrusted
to me, the Building Society deposited gigantic sums. By midday
an out-and-out scoundrel. Cunning as they come. The details of
escape were executed with technical perfection. The job done
and away, sensational achievement—and the day still only half
gone. *(He props his chin on the back of his fist.)* I am prepared
to welcome each and every eventuality with open arms. I possess
infallible signs that there's an answer for all demands made upon
me. I'm on the march—there's no turning back. I'm marching—
so no beating about the bush, out with the trumps—I have
staked sixty thousand on a single card—that calls for a trump.
I play too high to lose. No nonsense. Cards on the table. Show
your hand and hey presto! Got it? *(He laughs a croaking laugh.)*
Now it's your turn, lovely lady. That's your cue, silken lady.
Give it to me, shimmering lady, why you're letting the show
down. Stupid bitch. How did you get into the act? Fulfill your
natural obligations, bear children—and don't bother the
prompter!—Beg your pardon, you have a son. You are completely absolved. I withdraw my insinuations. Farewell and give
my best wishes to the manager. His sheep's eyes will smear you
with revolting slime, but don't you worry about that. The man
has been done out of sixty thousand. Terrible loss to bear. The
Building Society will have to cover him. I release you from all
your obligations towards me, dismissed, you can go.—Take my
thanks with you on your way—on the train.—What? No occasion to thank you? I think I have excellent cause to! Not worth
mentioning? You are joking, I owe you everything!—How so? —

I owe you my life!—For heaven's sake!—Me exaggerate? I was a robot, your rustling electrified me, shook me free. I leapt after you and landed in the focus of fantastic events. And with this load in my breast pocket I pay cash for all favors. *(With a nonchalant gesture.)* Now fade, you are already outbid and with your limited means—you mustn't forget your son, must you? — can expect no more! *(He pulls the bundle of notes out of his pocket and slaps it on the palm of his hand.)* I pay cash! The amount is in ready cash—payment precedes supply. Come on, now, what's offering. *(He looks into the field.)* Snow. Snow. Sunlight. Silence. *(He shakes his head and puts the money away.)* Pay for blue snow with this money—that would be a disgraceful piece of profiteering. No deal. I withdraw my offer. The deal is no good. *(Flinging out his arms.)* I must pay!—I have the money in cash!!—Where are goods worth total investment?! Sixty thousand—and the buyer to boot, body and soul? —*(Screaming.)* You must deliver the goods—you must give a fair deal—value for value!!!! *(Sun obscured by clouds. He climbs down from the fork.)* The earth is in labor—spring storms. It's coming. It's coming. I knew I did not call out in vain. The demand was urgent. Chaos is affronted—does not want to look small, alongside my colossal deed of this morning. I knew it, in such cases one must persevere! Attack hard—rip the cloak off the body and then you see something!—To whom do I raise my hat so politely? *(His hat is whipped off. The hurricane has lashed the snow from the branches. Remnants stick in the crown and form a human face with grinning jaws. A skeleton hand holds the hat.)* Have you been sitting behind me all the time eavesdropping? Are you an agent of the police? Not in the usual narrow sense. All-embracing! Existential Police? —Are you the definitive answer to my probing? Do you who stand there looking so threadbare want to suggest the final truth—that you're bankrupt? —That is rather feeble. Very feeble. In fact nothing!—I reject the information as being incomplete. Thanks for the help. Shut your rag and bone shop. I am not just anybody who can be bamboozled!—It's true the proceedings would be enormously simple. Your answer removes further complications. But I prefer complications. So fare you well—if you *can* in your condition!—I still have various things to settle. When one is on the march, one can't call on everyone. No matter how pressing the invitation. I can see I have a whole lot of calls to make before nightfall. You can't possibly be the first. More likely the last. And even then only as a last resort—it would hardly be a pleasure. But as I say—as a last resort—well, that's worth considering. Ring me again about midnight. Ask the exchange for my current number!—I'll be on the move all the time! Excuse me for being so formal. We are really much closer. Our relationship is intimate. I even believe you are inside me. So disentangle yourself from the branches penetrating you from all sides and slip right inside me. In my ambiguous position I don't like to leave traces. First of all give me my hat. *(He takes the hat from the branch which the storm bends toward him—bows.)* I see we have reached some sort of understanding. That is a beginning which inspires confidence and provides the necessary support in the whirl of the great events to come. I know how to appreciate that fully. My profound respects—*(Roll of thunder. A final gust of wind sweeps the shape from the tree. Sun breaks through. It is bright as at the beginning.)* I said right away it was just a passing apparition! *(Pulls his hat down over his face, turns up his coat collar and trots off through the cloud of snow.)*

Part 2

Living room at CASHIER'S *house. Window with withered geraniums. Two doors at the back, door right. Table and chairs. Piano.* MOTHER *sitting at the window.* FIRST DAUGHTER *embroidering at table.* SECOND DAUGHTER *practicing the Overture to Tannhäuser.* WIFE *comes and goes through the back door right.*

MOTHER: What are you playing now?
FIRST DAUGHTER: Why, it's the Overture to Tannhäuser.
MOTHER: "In a Monastery Garden" is a pretty piece too.
FIRST DAUGHTER: That's not what she got from the library this week.
WIFE: *(enters.)* Time I fried the chops.
FIRST DAUGHTER: Not nearly time yet, mother.
WIFE: No, it's not time I fried the chops yet. *(Exit.)*
MOTHER: What are you embroidering now?
FIRST DAUGHTER: I'm doing the scalloping.
WIFE: *(comes to* MOTHER.*)* We're having chops today.
MOTHER: Are you going to fry them now?

WIFE: It's not time yet. It's not even noon.
FIRST DAUGHTER: It's not nearly noon.
MOTHER: When he comes it's noon.
WIFE: Yes. *(Exit.)*
SECOND DAUGHTER: *(pricking up ears, listening.)* Father?
FIRST DAUGHTER: *(similarly.)* Father?
WIFE: *(comes.)* My husband?
MOTHER: My son?
SECOND DAUGHTER: *(opens door right.)* Father!
FIRST DAUGHTER: *(has stood up.)* Father!
WIFE: Husband!
MOTHER: Son!

(CASHIER *enters right, hangs up hat and coat.)*

WIFE: Where have you been?
CASHIER: In the cemetery.
MOTHER: Has somebody died suddenly?
CASHIER: *(pats her on the back.)* Well, you can die suddenly, but you can't be buried suddenly.
WIFE: Where have you come from?
CASHIER: From the grave. I have bored my brow through clods of earth. There's still ice clinging to me. It was quite an effort to get through. Quite an effort. I dirtied my hands a bit. You have to be nimble-fingered to extricate yourself. You lie deeply buried. Life keeps dumping loads of rubbish on you. Mountains of it are piled on top of you. Heaps of rubbish—till you're a giant rubbish tip. The dead lie the regulation six feet beneath the surface—the living are buried far, far deeper.
WIFE: You are frozen from head to foot.
CASHIER: Thawed out! Shaken by storms—springlike. It rushed and roared—I tell you it ripped the flesh off me down to the bare bones. Bones—bleached within minutes. Boneyard! At last the sun welded me together again. It was a complete rejuvenation. And here I am.
MOTHER: You've been out in the open?
CASHIER: In dreadful dungeons, mother! Arrested in bottomless pits beneath precipitously steep towers. Clanking chains deafened my ears! Darkness plucked my eyes out!
WIFE: The bank is closed. The manager has been drinking with you. Has there been a happy event in the family?

CASHIER: He has his eye on a new mistress. An Italian woman—fur—silk—from where the oranges grow. Wrists like ivory. Black hair—dark complexion. Diamonds. Genuine—all genuine. Tus-Tus—the ending sounds like Canaan. Fetch an atlas. Tus-canaan. Is there such a place? Is it an island? A mountain range? A swamp? Geography can tell us everything! But he will burn his fingers—be turned down—brushed off like a speck of dirt. There he lies—our fat little manager—twitching on the carpet—with his legs in the air!

WIFE: The bank isn't closed?

CASHIER: Of course not, my dear. Prisons never close. The steady flow of clients never ends. The eternal pilgrimage knows no limits, like sheep they go bounding in—to the slaughterhouse. A seething mass. There's no escape—unless you take a bold leap over their backs.

MOTHER: Your coat is torn at the back.

CASHIER: Look at my hat. Behold a tramp!

SECOND DAUGHTER: The lining is in shreds.

CASHIER: Put your hand in my pockets—right and left!

(FIRST DAUGHTER *pulls out a cuff.*)

(SECOND DAUGHTER *ditto.*)

CASHIER: Well?

BOTH DAUGHTERS: Your cuffs.

CASHIER: Without cuff links. The links I have here. Triumph of cold-bloodedness!—Overcoat—hat—yes, you can't go leaping over their backs without ripping something here and there. They grab at you—dig their nails in! Hurdles and fences—must have order. All men are equal. But one mighty leap—don't hesitate—and you are out of the pen—out of the treadmill. One mighty leap and here I am! Behind me: nothing—and ahead? (*He looks round the room.*)

(WIFE *stares at him.*)

MOTHER: (*semi-whisper.*) He is ill.

(WIFE *with quick decision to the door, right.*)

CASHIER: (*stops her. To one of the* DAUGHTERS.) Fetch my jacket. (DAUGHTER *through door left; comes back with braided velvet jacket. He puts it on.)* My slippers. *(The other* DAUGHTER *brings them.)* My smoking cap. *(*DAUGHTER *comes with embroidered cap.)* My pipe.

MOTHER: You shouldn't smoke, if you've been—

WIFE: *(silences her quickly.)* Shall I bring you a light?

CASHIER: *(dressed in indoor clothes: makes himself comfortable at the table.)* Light her up!

WIFE: *(flutters round him solicitously for a while.)* Is it drawing?

CASHIER: *(busy with pipe.)* I shall have to send it away for a thorough clean. There are probably accumulations of unused tobacco fragments in the stem. I have noticed some kind of blockage. I have to suck harder than should be necessary.

WIFE: Shall I remove it right away?

CASHIER: No, stay where you are! *(Puffing out mighty clouds of smoke.)* It'll do. *(To* SECOND DAUGHTER.*)* Play.

*(*SECOND DAUGHTER *obeys sign from* MOTHER, *sits at piano and plays.)*

CASHIER: What piece is that?

SECOND DAUGHTER: *(breathless.)* Wagner.

CASHIER: *(nods approval. To* FIRST DAUGHTER.*)* Are you sewing, mending, darning?

FIRST DAUGHTER: *(sitting down rapidly.)* I'm doing the scalloping now.

CASHIER: Practical.—And you, mama?

MOTHER: *(infected by the general unease.)* I was just having forty winks.

CASHIER: Peaceful.

MOTHER: Yes, my life has become peaceful.

CASHIER: *(to* WIFE.*)* And you?

WIFE: I'm going to fry the chops.

CASHIER: *(nods.)* The kitchen.

WIFE: I'll fry yours now.

CASHIER: *(as before.)* The kitchen.

*(*WIFE *exits.)*

CASHIER: *(To* FIRST DAUGHTER.*)* Open the doors wide.

*(*FIRST DAUGHTER *pushes the doors at the back open: right, the* WIFE *busy at the stove in the kitchen; left, the bedroom with the twin beds.)*

WIFE: *(at the door.)* Do you feel hot? *(Back to the stove.)*

CASHIER: *(looking round.)* Dear old grandmother at the window. Daughters at the table, embroidering, playing Wagner. Wife busy in the kitchen. Family life—within four walls. The cosy comfort of togetherness. Mother—son—child all assembled. Familiar magic weaves its spell. The parlor with its table and hanging lamp. Piano on the right. The tiled stove. The kitchen—daily bread. Morning coffee, midday chops. Bedroom: beds, in and out. Familiar magic. In the end—you're flat on your back—stiff and white. The table pushed against the wall there—a yellow coffin laid across it, removable mountings—some crepe round the lamp—and the piano isn't played for a year—

(SECOND DAUGHTER stops playing and runs sobbing into the kitchen.)

WIFE: *(at the door, trembling.)* She is still practicing her new piece.

MOTHER: Why doesn't she get out the music for "In a Monastery Garden"?

(CASHIER lets pipe go out. Begins to change his clothes.)

WIFE: Are you going to the bank? Have you got to go somewhere on business?

CASHIER: To the bank—business—no.

WIFE: Where do you mean to go, then?

CASHIER: That's a difficult question, my dear. I have clambered down from wind-swept trees to find an answer. I looked in here first. That was only natural. Everything is absolutely wonderful—I do not dispute its undoubted advantages, but it does not survive the supreme test. The solution does not lie here—so I know what I have to do. The answer here is negative. *(He is fully dressed now as before.)*

WIFE: *(shattered.)* Husband, how wild you look!

CASHIER: A tramp. I told you so. Don't scold! Better a ragged wanderer on the street—than a street with no wanderers on it at all!

WIFE: But we're just going to have lunch.

CASHIER: Chops; I smell them.

MOTHER: You don't mean you're going out—before lunch—?

CASHIER: A full stomach makes a man sleepy.

(MOTHER *flails around with her arms, falls backward.*)

FIRST DAUGHTER: Grandmama—
SECOND DAUGHTER: *(from the kitchen.)* Grandmama. *(Both fall on their knees beside her.)*

(WIFE *stands rigid.*)

CASHIER: *(walks over to armchair.)* Because a man leaves before lunch, she drops dead. *(He looks at the dead woman.)* Grief? Mourning? Floods of tears, sweeping all before. Are the bonds so close that when they snap fulfillment is found in intensest grief? Mother–son? *(He pulls the banknotes from his pocket and weighs them in his hand—shakes his head and pockets them again.)* No total paralysis in grief—no fulfillment so absolute that it streams from the eyes. Eyes dry—thoughts work on. I must hurry if I want to break through to valid truths! *(He puts his worn wallet on the table.)* Take note. These are my honorably earned wages. The remark may become important. Take note. *(Goes off right.)*

(WIFE *stands motionless.*)

BANK MANAGER: *(enters through door right.)* Is your husband home? —Has your husband been here? —I have to make a rather distressing announcement. He has absconded with the bank's money. We discovered his defection some hours ago. There's a matter of some sixty thousand deposited by the Building Society. I have refrained from reporting him to the police in the hope that he might think better of it. This is the most I can do. I came personally.—Your husband has not been here? *(He looks around, notices jacket, pipe, etc., all doors open.)* To all appearances— *(His eyes stop at the group by the window, nods.)* I see things have already reached an advanced stage. Well, in that case—*(He shrugs his shoulders, puts his hat on.)* There only remains the honest expression of my personal regret, of which I desire to assure you—apart from that, the consequences. *(Exit.)*
BOTH DAUGHTERS: *(crowd round* WIFE.*)* Mother—
WIFE: *(exploding.)* Stop screeching. Stop gaping at me. What do you want? Who are you? Brats—monkey-faces—what do I care about you? *(Flings herself across the table.)* My husband has left me.

(BOTH DAUGHTERS *shyly holding hands.*)

Sports Palace. Six-day cycle race. Arc light. In the haze roughly carpentered suspended wooden ramp. The JEWISH GENTLEMEN *acting as* STEWARDS *come and go. They are all indistinguishable; little scurrying figures, in dinner jackets, dumpy top hats tilted back, binoculars on leather straps round neck. Rumbling roar of wheels over boards. Whistles, shouts, catcalls from packed public above and below. Bands playing.*

A GENTLEMAN: *(entering.)* Is everything ready?
A GENTLEMAN: See for yourself.
A GENTLEMAN: *(through binoculars.)* The potted plants—
A GENTLEMAN: What's up with the potted plants?
A GENTLEMAN: I thought as much.
A GENTLEMAN: Well, what's the matter with the potted plants?
A GENTLEMAN: Who arranged them like that?
A GENTLEMAN: You're right.
A GENTLEMAN: Why, it's crazy.
A GENTLEMAN: Did nobody bother about how they were arranged?
A GENTLEMAN: Simply ridiculous.
A GENTLEMAN: Whoever did it must be blind.
A GENTLEMAN: Or asleep.
A GENTLEMAN: That's the only acceptable explanation.
A GENTLEMAN: What do you mean—asleep? This is only the fourth night.
A GENTLEMAN: The pots must be moved more to the side.
A GENTLEMAN: Will you see to it?
A GENTLEMAN: Right against the walls.
A GENTLEMAN: There must be a clear view of the whole track.
A GENTLEMAN: And the Royal Box.
A GENTLEMAN: I'll help you. *(All exit.)*

(A GENTLEMAN *comes in, fires a starting pistol. Exit.*)

(TWO GENTLEMEN *enter with red lacquered megaphone.*)

FIRST GENTLEMAN: How big is the prize?
SECOND GENTLEMAN: Eighty. Fifty to the first. Thirty to the second.

FIRST GENTLEMAN: Three laps. No more. We're exhausting the competitors.

OTHER GENTLEMAN: *(announces through megaphone.)* A prize of eighty pounds is offered from the bar—to be competed for immediately, over three laps: fifty pounds to the winner, thirty pounds for the runner-up. *(Clapping.)*

*(*SEVERAL GENTLEMEN *enter, one with a red flag.)*

ONE GENTLEMAN: Start them off now.

ANOTHER GENTLEMAN: Not yet—Number seven is changing over.

A GENTLEMAN: Start.

(A GENTLEMAN *lowers the red flag. Noise reaches a crescendo. Then clapping and whistling.)*

A GENTLEMAN: The little fellows have to win sometimes.

A GENTLEMAN: It's a good thing the big boys are holding back.

A GENTLEMAN: There's still a lot of work ahead of them tonight.

A GENTLEMAN: The tension among the riders is tremendous.

A GENTLEMAN: I can imagine.

A GENTLEMAN: You wait and see. Tonight will be decisive.

A GENTLEMAN: *(shrugging his shoulders.)* The Americans are still fresh.

A GENTLEMAN: Our lads will make them show what they are made of.

A GENTLEMAN: Anyway, it would make the Royal Visit worth while.

A GENTLEMAN: *(looking through binoculars.)* The Royal Box is clear now. *(All* GENTLEMEN *exit except one with megaphone.)*

A GENTLEMAN: *(with a ticket.)* The result.

A GENTLEMAN: *(through megaphone.)* Prize from the bar. Fifty for number eleven, thirty for number four.

(Victory fanfare from band. Whistles and clapping. The stewards' ramp is empty. ONE GENTLEMAN *enters with* CASHIER. CASHIER *in tails, evening cloak, top hat, white gloves, pointed beard; hair carefully parted.)*

CASHIER: Tell me how this works.

GENTLEMAN: I'll introduce you.

CASHIER: My name is not important.

GENTLEMAN: You have the right to be introduced to the Board.

CASHIER: I'll remain incognito.

GENTLEMAN: You are a lover of our sport?

CASHIER: I have not the slightest idea what it's all about. What are these fellows down there doing? I see an arena and the line of color snaking round it. Every so often one comes in and another falls out. Why?

GENTLEMAN: The riders race in pairs. While one is in—

CASHIER: The other chap is out having a good sleep?

GENTLEMAN: Being massaged.

CASHIER: And you call that a six-day cycle race?

GENTLEMAN: What do you mean?

CASHIER: You might just as well call it a six-day cycle rest. There's always one partner asleep.

A GENTLEMAN: *(enters.)* The ramp is reserved for the management.

FIRST GENTLEMAN: This gentleman offers a prize sum of one thousand pounds.

OTHER GENTLEMAN: Allow me to introduce myself.

CASHIER: On no account.

FIRST GENTLEMAN: The gentleman wishes to remain incognito.

CASHIER: Impenetrably.

FIRST GENTLEMAN: I have just been explaining some of the rules to him.

CASHIER: Yes. Don't you find it funny?

SECOND GENTLEMAN: In what way?

CASHIER: This six-day cycle rest.

SECOND GENTLEMAN: So one thousand pounds it is—over how many laps?

CASHIER: You decide.

SECOND GENTLEMAN: How much for the winner?

CASHIER: You decide.

SECOND GENTLEMAN: Eight hundred pounds and two hundred pounds. *(Through megaphone.)* Prize awarded by a gentleman who wishes to remain anonymous, over ten laps, to be run off immediately: eight hundred pounds for the winner—two hundred pounds for the runner-up. One thousand pounds in all. *(Mighty roar.)*

FIRST GENTLEMAN: Then tell me, if you regard the whole show as a mere joke, why do you award one thousand pounds in prizes?

CASHIER: Because the effect is marvelous.

FIRST GENTLEMAN: On the speed of the riders?

CASHIER: Rubbish.

A GENTLEMAN: *(coming in.)* Are you the gentleman who is putting up the thousand?

CASHIER: In gold.

GENTLEMAN: That would take too long.

CASHIER: What, to count? Watch me. *(Takes a roll out, tears it open, shakes the contents into his hand, checks the empty packet, throws it away and quickly counts the clinking gold coins into his cupped hand.)* Besides, it takes the weight off my pockets.

GENTLEMAN: Sir, I see you are an expert in these matters.

CASHIER: A mere trifle, sir. *(He hands over the sum.)* Take it.

GENTLEMAN: Received with thanks.

CASHIER: All part of the service.

A GENTLEMAN: *(enters.)* Where is the gentleman? Allow me—

CASHIER: Nothing.

A GENTLEMAN: *(with the red flag.)* I'll signal for the start.

A GENTLEMAN: This time the big stars will go flat out.

A GENTLEMAN: All the champions are in the race.

A GENTLEMAN: *(waving the flag.)* Start. *(Drops the flag. Wild howl starts up.)*

CASHIER: *(seizing two GENTLEMEN by the neck and bending their heads round backward.)* Now I shall answer your question. Look up!

A GENTLEMAN: What you have to follow are the changing phases of the struggle down below on the track.

CASHIER: Childish. Somebody has to be first, because he's better than the others.—The magic is revealed up there. In three tiers— one above the other—packed full with spectators there—the excitement rages. In the first tier—apparently the better class public still shows some restraint. Just stares, wide-eyed stares. One row higher you already have bodies beginning to move. And shout— that's the center balcony!—Right up in the Gods all restraints are dropped. Fanatical screams. Total abandon. The gallery for passion!—Just look at that group. Five entwined as one. Five heads on one shoulder. One demented body sprouting five pairs of arms. One man is in the center. He is being crushed—squeezed forward—there, see his bowler tumbling down—idly drifting down through the haze—to the center balcony. On to a lady's bosom. She is unaware of it. There it rests. Delightful! Delightful!

She'll never notice the hat, she'll go to bed with it, and wear the bowler on her bosom, year in, year out.

GENTLEMAN: The Belgian is putting his spurt on.

CASHIER: The center balcony is starting to scream. The hat has made the connection. The lady has crushed it against the rail. Great weals appear on her bosom. Lovely lady, you have to go to the rail, and have your bosom branded. It is inevitable: it is senseless to struggle. Caught up in that tangled mass of humanity you are pressed to the wall and must reveal what you are. Give yourself, your all—without a whimper!

GENTLEMAN: You know the lady?

CASHIER: Now look: up top the five are squeezing the man in the middle over the railing—he swings free plunges—there—sails down into the first row. Where is he? Choking to death somewhere? Eliminated—buried without trace. Nobody cares. A spectator—someone who dropped in—a chance visitor, no more among thousands and thousands!

A GENTLEMAN: The German is moving up.

CASHIER: The first rows are frantic now. That fellow has made the contact. Restraint has gone by the board. Dinner-jackets quiver. Shirt fronts split. Studs pop in all directions. Beards twitch, lips snarl, dentures rattle. Top and bottom and the middle rows are one. One single howl from all levels—without distinction. All distinctions are lost. That much has been accomplished.

GENTLEMAN: *(turning round.)* The German has it. What have you got to say to that?

CASHIER: Utter rubbish.

(Tremendous din. Clapping.)

A GENTLEMAN: A fabulous spurt.

CASHIER: Fabulous fiddlesticks.

A GENTLEMAN: We'll get the office to check the result. *(All exeunt.)*

CASHIER: *(holding on to this* GENTLEMAN.*)* Have you still any doubts?

GENTLEMAN: The Germans are bound to win.

CASHIER: That's unimportant. *(Pointing upward.)* That's where it is, there you have the compelling fact. There you have the ultimate compression of reality. Here we witness the dizzy, soaring heights of accomplishment. From the first rows right up to the Gods, fusion. Out of the seething dissolution of the individual comes the concentrated essence. Passion! All restraints—all differences melt away. Concealing coverings stripped off nakedness. Passion!—To break through here is to experience. Doors—gates fade away. Trumpets blare and walls crumble. No resisting— no modesty—no mothering—no childhood: nothing but pure passion! This is it. This is it. This is really worthwhile. This is worth the grab—that's your reward brought to you on a platter!

A Gentleman: *(coming in.)* The Ambulance Squad is working magnificently.

Cashier: The man who fell was ground to pulp?

A Gentleman: Trampled to death.

Cashier: There are bound to be deaths, where others live feverishly.

A Gentleman: *(through megaphone.)* Result of the prize awarded by the gentleman wishing to remain anonymous: eight hundred pounds won by Number Two; two hundred pounds by Number One.

(Mad applause. Fanfare.)

A Gentleman: The teams are exhausted.

A Gentleman: The tempo is visibly slackening.

A Gentleman: We must get their managers to keep things quiet on the track.

Cashier: A new prize!

A Gentleman: Later, sir.

Cashier: There must be no let-up in this situation.

A Gentleman: The situation is getting dangerous for the riders.

Cashier: Never mind about them. The public is bubbling with excitement. This must be exploited to the full. The conflagration must reach heights never before experienced. Fifty thousand pounds.

A Gentleman: You mean it?

A Gentleman: How much?

Cashier: I'm wagering everything on it.

A Gentleman: An incredible prize.

Cashier: And the effect must be incredible too. Alert the Ambulance Squads on all levels.

A Gentleman: We accept the offer. We'll have it contested when the Royal Box is occupied.

A Gentleman: Splendid.

A GENTLEMAN: Great idea.

A GENTLEMAN: The Royal Visit will undoubtedly be worthwhile now.

CASHIER: What does that mean: with the Royal Box occupied?

A GENTLEMAN: We'll discuss the conditions in the office. Thirty thousand the winner; fifteen thousand second; five thousand third.

A GENTLEMAN: The field will be blown sky-high tonight.

A GENTLEMAN: This will pretty well finish the racing.

A GENTLEMAN: Anyway, the Royal Box will be occupied.

(SALVATION ARMY GIRL appears. Laughter from spectators. Whistles. Cat calls.)

SALVATION ARMY GIRL: *(offering.)* The War Cry—a shilling, sir.

CASHIER: Another time.

SALVATION ARMY GIRL: The War Cry, sir.

CASHIER: What kind of rag are you hawking there?

SALVATION ARMY GIRL: The War Cry, sir.

CASHIER: You come too late. The battle is in full swing here.

SALVATION ARMY GIRL: *(with the collecting box.)* A shilling, sir.

CASHIER: You want to launch a war with a shilling?

SALVATION ARMY GIRL: A shilling, sir.

CASHIER: I'm subsidizing this war to the tune of fifty thousand.

SALVATION ARMY GIRL: A shilling.

CASHIER: For a wretched little skirmish. I only subsidize top performances.

SALVATION ARMY GIRL: A shilling.

CASHIER: I only carry gold.

SALVATION ARMY GIRL: A shilling.

CASHIER: Gold—

SALVATION ARMY GIRL: A—

CASHIER: *(roars at her through the megaphone.)* Gold—gold—gold!

(SALVATION ARMY GIRL exits.)

(Neighing laughter from the spectators. Clapping. Many GENTLEMEN enter.)

A GENTLEMAN: Would you care to announce the prize yourself?

CASHIER: I'll remain vaguely in the background. *(He gives him the megaphone.)* You announce it now. Give them the final convulsion!

A GENTLEMAN: *(through megaphone.)* A new prize offered by the same gentleman who wishes to remain anonymous. *(Cries of "Bravo!")* Total sum of fifty thousand *(deafening screams)*—five thousand to the third—*(screaming)*—fifteen thousand to the second—*(screaming reaches crescendo)* to the winner thirty thousand—*(ecstasy.)*

CASHIER: *(stands apart, nodding.)* This'll be it. This is the climax. Fulfillment. The howling gale of a spring hurricane. Surging wave of humanity. Unleashed—free. Curtains raised—pretenses lowered. Humanity. Free humanity. High or low—just man. No different levels, no social strata—no classes. Release from class and wage-slavery in passion sweeping to infinity. Not pure, but free! That will be the reward for my boldness. *(He pulls the bundle of notes out.)* Given gladly—account settled without hesitation.

(Sudden dead silence. National Anthem. The GENTLEMEN *have taken off their silk hats and stand with bowed heads.)*

A GENTLEMAN: If you'll hand me the money, we can have the race for your prize immediately.

CASHIER: What is the meaning of this?

GENTLEMAN: What, sir?

CASHIER: This sudden unexpected silence above and below?

GENTLEMAN: Not at all unexpected. His Royal Highness has entered the Royal Box.

CASHIER: His Royal Highness—the box.—

GENTLEMAN: Your considerable prize comes at a most opportune time.

CASHIER: I've no intention of throwing my money away!

GENTLEMAN: What do you mean?

CASHIER: It's too high a price to pay to subsidize grovelling lickspittles.

GENTLEMAN: Would you be kind enough to explain.

CASHIER: The flame that was raging just a moment ago has been stamped out by His Highness's patent leather boot. You must be mad, to think I'm crazy enough to throw sixpence to these dogs. Even that would be too much. A boot where the dog takes its tail between its legs, that's the prize offered!

GENTLEMAN: The prize is announced. His Royal Highness awaits in his box. The public too is waiting, quietly and respectfully. What does this mean?

CASHIER: If you cannot grasp the meaning of my words—then you cannot fail to gain the necessary insight, if I administer an unequivocal indication of my feelings. *(He bashes the* GENTLE-MAN's *silk hat over his head onto his shoulders. Exit.)*

(National Anthem again. Silence. People on ramp bow.)

Night Club. Chambre séparée. Still dark. Muted dance rhythms from orchestra.

*(*WAITER *opens the door, turns red light on.)*

*(*CASHIER *tails, cloak, scarf, gold-headed malacca cane.)*

WAITER: All right?
CASHIER: Perfectly.

*(*WAITER *takes cloak.)*

*(*CASHIER *at the mirror.)*

WAITER: How many places, sir?
CASHIER: Twenty-four. I'm expecting my grandmother, my mother, my wife, and various aunts. I'm celebrating my daughter's confirmation.

*(*WAITER *amazed.)*

CASHIER: *(to him in the mirror.)* Ass! Two! Or what do you pad these discretely lit alcoves for?
WAITER: Which brand do you prefer, sir?
CASHIER: You greasy fixer. My good friend, you can leave me to decide which bloom I'll pluck off the dance floor—bud or full-blown flower—short or slim. I shall not over-extend your inestimable services. Inestimable—or have you fixed rates?
WAITER: Which brand of champagne, sir?
CASHIER: *(clears throat.)* Er, Grand Marnier.
WAITER: That is a liqueur for after the champagne.
CASHIER: Oh—then I shall let myself be guided by you.
WAITER: Two bottles of Pommery. Dry?
CASHIER: Of course I'm dry.
WAITER: Extra dry?
CASHIER: None of your business, but I am; better make it three bottles. OK.
WAITER: *(with the menu.)* And for dinner.

CASHIER: Pinnacles!

WAITER: Oeufs pochés Bergère? Poulet grillé? Steak de veau truffé? Parfait de foie gras en croûte? Salade coeur de laitue?

CASHIER: Pinnacles—from start to finish, nothing but pinnacles.

WAITER: Beg your pardon, sir?

CASHIER: *(tapping him on the nose.)* Pinnacles are ultimate peaks of perfection. And that's what we must have from your pots and pans. The most delicate of delicacies. The menu of menus. As garnish for great events. That's your affair, my friend, I am not the cook.

WAITER: *(lays a larger menu card on the table.)* Ready to serve in twenty minutes. *(Arranges glasses etc.)*

(Through the half-open door heads with silk masks appear.)

CASHIER: *(talking into the mirror, with threatening finger.)* Wait, my little moths, I'll hold you up to the light directly. We'll discuss that when we have a seat together. *(He nods.)*

(Giggling masks disappear.)

(WAITER hangs a RESERVED *sign on the door. Exits.)*

CASHIER: *(pushes his top hat back, takes cigarettes out of gold case and lights up.)* To-re-ador, To-re-ador—the things one comes out with! The mind is simply loaded. Everything, just everything. Toreador—Carmen—Caruso. Read the junk somewhere—it stuck. Stored up. At this very moment I could give an account of the Baghdad Railway deal. The Crown Prince of Rumania marries the Tsar's second daughter. Tatiana. Right, let her marry. Happy honeymoon. The people need princes. Tat-Tat-iana— *(Exits, twirling cane.)*

(WAITER with bottles and ice-bucket: uncorks and pours. Exits.)

CASHIER: *(shooing in a female mask—red and yellow chequered harlequin costume fitting boyishly from top to toe and open at the bosom.)* Moth!

MASK: *(running round the table.)* Bubbly! *(Pours both glasses of champagne down her throat, falls into the sofa.)* Bubbly!

CASHIER: *(refilling.)* Liquid dynamite. Load your chequered body.

MASK: Bubbly!

CASHIER: Action stations, ready to fire!

MASK: Bubbly!

CASHIER: *(putting away the bottles.)* Empty. *(Joins* MASK *on sofa.)* Ready to fire.

(MASK leans over drunkenly.)

CASHIER: *(shakes her limp arms.)* Wake up, Moth.

(MASK limp.)

CASHIER: Give yourself a shake, pretty butterfly. You have licked the prickly yellow honey. Open your butterfly wings. Descend on me. Bury me, cover me up. In certain respects I have fallen out with the world of decent security—now you fall out and cover me with your body.

MASK: *(drunkenly.)* Bubbly.

CASHIER: No, my bird of paradise. You have taken on a sufficient load. You've had enough.

MASK: Bubbly.

CASHIER: Not another bubble. Or you'll get hazy. And do me out of all your glorious possibilities.

MASK: Bubbly.

CASHIER: Or haven't you any? Any at all? Look—if I take deep soundings: what have you got?

MASK: Bubbly.

CASHIER: You've certainly got that. I gave it to you. But what can you give me?

(MASK falls asleep.)

CASHIER: You want to sleep it off here? Little devil. I haven't the time for jokes of that kind. *(Stands up, fills a glass, throws it in her face.)* Rise and shine. Wakey! Wakey!

MASK: *(leaps up.)* Swine!

CASHIER: You have an unusual name. Unfortunately I am not in a position to reciprocate and give you my name. Well then, now we know you belong to one of the many branches of the pig family, clear out.

MASK: I'll make you pay for this.

CASHIER: More than reasonable, considering I've paid for everything so far.

(MASK exits.)

(CASHIER *drinks champagne. Exits.*)

(WAITER *enters, brings caviar; takes empty bottles away.*)

(CASHIER *enters with two black* MASKS.)

FIRST MASK: *(flinging the door shut.)* Reserved.
SECOND MASK: *(at the table.)* Caviar.
FIRST MASK: *(running up.)* Caviar.
CASHIER: Black like you. Eat it up. Stuff it down your throats. *(Seating himself between the two on the sofa.)* Talk Caviar. Sing Champagne. I can do without your brains. *(Fills the glasses, heaps the plates.)* You're not to speak. Not a syllable, not an exclamation. Silent as the fish, which spawned this black caviar over the Black Sea. Giggle, carry on, but don't talk. 'Cause nothing comes out of it anyway. At most you might have to get out of the sofa. I've cleared it once already.

(MASKS *look at each other giggling*)

CASHIER: *(grabbing the first one.)* What color are your eyes? Green-yellow? *(To the other.)* And yours? Blue-red? Charming game of eyeballs in the slits. Very promising. Must find out. I'll offer a prize for the prettiest!

(MASKS *laugh.*)

CASHIER: *(to the first.)* You are the more beautiful. You put up powerful resistance. Wait, I'll tear down the curtain and see the show!

(MASK *breaks away.*)

CASHIER: *(to the other.)* Do you have to conceal your identity? Your modesty is overwhelmingly attractive. You wandered into this dance hall by mistake. You are seeking adventure. Well, you have found the adventurer you were seeking. Off with your mask—let me see the peaches-and-cream complexion.

(MASK *moves away from him.*)

CASHIER: I've reached my goal. I sit trembling—my blood is pounding. This is it!—And now pay. *(Brings out wad of notes and splits it.)* Lovely mask, because you are lovely. Lovely mask, because you are lovely. *(Covering his eyes with his hands.)* One—two—three!

(MASKS raise their masks.)

CASHIER: *(looks, laughs.)* Cover up—cover up—cover up! *(Runs round the table.)* Horrors—horrors—horrors! Get out right now—I mean now—or—*(swings his cane.)*

FIRST MASK: Do you want us?

SECOND MASK: You want us—

CASHIER: I'll want you!!

(MASKS off.)

CASHIER: *(shuddering, drinks champagne.)* You hags! *(Exits.)*

(WAITER with new bottles. Exits.)

CASHIER: *(pushes the door open: dances in with a pierrette, whose cloak reaches down to her shoes. He leaves her standing in the middle of the floor and flings himself on the sofa.)* Dance!

(MASK stands still.)

CASHIER: Dance, spin. Dance, dance. Brains don't count. Beauty doesn't count. The dance is the thing—twisting—spinning. Dance! Dance! Dance!

(MASK comes to the table.)

CASHIER: *(waving her away.)* No pause. No letup. Dance.

(MASK stands still.)

CASHIER: Why don't you skip? Do you know what dervishes are? Dancing men. Alive while they dance. Dead when they stop. Death and dancing—erected at the turning points of life. Between—

(The SALVATION ARMY GIRL comes in.)

CASHIER: Hallelujah!

SALVATION ARMY GIRL: The War Cry.

CASHIER: A shilling.

(The SALVATION ARMY GIRL offers box.)

CASHIER: When do you expect me to jump into your box?

SALVATION ARMY GIRL: The War Cry.

CASHIER: You really expect me to, don't you?

SALVATION ARMY GIRL: A shilling.
CASHIER: All right—when?
SALVATION ARMY GIRL: A shilling.
CASHIER: You're hanging on to my coattails, aren't you?

(SALVATION ARMY GIRL *shakes the box.*)

CASHIER: And I'll shake you off again!

(SALVATION ARMY GIRL *shakes.*)

CASHIER: All right! *(To* MASK.*)* Dance!

(SALVATION ARMY GIRL *off.*)

(MASK *comes to the sofa.*)

CASHIER: Why do you sit in the corners of the rooms, why don't you dance in the middle of the floor? That's what drew my attention to you. The others are all leaping about and you stay still. Why do you wear long skirts, when all the others show as much of their legs as schoolboys?
MASK: I don't dance.
CASHIER: You don't dance like the others.
MASK: I cannot dance.
CASHIER: Not to the music—following the rhythm. That's stupid anyway. You know other dances. You conceal something beneath your skirts.—Your special kicks, not to be confined within the structures of rhythms and steps. Whirling movements of far greater tempo, that's what you go in for. *(Pushing everything off the table onto the carpet.)* There is your dance floor. Jump up. Boundless tumult within the narrow confines of this table. Jump up. Leap from the carpet. Effortless. Soaring off the springs which lie coiled in your feet. Leap. Prick your heels. Arch your thighs. Let your dress swirl round your dancing limbs!
MASK: *(nestling up to him on the sofa.)* I cannot dance.
CASHIER: You are whipping me up to a state of high tension. You don't know what's at stake. You shall know. *(He shows her the notes.)* Everything!
MASK: *(slides his hand down her leg.)* I can't.
CASHIER: *(leaps up.)* A wooden leg! *(He grabs the ice bucket and rams it on her head.)* We'll make it sprout. I'll water it!
MASK: I'll teach you—

CASHIER: Exactly what I'm here for.
MASK: Wait here. *(Exits.)*

(CASHIER leaves a note on the table, takes cloak and stick, hurries off. GENTLEMEN in evening dress enter.)

A GENTLEMAN: Where is the fellow?
A GENTLEMAN: We'll give him what for.
A GENTLEMAN: Stealing our girls—
A GENTLEMAN: Showing off with champagne and caviar—
A GENTLEMAN: Then insulting them—
A GENTLEMAN: We'll give the fellow a piece of our mind.
A GENTLEMAN: Where is he?
A GENTLEMAN: Cleared out!
A GENTLEMAN: Taken off!
A GENTLEMAN: The Gentleman smelled trouble.
A GENTLEMAN: *(discovering the note.)* Look at the size of this note!
A GENTLEMAN: Wow!
A GENTLEMAN: He's sure got some nerve.
A GENTLEMAN: Is that to pay the bill?
A GENTLEMAN: Who cares? He's done a disappearing trick. We'll make the note disappear too. *(Puts it in his pocket.)*
A GENTLEMAN: That'll be our compensation.
A GENTLEMAN: For stealing our girls.
A GENTLEMAN: Let's dump the tarts.
A GENTLEMAN: They're sozzled anyway.
A GENTLEMAN: They'll only soil our evening suits.
A GENTLEMAN: We'll go to a brothel and rent the place for three days.
ALL: Bravo! Let's go. Let's blow. Look out, here comes the waiter.

(WAITER with loaded tray; dismayed at the sight of the table.)

A GENTLEMAN: Looking for somebody?
A GENTLEMAN: Carry on serving him under the table. *(Laughter.)*
WAITER: *(bursting out.)* The champagne—the supper—the private room—nothing paid for. Five bottles of Pommery—two helpings of caviar—two special suppers—I have to cover the lot. I have a wife and children. I've been out of work for four months. I had contracted a weak lung. You won't see me ruined, gentlemen?

A GENTLEMAN: What's your lung got to do with us? We've all got a wife and family. What do you want of us? Did we slip off without paying? What are you talking about?

A GENTLEMAN: What sort of place is this anyway? Where exactly are we, here? This is a low clip joint, for sure. You entice people into such company? We are respectable people, we pay for what we drink. Eh? What? Eh?

A GENTLEMAN: *(who has changed the door key from inside to outside.)* Look behind you. This is how we pay. *(Gives the* WAITER, *who has turned round, a push in the back.)*

*(*WAITER *staggers forward, collapses on the carpet.)*

*(*GENTLEMEN *exeunt.)*

WAITER: *(gets up, runs to the door, finds it locked. Hammering the wood with his fists.)* Let me out—you don't have to pay— I'm going to throw myself into the river.

Salvation Army Hall, seen in depth. Backed by yellow curtain with black cross sewn on, big enough to take a man. On the platform right, Penitents' Bench—on left the brass band instruments, kettle drums, etc. Closely packed rows of benches. Hanging light bracket over everything with tangle of wires for electric light bulbs. Entrance front. Music of Salvation Army Band. From one corner, clapping and laughter.

Salvation Army Girl goes over and sits down beside the trouble-maker—a clerk—takes his hands and talks to him in an earnest whisper.

VOICE: *(from the other corner.)* Closer, closer.

*(*SALVATION ARMY GIRL *goes to this fellow, a young* WORKMAN.*)*

WORKMAN: Well, what do you want?

*(*SALVATION ARMY GIRL *looks at him solemnly, shaking her head. Laughter.)*

SALVATION ARMY OFFICER: *(a woman, appears on platform.)* I've a question I want to put to you.

(Some "SSSh" for silence.)

OTHERS: *(amused.)* Speak louder. No, don't. Music. Bring on the band. Bring on the cherubs with trumpets.

VOICE: Begin.

ANOTHER VOICE: No, don't.

OFFICER: Why are you sitting down there on these benches?

ANOTHER VOICE: Why not?

SALVATION ARMY OFFICER: You've filled every single place. You're packed in, each one hard up against the next. And yet there is one bench empty.

VOICE: Nothing doing.

SALVATION ARMY OFFICER: Why do you stay down there, where you have to press and crush? Isn't it unpleasant, to sit in a crowd? Who knows his neighbor? You rub knees with him and maybe he is sick. You look into his eyes—and maybe murderous thoughts lurk behind them. I know there are many sick and sinful people in this room. The sick and the sinful come in and sit down with everybody else. Therefore I warn you! Beware of the man sitting beside you on these benches. These benches are full of the sick and sinful.

VOICE: Oh, Mum, she's getting at me.

SALVATION ARMY OFFICER: I know it and so I advise you: steer clear of your neighbor. That is the advice we are given. Sickness and crime are so widespread in this asphalt jungle. Who is there among you who is not festering? Your skin can be white and smooth, but your eyes proclaim you. You have eyes, but not to see with—your eyes are open, only to betray you. You betray yourselves. You are no longer free of the great plague: the risk of infection is great. You have been keeping bad company too long. So if you do not wish to be like your neighbor in this asphalt jungle, step forward from these benches. This is the last warning. Repent! Repent! Come up, come up to the stool of repentance. Come to the stool of repentance. Come to the stool of repentance.

(Salvation Army band starts up.)

*(*SALVATION ARMY GIRL *brings in the* CASHIER.*)*

*(*CASHIER *excites some attention in his tails.*)*

*(*SALVATION ARMY GIRL *shows him to a seat, sits beside him and explains things to him.*)*

*(*CASHIER *looks round in amusement.*)*

(Bands stops. Ironical applause, loud and long.)

SALVATION ARMY OFFICER: *(stepping forward on the platform again.)* Let our young comrade tell you how he found the path to repentance.

*(*YOUNG SALVATION ARMY MAN *steps forward onto the platform.)*

VOICE: You look just the type. *(Laughter.)*

YOUNG SALVATION ARMY MAN: I want to tell you of my sin. I led a life with no thought for my soul. I lived only for my body. I set it up in front of my soul, if you like, and made my body stronger and bigger. My soul was completely absorbed by it. I sought fame through my body and failed to see that this only magnified the shadow under which my soul was languishing. My besetting sin was sport. I practiced and practiced, never stopping to consider what I was doing or why. I was conceited about the speed of my feet on the pedals, the strength of my arms on the handlebars. When applause engulfed me I forgot everything. I redoubled my efforts and became the national sporting champion. My name was on every hoarding, every billboard and on millions of colored handouts. Then I became world champion. At last my soul cried out in protest. It lost patience. In one big race I fell. I was only slightly injured. My soul wanted me to have time for repentance. My soul gave me the strength to find a way out. I stepped forward from the benches in this room— up to the stool of repentance. Only then did my soul have peace to speak to me. And what it tells me I cannot tell you here. It is too beautiful and my words are too weak to give you a picture of it. You must come forward yourselves, and hear it within yourselves. *(He steps aside.)*

*(*VOICE *dirty laugh.)*

*(*OTHERS *shush for silence.)*

SALVATION ARMY GIRL: *(to* CASHIER.*)* Do you hear him?

CASHIER: Leave me alone.

SALVATION ARMY OFFICER: You have heard the testimony of our comrade. Doesn't it sound tempting? Can anyone gain anything more lovely than his soul? And it's so easy, because it is there inside all of you. You only have to give it peace. It just wants to sit quietly beside you. This bench is its favorite seat. There must be somebody among you who has sinned like our comrade. Our comrade wants to help him. He has prepared the way for him. Come now. Come to the stool of repentance. Come to the stool of repentance. Come to the stool of repentance. *(Silence reigns.)*

(One powerful young man, his arm in a sling, stands up in one corner, crosses the room smiling embarrassedly and climbs up to the platform.)

(VOICE utters an obscenity.)

ANOTHER VOICE: *(indignantly.)* Who was the filthy swine who said that?

(Cause of disturbance stands up and heads for the door in shame.)

VOICE: That's him.

(SALVATION ARMY GIRL hurries to him and leads him back to his place.)

VOICE: Don't handle him so gently.
SEVERAL: Hear, Hear!
PENITENT: *(on the platform, awkward at first.)* This city of asphalt has erected a stadium. I was a rider in that stadium. I am a professional cyclist. In the Six-Day Cycle Race. On the second night I was rammed by another cyclist. I broke my arm. I had to scratch from the race. The race rages on—I have peace. I have time to think things out in peace. I have been racing all my life without pause for thought. I want to think everything out—everything. *(Loud.)* I want to think of my sins at the stool of repentance. *(Led there by a soldier, he sinks down on the bench. Soldier stays close beside him.)*
SALVATION ARMY OFFICER: A soul has been saved!

(Salvation Army band plays. The soldiers scattered round the room have all leapt up and rejoice, arms upstretched. Band stops.)

SALVATION ARMY GIRL: *(to CASHIER.)* Do you see him?
CASHIER: The Six-day Cycle Race.
SALVATION ARMY GIRL: What are you muttering?
CASHIER: My own story. My own story.
SALVATION ARMY GIRL: Are you ready?

CASHIER: Be quiet, will you?

SALVATION ARMY OFFICER: *(appearing on platform.)* Now this comrade wants to testify. *(Somebody hisses.)*

MANY: *(shout.)* Quiet!

SALVATION ARMY GIRL: *(appearing on platform.)* Whose sin is my sin? I want to tell you about myself without shame. I come from a home in which things were sordid and dissolute. The man— he was not my father—was an alcoholic. My mother consorted with fine gentlemen. She gave me as much money as I wanted. He gave me more beatings than I wanted. *(Laughter.)* Nobody looked after me, least of all did I look after myself. So I became a lost woman. For I didn't know then that the wild state of affairs at home was meant to make me pay all the more attention to my soul—and devote myself entirely to it. I learned that in one night. I had a man with me and he wanted me to put the lights out in my room. I switched the lights out though it was not what I was accustomed to. Later when we were together I understood why he wanted it that way. For I felt only a man's trunk against me, his legs had been amputated. I was not meant to see that before. He had wooden legs, which he had secretly removed. At that point, horror seized me and never let me go. My body I now detested—only my soul could I love. Now I only love my soul. It is so perfect it's the loveliest thing I know. I know too much about my soul to be able to tell you everything. If you ask your soul, it will tell you everything—everything. *(She steps down.)*

(Silence in the hall.)

SALVATION ARMY OFFICER: *(coming forward.)* You have heard the testimony of our sister. Her soul offered itself to her. She did not turn it away. Now she can talk of it with joy. Does not anyone among you feel his soul offering itself to him? Let it come to you. Let it. Let it speak and tell all, at this bench it is undisturbed. Come to the stool of repentance. Come to the stool of repentance.

(Movement among the benches, people look round.)

PROSTITUTE: *(elderly, right at the front, begins to speak from the floor of the hall.)* What do you think of me, ladies and gentlemen? I only came in here for shelter, because I was tired out walking the streets. I'm not a bit embarrassed. I don't know this place at all. This is my first time. Pure chance brings me here. *(Up on platform now.)* But you're wrong, ladies and gentlemen, if you think I could wait to be asked a second time. Thanks, but that's expecting too much. Well, you can see what I am—come on—look me over good and proper—size me up—use your eyes as much as you like. I'm not degrading myself in any way. I'm not a bit embarrassed. You won't get the chance to enjoy this spectacle more than this once. You'll be bitterly disappointed if you think you can buy my soul off me too. That I've never sold yet. I might have been offered a lot, but my soul was just not for sale. I'm obliged for all the compliments, ladies and gentlemen. You'll never come across me on the streets again. I've not a minute to spare for you lot—my soul gives me no peace. Thanks again, ladies and gents, I'm not a bit embarrassed, not a bit. *(She has taken off her hat. The soldier leads her to the stool of repentance.)*

SALVATION ARMY OFFICER: A soul has been saved!

(Salvation Army band. Jubilation of the Soldiers.)

SALVATION ARMY GIRL: *(to* CASHIER.*)* Do you hear it all?
CASHIER: My story. My story.
SALVATION ARMY GIRL: What are you muttering to yourself?
CASHIER: The wooden leg.
SALVATION ARMY GIRL: Are you ready?
CASHIER: Not yet, not yet.
MAN: *(standing in the middle of the hall.)* What is my sin? I want to hear my sin.
SALVATION ARMY OFFICER: *(appearing on platform.)* Our comrade will tell you.
VARIOUS VOICES: Sit down. Quiet. Let him talk.
ELDERLY SALVATION ARMY MAN: Let me tell you my story. It is an everyday story, no more. That's why it became my sin. I had a pleasant home, a contented family, a comfortable job—mine was just a normal humdrum life. When I sat in the evening at the table under the lamp and puffed away at my pipe, with my family round about me, then I was content. I never wanted my life to change. And yet it did. I don't remember what started it—perhaps I never knew. The soul can make its presence felt without great upheavals. It bides its time and takes its chance.

Anyway, I could not ignore its warning. My sloth struggled against it at first, I know, but the soul was mightier. I felt that more and more. The soul alone could procure me lasting contentment. And contentment had been my goal all my life. Now I can find it no more at the table with the lamp and with the long pipe in my mouth. I find it only at the stool of repentance. That's my everyday story. *(He steps aside.)*

SALVATION ARMY OFFICER: *(appearing on platform.)* Our brother has told you—

MAN: *(coming forward ahead.)* My sin! *(On platform.)* I'm the father of a family, I have two daughters. I have a wife. I still have my mother. We all live in three rooms. It is quite cozy at our place. My daughters—one of them plays the piano—one of them does embroidery. My wife cooks. My mother waters the flowers in the window box. It's really as cozy as can be at our place. The quintessence of coziness. It is wonderful at our place—splendid—a real model home—so practical—like the ads.—*(Changes.)* It is sickening—horrible—it stinks—it is pathetic, absolutely one-hundred-per-cent pathetic, with the piano playing—the embroidery—the cooking—watering plants—*(Exploding.)* I have a soul! I have a soul! I have a soul! *(He staggers to the stool of repentance.)*

SALVATION ARMY OFFICER: A soul has been saved!

(Salvation Army band. Great tumult in the hall.)

MANY: *(standing up after the band finishes, even standing on the benches.)* What is my sin? What is my sin? I want to know my sin! I want to know my sin!

SALVATION ARMY OFFICER: *(appearing on platform.)* Our comrade will tell you.

(Deep silence.)

SALVATION ARMY GIRL: Do you see him?

CASHIER: My daughters. My wife. My mother.

SALVATION ARMY GIRL: Why do you keep muttering and whispering?

CASHIER: My own story. My own story.

SALVATION ARMY GIRL: Are you ready?

CASHIER: Not yet. Not yet. Not yet.

MIDDLE-AGED SALVATION ARMY MAN: *(stepping forward.)* My soul had no easy victory. It had to seize hold of me and shake me up. In the end it used the strongest possible means. It sent me to prison. I had stolen from the money that was entrusted to me, embezzled a large sum. I was caught and sentenced. There in my cell I had peace. That's what the soul had been waiting for. Now at last it could speak freely to me. And I had to listen to it. The most wonderful time of my life was in that lonely cell. When I came out, I wanted only to commune with my soul alone. So I looked for a quiet place. I found it at the stool of repentance and find it daily, whenever I want to enjoy a glorious hour! *(He steps aside.)*

SALVATION ARMY OFFICER: *(appearing on platform.)* Our comrade has told you of his glorious hours at the stool of repentance. Who is there among you who longs to free himself of this sin? Whose sin is this, from which he escapes here in joyousness? Here is peace for him. Come to the stool of repentance.

ALL: *(in the hall screaming and gesticulating.)* That is nobody's sin here! That is nobody's sin here! I want to hear my sin!! My sin!! My sin!! My sin!

SALVATION ARMY GIRL: *(piercingly.)* What are you shouting?

CASHIER: The bank. The money.

SALVATION ARMY GIRL: *(urgently.)* Are you ready?

CASHIER: Now I am ready.

SALVATION ARMY GIRL: *(taking his arm.)* I'll lead you there. I'll stand by you. I'll always stand by you. *(Ecstatically, into the hall.)* A soul wishes to proclaim itself. I have sought this soul. I have sought this soul. *(Din ebbs. Silence hums.)*

CASHIER: *(on platform, GIRL by his side.)* I have been searching since this morning. Something triggered this search off. It was a total upheaval with no possibility of return—all bridges burned. So I have been on the march since morning. I don't want to detain you with stations that did not detain me. They were none of them worth my decisive revolt. I marched on stoutly—with critical eye, groping finger, selective mind. I passed it all by. Station after station disappeared behind my wandering back. This wasn't it, that wasn't it, nor the next, the fourth, the fifth. What is it? What is there in life really worth sacrificing everything for? This hall! Drowned in music, packed with benches. This hall! From these benches rises up—with roar of thunder—

fulfillment. Freed from dross it rises liberated aloft in praise—molten out of the twin glowing crucibles: confession and repentance. There it stands like a gleaming tower—sure and bright: confession and repentance! You cry fulfillment, to you I shall tell my story.

SALVATION ARMY GIRL: Speak. I'll stand by you. I'll always stand by you.

CASHIER: I have been on the road since this morning. I confess: I embezzled money entrusted to me. I am a cashier in a bank. I took quite a sum: sixty thousand pounds! I fled with it to the asphalt city. By now I'm certainly being hunted—a reward has probably been put on my head. I am not hiding anymore, I confess. Not all the money from all the banks in the world can buy anything of real value. You always get less than you pay for. The more you pay, the less you get. Money diminishes value. Money conceals the genuine—of all frauds money is the most miserable. *(He pulls it out of his tail pockets.)* This hall is the fiery furnace, heated by your contempt for all mean things. I throw it to you, to trample beneath your feet. That's some of the fraud removed from the world. I shall pass through your benches and give myself up to the first policeman: after the confession I seek atonement. Thus it is consummated. *(With his kid gloves he flings notes and gold coins into the hall. The notes flutter down on the bewildered company, the coins roll on the ground between them. Then fierce battle for the money is joined. The meeting becomes one struggling heap. From the platform the bandsmen abandon their instruments and dive in. Benches are overturned, hoarse shouts resound, fists punch into bodies. Finally the tangled mass heaves to the door and rolls out.)*

(SALVATION ARMY GIRL who has taken no part in the fight, stands alone in the middle of the upturned benches.)

CASHIER: *(looks at the GIRL with a smile.)* You stand by me—you'll always stand by me! *(He notices the abandoned instruments, takes two drumsticks.)* Onward! *(Short drum roll.)* From station to station. *(Drums a few rolls followed by single beats.)* Masses left behind us? Crowd dispersed. Vast emptiness. We've made space. Space! Space! *(Drum roll.)* A girl stands there, emerging from departing waves—upright—steadfast! *(Drum roll.)* Maid and man. Ancient gardens re-opened. Cloudless sky.

Voice from the silence of the tree-tops. All is well. *(Drum roll.)*
Maid and man—eternal constancy. Maid and man—fullness in
the void—beginning and end—seed and flower—sense and aim
and goal. *(Drumbeat after drumbeat, then endless roll.)*

*(SALVATION ARMY GIRL steps back gradually to the door,
disappears.)*

(Drum roll dying away.)

SALVATION ARMY GIRL: *(flings door open. To POLICEMAN, pointing to CASHIER.)* There he is. I pointed him out to you. I've
earned the reward!
CASHIER: *(letting the sticks drop from his raised hands.)* Here I
stand. I stand above you. Two are too many. There's space for
one only. Loneliness is space; space is loneliness. Coldness is
sun. Sun is coldness. The fevered body bleeds. The fevered body
shivers. Bare fields. Ice spreading. Who can escape? Where is the
way out?
POLICEMAN: Are there any other doors?
SALVATION ARMY GIRL: No.

(CASHIER fumbles for something in his pocket.)

POLICEMAN: He has his hand in his pocket. Turn the light out. We
present too much of a target.

(SALVATION ARMY GIRL obeys.)

*(All lights on the chandeliers out except one. Single bulb lights up
the bright wires of the crown in such a way that they seem to make
a human skeleton.)*

CASHIER: *(burying his left hand in his breast pocket, grabbing a
trumpet with the right and blowing a fanfare to the chandelier.)*
Discovered! *(Fanfare.)* Rejected amid the snow-laden tree this
morning—welcomed now amid the wire-mesh of the chandelier.
(Fanfares.) I announce my arrival to you. *(Fanfare.)* My path is
behind me. In steep curves I pant upwards. I have exhausted my
strength. I have not spared myself! *(Fanfares.)* I have taken the
difficult way and could have had it so easy—up in the snow-
laden tree, when we were sitting on the same branch. You should
have urged me a little more forcefully. A little spark of enlightenment would have helped me and spared me all that trouble. So

ridiculously little intelligence is needed! *(Fanfare.)* Why did I climb down? Why did I take that path? Where else am I still going? *(Fanfares.)* At the start he is sitting there—stark naked! At the end he is sitting there—stark naked! From morning to midnight I chase round in a frenzied circle—his beckoning finger shows the way out—where to? *(He shoots the answer into his shirt front. The trumpet dies out at his lips with a fading note.)*

POLICEMAN: Switch the light on again.

(GIRL does so. At that moment all the bulbs explode.)

(CASHIER has fallen back with outstretched arms against the cross sewn onto the curtain. His dying cough sounds like an Ecce—his expiring breath like a whispered—Homo.)

POLICEMAN: There must have been a short circuit.

(It is quite dark.)

Translated by J. M. Ritchie

Ernst Toller

Masses and Man

*A Fragment of the Social Revolution
of the Twentieth Century*

TO THE WORKERS

Dramatis Personae

Working Men and Women	An Officer
The Woman (Sonia)	A Priest
Her Husband (a State Official)	Two Girl Prisoners
The Nameless One	

In Sonia's dream pictures:

Sonia	The People's Sentries
The Guide	The Nameless One
The State Official	Prisoners
Bankers	Shadows

*The second, fourth, and sixth scenes are dream pictures; the first,
third, fifth, and seventh are visionary abstracts of reality.*

TRANSLATOR'S NOTE

The stage directions in square brackets, which I have supplied in
a few places where the text does not immediately explain itself,
are based on the original Berlin production.

First Picture

SCENE.—*The back room of a workmen's tavern is indicated. In the middle a clumsy table. A* WOMAN *and some* WORKMEN *sit around it.*

FIRST WORKMAN: Pamphlets have been distributed:
  We assemble in the large hall.
  Early tomorrow the factories will close,
  The masses are in ferment,
  Tomorrow will decide.
  (To the WOMAN) Comrade, are you ready?
THE WOMAN: I am ready.
  With every breath power grows in me.
  How I have longed and waited for this hour,
  When heart's blood turns to words
  And words to action!
  Often I have been stricken—
  Clenched my hands with rage and shame and pain!
  When the vile papers bawl of victory
  A million hands take hold of me,
  A million voices shriek:
  You, you, are guilty of our death!
  Yes, every horse whose flanks tremble and foam
  Dumbly accuses me—accuses.
  If I tomorrow sound the trumpet of the Judgment
  And if my conscience surges through the hall—
  It is not I who shall proclaim the strike;
  Mankind is calling, strike! and Nature, strike!
  I think the dog who leaps to greet me at my door
  Barks, strike!
  I think the flowing river hisses, strike!
  My knowledge is so strong. The masses—
  In resurrection, freed
  From wordy snares woven by well-fed gentlemen—
  Shall grow to be
  The armies of humanity;
  And with a mighty gesture
  Raise up the invisible citadel of peace . . .
  Who bears the flag, the red flag,
  Flag of beginnings?

SECOND WORKMAN: You. They follow you.

(Silence flickers.)

THE WOMAN: If only all our agents keep the secret!
   You think that the police know nothing?
   But what if troops surround the hall?
FIRST WORKMAN: Whatever the police may know,
   They do not know our final purpose.
   Once that the masses fill the hall
   They'll be a mighty flood which no police
   Can shape to little splashing fountains.
   Moreover the police are growing cautious;
   No longer drunk with power, they waver.
   The troops are with us—
   There are Soldiers' Councils everywhere.
   Tomorrow is decisive, comrade.

(There is a knock at the door.)

   Betrayed!
SECOND WORKMAN: But they must not take *you!*
FIRST WORKMAN: Only one door!
SECOND WORKMAN: Go by the window.
FIRST WORKMAN: The window gives upon a light shaft.
THE WOMAN: So near the battle—

(Louder knocking. The door opens. The WOMAN'S HUSBAND *enters. His coat collar is turned up over his face. He looks round quickly and raises his bowler.)*

   This is—a friend.
   Nothing to be afraid of . . .
   You come to me—
   You find me.
THE HUSBAND: Good evening.
   (Softly) Please do not introduce me,
   But may I speak to you?
THE WOMAN: Comrades . . .
THE WORKMEN: Good night—
   Until tomorrow!
THE WOMAN: Good night. Until tomorrow!

(The WORKMEN *go out.)*

THE HUSBAND: You realize
I do not come here as a helper.
THE WOMAN: Forgive my budding, momentary dream.
THE HUSBAND: Only your conduct, which dishonors me,
Forced me to come.
THE WOMAN: The honor of a citizen imperiled by my actions?
Strange!
Then has the vote been taken?
Does the majority
Threaten to oust you from its ranks?
THE HUSBAND: I beg you, do not jest.
For I obey considerations which you flout;
The code of gentlefolk
Is binding on me.
THE WOMAN: Stamping you and your like
To formulae!
THE HUSBAND: Commanding our submission, our self-
discipline . . .
You do not grasp my words.
THE WOMAN: I see your eyes.
THE HUSBAND: Do not confuse me.
THE WOMAN: You—you . . .
THE HUSBAND: To be brief,
I am about to limit your activities.
THE WOMAN: You . . .
THE HUSBAND: The urge you feel to help society
Can find an outlet in our circles.
For instance,
You could found homes for illegitimate children.
This is a reasonable field of action,
A witness to the gentle nurture which you scorn.
Even your so-called comrade–workmen
Despise unmarried mothers.
THE WOMAN: Go on, go on.
THE HUSBAND: You are not free to act.
THE WOMAN: I *am* free.
THE HUSBAND: I may expect some slight consideration,
Some tactfulness, if not some understanding.
THE WOMAN: I care for nothing
But the work we have to do.
I serve this work; and, understand me,

I *must* serve it.

THE HUSBAND: Let me dissect your motives:
The wish for wide activities
Governs your conduct.
I do not say the motives that determine
This wish are anything but noble.

THE WOMAN: How every word you utter hurts me . . .
You know the pictures of Madonnas
In peasant homes?
With hearts, sword-pierced, bleeding dark tears;
Those ugly, pious, tender pictures,
So simple-minded and so great . . .
You—you . . .
Can you talk of my ambitions?
What an abyss opens between us!
No idle wish has so transformed my fate;
It was the bare necessity,
The need stored in my deepest being,
The need to be a human creature.
Necessity—oh! understand—*necessity* transforms me—
Not mood, not occupation for an idle hour,
Need to be human, sways me.

THE HUSBAND: Need? And have you a right
To speak of need?

THE WOMAN: Oh let me be . . . my man,
I hold you, kiss your eyes.
You . . . speak no more.

THE HUSBAND: I would not willingly torment you—
This place—Can we be overheard?

THE WOMAN: Although a comrade hear us—
They need no code of honor
To be considerate.
If only you could understand them, feel their need—
Which is *our* need—must be!
You have abased them;
And their humiliation
Dishonors you.
So you have written your own doom . . .
Hold back the pity in your eyes!
I am not sentimental or neurotic.

No, I belong to them because fine feelings
And wretched little hours appointed to good works
Can only soothe our vanity and weakness!
I tell you, there are comrades
Who blush for you—
Unless they laugh aloud,
As I laugh now!

THE HUSBAND: Then you must know the truth:
The secret service knows—
The authorities are watching you.
Wife, I have sworn allegiance to the State—
You cripple my career.

THE WOMAN: And so—?

THE HUSBAND: I tell you frankly
That I shall suffer for your actions;
Which, I assure you, touch my feelings also—
The more that you will harm the State
As well as my career—
For you support the enemy in our midst.
That gives me grounds for a divorce.

THE WOMAN: In that case—if I harm you—
If I am a hindrance on your path—

THE HUSBAND: There is still time.

THE WOMAN: In that case—
I am ready.
I bear the blame of my own actions.
You need not fear that the divorce will harm you.
You . . .
You . . . my arms reach for you
In my great need.
My blood is blossoming for you—
Without you I shall be a faded leaf.
You are the dew that causes my unfolding,
You are the mighty March wind throwing torches
Into my thirsty veins . . .
There have been nights and cries of budding boys
Rearing and prancing in the flush of youth.
Oh! carry me away into the fields, the parks, the alleys.
So humbly I will kiss your eyes . . .
I think I shall be weak without you,

Boundlessly weak . . .
Forgive me, *this* is weakness.
I see your case and you are justified.
For, look, tomorrow I shall stand before the masses,
Tomorrow I shall speak.
I shall attack the State
To which you have sworn loyalty;
Tomorrow
I shall tear down the mask
That hides grimacing murder.
THE HUSBAND: But this is treason
    To the State!
THE WOMAN: Your State makes war,
    Your State betrays the people,
    Your State robs, squeezes and oppresses
    The disinherited,
    The people.
THE HUSBAND: The State is sacred, war keeps it alive;
    Peace is a phantom of neurotics
    And war only a broken truce of arms.
    War is the rule, the constant life of States,
    Threatened, without, within, by enemies.
THE WOMAN: How can a body live
    Eaten by pestilence and fire?
    You have not seen the naked body politic—
    The worms devouring it,
    The private purses battening on human lives.
    You have not seen . . . I know, you have sworn loyalty;
    You do your duty and your conscience is at rest.
THE HUSBAND: Is this your last decision?
THE WOMAN: My last decision.
THE HUSBAND: Then—good night.
THE WOMAN: Good night.

       (As the HUSBAND *is about to go.)*

May I go with you?
Today for the last time . . .
Or am I shameless?
Or am I shameless—
Shameless to my last drop of blood?

(The WOMAN *follows her* HUSBAND. *The stage darkens.)*

Second Picture

(A DREAM PICTURE.)

The Interior of the Stock Exchange is indicated. At the desk the OFFICIAL RECORDER. *Round him* BANKERS *and* BROKERS. *The* RE-CORDER *has the face of the* HUSBAND.

THE RECORDER: I record.
FIRST BANKER: Munition factories—
  350.
SECOND BANKER: Make it
  400.
THIRD BANKER: I sell
  At 400.

(The FOURTH BANKER *drags the* THIRD *forward. In the background there is a murmur of bidders and sellers.)*

FOURTH BANKER *(to* THIRD BANKER*):* Heard the news?
  Retreat imperative.
  The great offensive
  Is going to fail.
THIRD BANKER: And the reserves?
FOURTH BANKER: The stuff
  Is poor in quality.
THIRD BANKER: The food inadequate?
FOURTH BANKER: That also.
  Although
  Professor Uhde thinks
  That ninety-five percent of rye
  Is a luxurious diet.
THIRD BANKER: And leadership?
FOURTH BANKER: Is excellent.
THIRD BANKER: Not enough alcohol?
FOURTH BANKER: The distilleries
  Work at high pressure.
THIRD BANKER: Then what is lacking?
FOURTH BANKER: The General at headquarters

Has sent for ninety-three professors,
Including the official Gluber
Who's in our pocket—
Results are rumored.
THIRD BANKER: Which are?
FOURTH BANKER: To be kept dark
In bourgeois circles.
THIRD BANKER: Does a perverted love
Weaken the troops?
FOURTH BANKER: Strangely, no.
For man hates man.
There is a lack.
THIRD BANKER: What's lacking?
FOURTH BANKER: The mechanism of life
Has been revealed.
THIRD BANKER: What's lacking?
FOURTH BANKER: The masses
Require incentive.
THIRD BANKER: What's lacking?
FOURTH BANKER: Just love.
THIRD BANKER: That's quite enough!
And so the war
Our instrument,
Our mighty instrument,
Which pulls the strings—
That Kings and States,
Ministers, Parliaments,
The Press, the Church,
Must dance—
The round world over,
The oceans over,
Dance—
Our war is lost,
You say, is lost!
Is that the balance?
FOURTH BANKER: No, you miscalculate.
The flaw is found,
Accounts will balance?
THIRD BANKER: How so?
FOURTH BANKER: Quite internationally.
THIRD BANKER: Is that known?

FOURTH BANKER: The contrary.
  We dress it up—
  It's purely patriotic
  And independent
  Of our depreciated currency.
THIRD BANKER: Well underwritten?
FOURTH BANKER: The biggest banks
  Support the enterprise.
THIRD BANKER: And profits?
  Dividends?
FOURTH BANKER: Come rolling in
  Most steadily.
THIRD BANKER: It sounds a good thing;
  What's the product?
FOURTH BANKER: We call it
  Convalescent Home
  For strengthening the will to victory:
  In fact it is
  State-managed brothel.
THIRD BANKER: Splendid! I'll take up
  One hundred thousand.
  One more question:
  Who organizes?
FOURTH BANKER: Experienced generals,
  Connoisseurs
  Of tested regulations.
THIRD BANKER: Is the system
  Planned?
FOURTH BANKER: By regulation,
  As I said.
  Three prices
  And three categories.
  Brothel for officers,
  Stay overnight.
  Brothel for non-coms,
  Stay one hour.
  And the third brothel,
  Men in the ranks,
  Stay fifteen minutes.
THIRD BANKER: I thank you.
  When does the market open?

FOURTH BANKER: At any moment.

(There is a noise in the background. The THIRD *and* FOURTH BANKERS *retire to the background.)*

THE RECORDER: Newly admitted:
  National Convalescent Home,
  Limited Company.
FIRST BANKER: I have no commission to buy.
SECOND BANKER: The dividends do not tempt me.
THIRD BANKER: I will take up
  One hundred thousand
  At par.
THE RECORDER: I record.
FOURTH BANKER: I, the same number.
FIRST BANKER *(to* SECOND BANKER*):* He's a cool bidder.
  What do you think?
SECOND BANKER: A telegram!
  The battle
  On the western front
  Is lost.
FIRST BANKER: Gentlemen!
  The battle
  On the western front
  Is lost!

(Calls, shouting, screeching.)

VOICES: Lost!
VOICE: Munition factories
  Are offered
  At one fifty.
VOICE: Liquid Firethrower Trust.
  On offer.
VOICE: War Prayerbook Limited.
  On offer.
VOICE: Poison-gasworks.
  On offer.
VOICE: War loan
  Is on offer.
THIRD BANKER: I take up another
  One hundred thousand.
VOICE: Oho!

In such a slump?

VOICE: Who was it said the battle
  Is lost?

VOICE: Is the news true?
  Or meant to rig the market?
  He coolly takes up
  Twice one hundred thousand!

SECOND BANKER: It's a bear drive.
  I'll buy at
  One fifty.

VOICE: I'll make it
  Two hundred.

VOICE: I'll buy at
  Three hundred.

VOICE: Who'll sell at
  Four hundred?
  I'm bidding.

THE RECORDER: I record.

FOURTH BANKER *(to* THIRD BANKER*):* The sly fox guesses!

THIRD BANKER: Forgive the question,
  Our most powerful instrument
  Is saved?

FOURTH BANKER: How can you doubt it?
  The mechanism of life
  Is simple.
  There was a leakage;
  Now discovered.
  And stopped.
  These passing fluctuations of our stock
  Are negligible—
  Essential:
  The stability
  Of the mechanic law.
  In consequence
  Our system saved!

THE RECORDER: I record.

(THE GUIDE *enters. His face magically resembles that of the* WOMAN; *on it, lines of death and lines of intensest life are interwoven. He leads the* WOMAN.)

THE GUIDE: Gentlemen,

You record
Too hastily.
Your system governing the blood in human veins!
Your system working upon human creatures!
There's a flaw in your system:
Human nature.
One spurning foot
And the whole mechanism
Is a broken plaything.
So beware!

(To the WOMAN.*)*

Speak, you.
THE WOMAN *(softly):* Gentlemen,
These are men and women.
I say again
Are *men* and *women*.

(The GUIDE *and the* WOMAN *fade, as paling shadows. Sudden silence.)*

THIRD BANKER: Did you hear?
A mine disaster,
It seems.
People in want.
FOURTH BANKER: Then I suggest
A charitable entertainment,
A dance around the desk
Of the Exchange.
A dance
To cope with want;
The proceeds to the poor,
Gentlemen, if you please,
A dance!
I will contribute
A share
In the War Convalescent's Home,
Limited.
VOICE: But women?
FIRST BANKER: As many as you wish.

Just tell the porter
To order five hundred
Accomplished girls.
Meanwhile—
THE BANKERS: We will contribute,
We will dance,
The proceeds go
To the poor!

(*Music of clinking gold coins. The* BANKERS *in top hats dance a fox-trot round the desk. The stage darkens.*)

Third Picture

The stage remains darkened. CHORUS OF THE MASSES (*as from far off*).

THE MASSES: We, from eternity imprisoned
In the abyss of towering towns;
We, laid up on the altar of mechanic
And mocking systems; we,
Whose face is blotted in the night of tears,
Who from eternity are motherless—
From the abysses of the factories we cry:
When shall we live in love?
When shall we work at will?
When is deliverance?

(*The stage grows lighter. A large hall is indicated. On the platform, a long narrow table. The* WOMAN *sits on the left. Working men and women closely packed in the hall.*)

GROUP OF YOUNG WORKING WOMEN: So battle breeds fresh
battle!
No longer let us dally with our masters,
No longer turn aside nor weaken in our purpose,
But let a body of comrades
Sow the machines with dynamite;
And factories shall scatter in the air
Tomorrow.
For the machines
Herd us like beasts for slaughter—

Machines
Hold us cramped in a vice—
Machines
Day by day beat
Out of our bodies
Rivets and screws—
Point three inch screws—point five inch screws—
Till our eyes wither and our hands decay
Upon our living bodies.
Down with the factories! Down
With the machines!

SINGLE VOICES *(shouting in the hall):* Down with the factories!
Down
With the machines!

THE WOMAN: I too was blind and desperate,
Battered, devoured, tormented by machines;
I shouted: Tear them down! . . .
It was a dream.
And evil is the dream that blurs your eyes,
You children, scared with darkness!
For see, this is the twentieth century;
The case is judged, is settled.
Machines can never be undone.
Scatter the earth with dynamite
And let a single night of action
Blow factories to nothing—
Before spring comes
They will have risen again
More cruel than before.
Factories may no longer be the masters
And men the means.
Let factories be servants
Of decent living;
And let the soul of man
Conquer the factories.

GROUP OF YOUNG WORKING MEN: Then let us perish with the
factories.
We waste ourselves with words of hate and fury.
The masters build their palaces, while our brothers
Rot in the trenches.

Meadows and dancing, colors, play,
Blossom about us—in our nights
We read of it and howl to heaven.
A craving lives in us for knowledge . . .
But when *they* took the best of life
It turned to evil . . .
Sometimes we touch it in the theaters—
So tender and so fine, it mocks
Us with its beauty.
They have destroyed our youth in schools,
Our souls are broken and our lives
Shout want—raw want.
We are the steaming stench of want.
What else are we today?
We will not wait!

GROUP OF FARM LABORERS: We have been hounded off our
mother earth.
Rich masters buy the land
As they buy venal women;
Make sport of her—
Our blessed mother earth;
Thrust our rough arms
Into munition factories,
Where we, uprooted, wither.
Joyless towns break our strength.
We want the land!
The land for all!

THE MASSES IN THE HALL: The land for all!

THE WOMAN: When I passed through the poor quarters,
Where grey rain drips
Through shingled roofs
And fungus grows on bedroom walls,
A sick man stuttered:
The street is better—almost better—
We live in sties, don't we? in sties!
His eyes were shy
And I was shamed with him . . .
But would you know the way, brothers,
The only remedy for us
Weak ones.

Who hate the cannons?
Strike! Not a hand's turn more!
To strike is action.
Then, strong as rocks,
We weak ones need no violence
To burst our chains;
There is no weapon made
Can conquer us!
Call up our voiceless armies! Call
A strike!
Hear me:
I call a strike!
These six years past
Moloch devours our bodies,
And in our streets
Women with child break down—
Whom hunger makes too weak to carry
The burden of the unborn.
Out of your homes this bitter want,
Pestilence, madness, and raw hunger glares:
But over there, see, over there,
The money bags spue forth their orgies
And hard-won victories are drowned
In foaming wine.
The thrills of luxury dance fatefully
Round golden altars.—But out there,
See the pale faces of your brothers
And feel their bodies clammy in the chill
Of evening!
Do you smell corruption?
Do you hear screams?
Tell me, do you hear them cry:
"Your turn has come!
We powerless, we
Chained to the guns,
We shout to you:
You! Bring us help!
You! build a bridge for us!" . . .
Hear me: I call a strike!
Who henceforth feeds munition works,

Betrays his brother—
More than betrays—
Slays his own brother!
And you, women!
Remember the old legend
Of women stricken with eternal barrenness
For forging arms!
Think of your men who suffer!
I call a strike!
THE MASSES IN THE HALL: We call a strike!
We call:
Strike!

(*The* NAMELESS ONE *comes out of the Masses, hurries to the platform and stands to the right of the table.*)

THE NAMELESS: He who would build a bridge
Must look to his foundations.
A strike today
Is but a bridge without the piles.
We need more than a strike.
To strike, at best
Will force a peace this once;
A truce, no more.
War must be ended
For all eternity!
But first, a last, most ruthless fight!
What use to end the war?
The peace you will create
Still leaves your fate unaltered.
On this side lies a show of peace
And the old doom for you,
On that, a battle and a new
Order on earth.
You fools, break the foundations!
Break,
I say, break the foundations!
Then let the moldering house bolstered with gold
Be swept away by the avenging flood.
The system that we build will be more habitable;
The factories belong to workers

And not to my lord Capital.
The time is past when our bowed backs
Perched him up greedily to scan for distant treasure,
Plot wars to enslave foreign folk
And instigate the screech of lying papers:
"Your country! For your country!"—
Drowning their truer tune:
"For me! for me!"—
That time is past!
The masses of all countries cry together:
The factories belong to workers; and the power
To workers.
All is for all!
I call more than a strike,
I call: a war!
I call: the Revolution!
Our enemy up there
Cares not for pretty speeches.
Your power to match his power!
Force . . . force!
A VOICE: Arms!
THE NAMELESS: Yes, arms are all you need,
    Storm the town hall and fetch them;
    And let your war-cry be:
    Victory!
THE WOMAN: Hear me!
    I will not—
THE NAMELESS: Be silent, comrade!
    Handclasping, prayers, and passionate pleas
    Beget no children;
    Consumptives are not cured with slops and soups;
    To fell a tree one needs
    The ax.
THE WOMAN: Hear me!
    I will not have fresh murder.
THE NAMELESS: Be silent, comrade—
    What do *you* know?
    I grant you feel our need.
    But have you stood ten hours together in a mine,
    Your homeless children herded in a hovel?

Ten hours in mines, evenings in hovels,
This, day by day, the fate of masses.
You are not Masses!
I am the Masses!
Masses are fate.
THE MASSES IN THE HALL: Are fate. . . .
THE WOMAN: Only consider—
Masses are helpless,
Masses are weak.
THE NAMELESS: How blind you are!
Masses are master!
Masses are might!
THE MASSES IN THE HALL: Are might!
THE WOMAN: My feelings urge me darkly—
But yet my conscience cries out: No!
THE NAMELESS: Be silent, comrade,
For the Cause!
The individual, his feelings and his conscience,
What do they count?
The Masses count!
Consider this
One single bloody battle; then,
For ever peace.
No mockery of peace, as formerly,
Concealing war—
War of the strong upon the weak,
The war for loot, the war for greed!
Consider this:
An end to misery!
Consider:
A crime fades to a fairy story
In this the dawn of freedom for all peoples.
Think you I counsel lightly?
War is necessity for us.
Your words will split us—
For the Cause
Be silent.
THE WOMAN: You . . . are . . . the Masses.
You . . . are . . . right.
THE NAMELESS: Lay the foundations of the bridge!

Whoever stands across our path,
Be trodden down!
Masses are deeds!
THE MASSES IN THE HALL *(rushing out):* Deeds!

(The stage darkens.)

Fourth Picture

(A DREAM PICTURE.)

A courtyard surrounded by high walls is indicated. Night. In the middle of the court, standing on the ground, a lantern dribbles scanty light. From the corners of the courtyard the PEOPLE'S SENTRIES *appear.*

FIRST SENTRY *(sings):* My mother bore me—
  In a ditch one night.
  Lalala *la*
  Hm, hm.
SECOND SENTRY: Father spawned and ignored me
  In his cups one night.
ALL THE SENTRIES: Lalala *la*
  Hm, hm.
THIRD SENTRY: Three years they shore me—
  'Tis a jailbird's plight.
ALL THE SENTRIES: Lalala *la*
  Hm, hm.

(From anywhere, the NAMELESS *approaches with ghostly, noiseless steps. Stands beside the lantern.)*

FIRST SENTRY: My father maintained me—
  But forgot to pay.
ALL THE SENTRIES: Lalala *la*
  Hm, hm.
SECOND SENTRY: My mother—in pain she
  Walks the streets, as they say.
ALL THE SENTRIES: Lalala *la*
  Hm, hm.
THIRD SENTRY: The bourgeois complained of me
  On election day.
ALL THE SENTRIES: Lalala *la*

Hm, hm.

THE NAMELESS: Open the ball,
  I give you a tune.
SENTRIES: Halt! Who goes there?
THE NAMELESS: Did I ask you
  For your names,
  Who are nameless?
SENTRIES: Give us the password.
THE NAMELESS: Masses are nameless.
SENTRIES: Are nameless,
  As we all.
THE NAMELESS: I open your ball—
  I, herald of action.

(The NAMELESS begins to play a concertina. Provocative rhythms, now sensually soothing, now stormily passionate. A MAN CON-DEMNED TO DEATH, wearing a rope round his neck, steps out of the darkness.)

THE CONDEMNED: In the name of all those
  Condemned to die:
  We beg a last mercy:
  Invite us to dance.
  Dance is the kernel
  Of all things:
  Life,
  Born of a dance,
  Urges to dance—
  Dance of desire,
  Dance of the years
  And dance of death.
SENTRIES: The last request
  Of the condemned
  Must always be fulfilled!
  So we invite you.
THE NAMELESS: Come! Here we are all alike
  Shadows.
THE CONDEMNED: All those condemned to death!
  Put down your coffins
  And stand up
  For the last dance.

(Others condemned to death, wearing ropes round their necks, come out of the darkness [with harlots]. They dance with the SEN-TRIES around the NAMELESS.)

SENTRIES *(singing):* In a ditch she bore me . . .
  He spawned and ignored me. . . .

　　　　(They go on dancing. After a short time:)

  In jail they shore me. . . .

(They go on dancing. The NAMELESS suddenly breaks off. The harlots and the condemned run into a corner of the yard. Night swallows them. The SENTRIES resume their posts. Silence gathers about the NAMELESS. The GUIDE, in the shape of a SENTRY, has come through the wall. He holds the WOMAN close to him.)

THE GUIDE: The road is hard to go,
  But the road's end
  Rewards you.
  Look there,
  The play is just beginning.
  If the sensation tempts you,
  Take a part.

(A SENTRY brings in the PRISONER [face of the HUSBAND] and leads him to the NAMELESS.)

THE NAMELESS: Condemned
  By the tribunal.
SENTRY: He condemned
  Himself.
  He fired on us.
PRISONER: Death!
THE NAMELESS: Are you afraid?
  Listen—
  Sentry, speak out:
  Who taught us
  The death sentence?
  Who armed us?
  Who cried "hero," and "noble deeds"?
  Who hallowed violence?
SENTRY: Schools.

Barracks.
War:
Everlasting.
THE NAMELESS: Force! . . . Force!
  Why did you shoot?
PRISONER: I swore allegiance
  To the State.
THE NAMELESS: Then you die
  For *your* Cause.
SENTRIES: Stand up—
  Back to the wall.
THE NAMELESS: Rifles loaded?
SENTRIES: Loaded.
PRISONER *(at the wall):* O life!
  Life!

    (The WOMAN *tears herself away from the* GUIDE.*)*

WOMAN: Hold fire!
  That is my husband.
  Forgive him
  As I forgive him humbly.
  Forgiveness is so strong,
  Beyond all struggle!
THE NAMELESS: Do *they* forgive
  Us?
WOMAN: *Do they wage war*
  For men and women?
  Do they fight
  For all mankind?
THE NAMELESS: Only the Masses count.
SENTRIES: Back to the wall!
SENTRY: Pardon is weakness . . .
  I fled from our enemies
  Yesterday.
  They had lined me up, back to the wall,
  Scarred with their lashes.
  Beside me the man
  Appointed to kill me.
  With my own hands they compelled me
  To dig my own grave.
  The photographers waited to brand their plates

Greedy for murder. . . .
I spit upon the Revolution
If we are to be fooled
And mocked by murderers.
I spit upon the
Revolution.
SENTRIES: Back to the wall!

(The face of the PRISONER turns into the face of a SENTRY. The WOMAN speaks to a SENTRY.)

THE WOMAN: Yesterday
You stood up
Back to the wall.
Today you are standing
Back to the wall.
You are he who today
Stands, back to the wall.
Man, you are he!
Know yourself, man.
You are he!
SENTRY: Only the Masses count.
THE WOMAN: Only Man counts.
ALL THE SENTRIES: Only the Masses count.
WOMAN: I offer up
Myself
To mankind.

(Ugly laughter from the SENTRIES.)

WOMAN *(stands beside her HUSBAND)*: Then shoot me!
I renounce.

(The stage darkens.)

Fifth Picture

The hall is indicated. Dawn creeps through the windows. A dreary light falls on the platform. The WOMAN sits to the left of the long table. The NAMELESS to the right. At the doors of the hall are the PEOPLE'S SENTRIES. In the hall isolated working men and women crouch at the tables.

THE WOMAN: Has any news
　Come this last hour?
　I slept. Forgive me, comrade.
THE NAMELESS: Message comes after message.
　Battle is battle, bloody play
　Of forces and cool judgment.
　Before midnight we occupied the station;
　At one, lost it again.
　And now our forces
　Again advance to the assault.
　We hold the post office
　And at this moment
　The wires are giving out
　News to all peoples of our deeds
　Done for the Cause.
WOMAN: Our work, our Cause!
　O holy words!
NAMELESS: Holy words, comrade!
　They call for steely armor,
　They call for more than burning, tender-hearted speech,
　They call for ruthless war.

(For whole seconds silence flickers in the hall.)

WOMAN: Comrade, even now
　I cannot bear it.
　Battle with violence enslaves.
THE NAMELESS: Battle with spiritual force
　Also enslaves.
　Do not be startled, comrade,
　I grasp naked realities.
　If I believed as you believe
　I should become a monk
　Vowed to eternal silence.

(Silence is about to settle heavily upon the hall. FIRST WORKMAN
comes in.)

FIRST WORKMAN: I am to report:
　We have advanced three times
　Against the station.
　The square is heaped with dead.

The enemy is well entrenched and armed
With liquid flame, mines, poison gas.
THE NAMELESS: Three times you advanced.
The fourth time?
FIRST WORKMAN: The fourth time never came—
The enemy
Ventured a sortie.
THE NAMELESS: You held your ground.
Do you need reinforcements?
FIRST WORKMAN: We are shattered.
THE NAMELESS: We must expect such checks.
Listen: Go to the thirteenth district.
The reserves are there.
Go—hurry!

(Workman goes.)

THE WOMAN: Men have been killed, he said,
Hundreds of men,
Killed.
Did I not cry to heaven against war
Yesterday—and today
Suffer my brothers to be done to death?
THE NAMELESS: There is confusion in your views.
In yesterday's war we were slaves.
THE WOMAN: And today?
THE NAMELESS: In today's war we are free.

(Silence is feverish.)

THE WOMAN: In both wars ... people ...
In both wars ... Man. ...

(Silence reels. A SECOND WORKMAN rushes in.)

SECOND WORKMAN: The post office is lost!
Our men in flight!
No quarter from the enemy!
Prisoners' fate is death!

(FIRST WORKMAN hurries in.)

FIRST WORKMAN: I come from the thirteenth district—
My effort failed.
The streets are barricaded,

The district has surrendered,
Our men are handing over
Their arms.

THIRD WORKMAN: The town is lost!
Our work has failed!

THE WOMAN: Is doomed to fail.

THE NAMELESS: Once more: be silent, comrade!
Deeds cannot fail.
Although our forces be too weak today,
Tomorrow fresh battalions thunder.

(FOURTH WORKMAN *screams into the hall.)*

FOURTH WORKMAN: They are advancing!
O horrible butchery!
My wife is shot! My father
Shot!

THE NAMELESS: They have died for the Masses. . . .
Up with the barricades!
We still defend!
Our blood shall bear fruit!
Let them come!

(WORKMEN *rush into the hall.)*

FIFTH WORKMAN: They are mowing down the people:
Men, women, children—all!
Never surrender, to be killed
Like captive cattle!
They are mowing down the people.
We must arm.
The laws of warfare saved the soldiers,
But *we* are shot down like wild beasts
Escaped from cages.
A price is on our heads.
But we have arms
And bourgeois prisoners.
I have ordered
Half to be shot—
The other half
Forms our shock troops.

THE NAMELESS: You avenge your brothers . . .

The Masses are revenge for the injustice
Of centuries.
The Masses are revenge!
THE WORKMEN: Revenge!
THE WOMAN: Stop! You are crazed with battle.
I bar your path.
The masses should be people bound together
By love.
Masses should be community.
Community is not revenge.
Community destroys the ground
And the foundation of all wrongs
And plants a seed of justice.
Humanity, taking revenge,
Shatters itself. . . .
Half of them shot?
That was not self-defense—
Blind rage—not service to the Cause!
Do you kill men
In the same spirit as the State
Killed men?
Those men outside
Are under my protection!
I was prepared to silence
My conscience, for the Masses.
I cry:
Shatter the system!
But you would shatter
Mankind.
No, I cannot keep silence, not today!
Those prisoners are men,
Born in the blood of groaning mothers—
Are men, immutably our brothers—
THE NAMELESS: For the last time: Silence, comrade!
Force! Force!
They do not spare our bodies:
This bitter battle is not to be won
By pious sentiments—
Pay no attention to this woman—
It is the idle babble of her sex.

THE WOMAN: I call a halt!
  And you . . . who are you?
  Does lust of power, caged for centuries,
  Impel you?
  Who . . . are you?
  O God . . . who are . . . you?
  Slayer or Savior?
  Slayer . . . or . . . Savior?
  Nameless—your face?
  You are . . .?
THE NAMELESS: The Masses!
THE WOMAN: You . . . Masses!
  You are more than I can bear!
  I shield the men outside.
  I have been many years your comrade;
  I know that you have suffered more than I.
  I have grown up in sunlit rooms,
  Have never known the pangs of hunger,
  Nor heard the crazy rattle of decaying walls;
  Yet I feel with you,
  Know you.
  Look, I come as a begging child,
  In all humility. O hear me:
  Break the foundations of injustice,
  Destroy the secret chains of servitude—
  But throw away
  The weapons of the moldering centuries!
  Revenge is not the will to new and living forms,
  Revenge is not the Revolution;
  Revenge is but the ax that splits
  The crystal, glowing, angry, iron will
  To Revolution.
THE NAMELESS: How dare you, woman of your class,
  Poison this hour of fate?
  I find another meaning in your words:
  You shield your friends and first companions.
  That is your deeper motive:
  Treason! you betray.

(The MASSES *in the hall crowd angrily round the* WOMAN.*)*

A Shout: Intelligentsia!
A Shout: Stand her
  Back to the wall!
  Let her be shot!
The Nameless: To shield the prisoners is treason.
  This is the hour for action,
  For ruthless action.
  Who is not for us, is against.
  Masses must live.
The Masses in the Hall: Must live!
The Nameless: I arrest you.
The Woman: I shield ... my friends ... my first companions?
  No, I am shielding you!
  You, who yourselves
  Have lined yourselves up to be shot.
  I shield our souls!
  I shield mankind ... to all eternity, mankind!
  Insane denouncer—
  You read fear into my words?
  I never chose so basely—
  Oh, you lie ... you lie. ...

> *(A Workman enters the hall.)*

Workman: A prisoner is shouting
  And shouting again
  For our woman leader.
The Nameless: That is proof.
The Woman: Once more ... you lie.
  Who wants to see me ... who?
  Perhaps my husband.
  Never again could I betray you for his sake.
  You, only you, betray yourselves—
  I know no more than that.

(The Nameless *leaves the platform and disappears among the* Massses *in the hall.* Workmen *press in from outside.)*

Workmen: Lost.
Shouts: Flee!
  Fight!

(Single shots heard outside. The Workmen *throng about the door.)*

SHOUTS: The door is bolted!
Trapped like hares!

(*Silence, awaiting death.*)

SHOUT: To die!

(*Someone begins to sing the Internationale [or the Marseillaise]; the rest join in. Mightily.*)

(*Suddenly, a brief volley of machine-guns. The song breaks, crumbles. The principal and side entrances are burst open. Soldiers with rifles leveled stand in the doorways.*)

OFFICER: Resistance useless.
Hands up!
Hands up, I say!

[*One by one they put up their hands.*]

Where is your leader?

[*To the* WOMAN.]
Put up your hands.
You disobey?
Put on the handcuffs.

(SOLDIERS *handcuff the* WOMAN. *The stage darkens.*)

Sixth Picture

(A DREAM PICTURE.)

SCENE.—*Boundless space. In its kernel a cage on which a ball of light plays. A* PRISONER *crouching in the cage (the face of the* WOMAN). *Beside the cage the* GUIDE *in the form of a* WARDER.

THE PRISONER: Where am I?
THE WARDER: In the showhouse of humanity.
THE PRISONER: Drive away the shadows.
THE WARDER: Only you can drive them away.

(*From anywhere, gray, headless shadows.*)

FIRST SHADOW: Do you know me,

My slayer?
I was shot.
THE PRISONER: I am not
Guilty.

>   *(From anywhere, gray, headless shadows.)*

SECOND SHADOW: Me also
You have slain.
THE PRISONER: You lie.

>   *(From anywhere, gray, headless shadows.)*

THIRD SHADOW: And me
You have slain.
FOURTH SHADOW: And me.
FIFTH SHADOW: And me.
SIXTH SHADOW: And me.
THE PRISONER: Warder!
O Warder!

>   *(The* WARDER *laughs.)*

THE WOMAN: I did not will
This blood.
FIRST SHADOW: But you kept silence.
SECOND SHADOW: Kept silence at the storming
Of the town hall.
THIRD SHADOW: Kept silence at the theft
Of weapons.
FOURTH SHADOW: Kept silence through the battle.
FIFTH SHADOW: Kept silence at the calling up
Of the reserves.
SIXTH SHADOW: You are guilty.
ALL SHADOWS: Guilty.
THE PRISONER: I wished to save the others
From death.
FIRST SHADOW: You deceive yourself. Before then
We were shot.
ALL SHADOWS: You
Are our slayer.
THE PRISONER: Then am I—
SHADOWS: Guilty.
Thrice guilty.

THE PRISONER: I ... am ... guilty.

(The SHADOWS *pale. From anywhere* BANKERS *in top hats.)*

FIRST BANKER: Shares in guilt
  On offer
  At par.
SECOND BANKER: Shares in guilt
  No longer valid.
THIRD BANKER: A bad investment,
  Shares in guilt.
  A scrap of paper.
BANKERS: Shares in guilt
  Booked as a loss.

(The PRISONER *sits up.)*

THE PRISONER: I ... am ... guilty.

(The BANKERS *fade.)*

THE WARDER: You fool!
  You sentimentalist!
  Were they alive
  They'd dance about the gilded altar,
  Where thousands offered sacrifice.
  You too.
THE PRISONER: I am guilty
  Being man!
THE WARDER: Masses are guilty.
THE PRISONER: Then am I doubly
  Guilty.
THE WARDER: All life is guilt.
THE PRISONER: But then, it *had* to be
  That I am guilty?
THE WARDER: Each lives his life.
  Each dies his death.
  As trees and flowers,
  So do men
  Grow in a preordained
  And fated form.
  A form created in unfolding
  And in its own destruction
  Still created. Find the answer

For yourself.
But life is all
That is.

(From anywhere, prisoners in convicts' clothes surround the Pris-
oner. A pointed cap on their heads, to which is fastened a scrap
of cloth with slits for the eyes, covering their faces. On the breast
of every prisoner is a number. With monotonous and soundless
rhythm they march in a square about the cage.)

THE PRISONER: Who are you?
  Numbers,
  Without a face!
  Who are you?
  Masses
  Without a face!
A DISTANT MUFFLED ECHO: Masses . . .
THE PRISONER: God!
ECHO *(receding)*: Masses . . .

                    (Silence drips.)

THE PRISONER *(screams out)*. Masses are fate.
  Masses are guiltless.
THE WARDER: Man is guiltless.
THE PRISONER: God is guilty.
ECHO *(far away)*: Guilty—
  Guilty—
  Guilty—
THE WARDER: God is in you.
THE PRISONER: Then I will overcome this God.
WARDER: Worm!
  You blaspheme
  God.
THE PRISONER: Is it I
  Who blasphemes God?
  Or does God blaspheme
  Mankind?
  This law,
  This horror, this inexorable guilt,
  Entangling man with man!
  God,
  Summoned to Justice,

I accuse!
ECHO *(far away):* To Justice.

(The marching PRISONERS *stand still. Their arms shoot upward.)*

THE PRISONERS: We accuse.

(The PRISONERS *fade.)*

THE WARDER: You are made whole.
  Now leave the cage.
THE PRISONER: I am free?
THE WARDER: Unfree!
  Free!

(The stage darkens.)

Seventh Picture

A PRISONER'S *cell is indicated. Small table, bench and iron bedstead let into the wall. Small barred window with opaque glass. The* WOMAN *sits at the table.*

THE WOMAN: O path through the ripe wheat-fields
  In August days . . .
  Wandering in the wintry mountains
  Before dawn. . . .
  Tiny beetles in the breath of noon . . .
  O world. . . .

(Silence spreads gently about the WOMAN.)

Did I crave a child?

(Silence stirs.)

O cleft and struggle of all living!
  Welded to husband—welded to work.
  To husband—to foe . . .
  To foe?
  Bound to the foe?
  Bound to myself?
  That he would come. I need conviction.

(The cell is unlocked. The HUSBAND *enters.)*

THE HUSBAND: Woman, I come. . . .
  Come! Since you called me.
THE WOMAN: Husband!
  Husband. . . .
THE HUSBAND: I bring you good news.
  Your name—my name—is safe from smirching.
  The investigations showed you guiltless
  Of the crime of murder.
  Take courage, your death sentence is not yet confirmed.
  For all your crime against the State,
  Right-thinking people respect motives,
  High principles and honor.
THE WOMAN *(sobs softly):* I am guiltless . . .
  Guiltlessly guilty . . .
THE HUSBAND: Yes, you are guiltless.
  To the right-thinking, that is certain.
THE WOMAN: To the right-thinking!
  In my raw sorrow
  I am glad that no disgrace
  Falls on your name.
THE HUSBAND: I knew that you were guiltless.
THE WOMAN: Yes, you knew . . .
  Respect for motives—so respectable you are—
  I see you now so clearly!
  Yet you are guilty—husband,
  You—guiltier than I of death.
THE HUSBAND: Woman, I came to you . . .
  Woman . . . your word is hate.
THE WOMAN: Hate? Not hate.
  I love you—love you in my bones and blood.
THE HUSBAND: I warned you of the Masses.
  Who stirs the Masses, stirs up hell.
THE WOMAN: Hell? Who created hell—
  Conceived the tortures of your golden mills
  Which grind, grind out your profit, day by day?
  Who built the prisons? Who cried "holy war"?
  Who sacrificed a million lives of men—
  Pawns in a lying game of numbers?
  Who thrust the masses into moldering kennels,
  That they must bear today

The filthy burden of your yesterday?
Who robbed his brothers of their human face,
Made them mechanic,
Forced and abased them to be cogs in your machines?
The State! You!
THE HUSBAND: My life is duty.
THE WOMAN: Oh yes, duty, duty to the State
You are—respectable!
I see you clearly. . . .
You! tell right-thinking people
That they are never right.
Guilty they are—
Guilty are we all . . .
Yes, I am guilty—guilty to myself—
Guilty before mankind.
THE HUSBAND: I came to you. . . .
Do you sit here in judgment?
THE WOMAN: Yes, here, a court of judgment
Comes to be.
I, the accused, I am the judge,
I prosecute, I pronounce guilty
And I absolve . . .
For in the end, this guilt—
Oh! do you guess who bears the final guilt?—
Since of necessity,
Man must desire to do:
And deeds grow red with blood of men—
Man must needs will to live:
And seas of blood rise round him—
Oh! do you guess who bears the final guilt? . . .
Give me your hand,
Beloved of my blood,
For I have overcome myself—
Myself and you.

(The HUSBAND *shudders. Thoughts distort his face. He stumbles out.)*

THE WOMAN: Give me your hand,
Give me your hand, my brother—
You too, my brother . . .

You . . . gone . . . you needs must go . . .
The last road leads across the snowfields.
The last road knows no guide.
The last road is motherless,
The last road is loneliness.

(*The door is opened. The* NAMELESS *enters.*)

THE NAMELESS: Have you recovered from delusion?
Have you dispersed your dreams?
Has the sharp knife of understanding pierced your heart?
Did the judge say "mankind" and "I forgive you"?
The lesson has been wholesome
And I congratulate you on conversion.
Now you're for us again.
THE WOMAN: You? Who sends you?
THE NAMELESS: The Masses.
THE WOMAN: Then I am not forgotten?
The message—the message?
THE NAMELESS: I am to bring you freedom.
THE WOMAN: Freedom!
Life! . . .
We are to escape? Is all prepared?
THE NAMELESS: Two warders have been bribed.
The third, him at the gate, I shall strike down.
THE WOMAN: Strike down . . . for me . . .?
THE NAMELESS: No, for the Cause.
THE WOMAN: I have no right
To gain my life by this man's death.
THE NAMELESS: The Masses have a right to you.
THE WOMAN: What of the warder's right?
The warder is a man.
THE NAMELESS: As yet there are no men.
On this side men of the Masses,
On that side men of the State.
THE WOMAN: To be a man is plain, is primal.
THE NAMELESS: Only the Masses are holy.
THE WOMAN: The Masses are not holy.
Force made the Masses,
Injustice of possession made the Masses.
The masses are instinct, necessity,
Are credulous humility,

Revenge and cruelty,
The Masses are blind slaves
And holy aspiration.
The Masses are a trampled field,
A buried people.
THE NAMELESS: And action?
THE WOMAN: Action and more than action!
To deliver—
Set free in Masses their humanity,
Set free in Masses their community.
THE NAMELESS: The rough wind at the gate
Will cure you!
Hurry!
The time is short.
THE WOMAN: You are not release.
You are not redemption.
I know you, who you are.
"Strike down!" Yes, you eternally strike down.
You are the bastard child of war,
You poor new hangman and high executioner.
Your watchwords of salvation: "death" and "extirpate"!
Throw off your mantle of fine words—
It is worn thin as paper!
THE NAMELESS: The murder-chiefs fight for the State.
THE WOMAN: They do not kill for joy of killing;
They, like you,
Believe their mission.
THE NAMELESS: They fight for the oppressor-state,
We for mankind.
THE WOMAN: You murder for mankind,
As they, deluded, murdered for their State.
Some even thought
That by their State, their Fatherland,
They might redeem the earth.
I see no difference.
These murder for one country,
And for all countries, those.
These kill men for a thousand men,
And those for millions.
Who takes life for the State,

Him you call hangman.
Who takes life for humanity,
Him you enwreathe,
Call moral, a good citizen, a noble and great man.
You even speak of healing force, of holy violence!
THE NAMELESS: Indict those others, indict life.
Shall I allow more millions to be enslaved,
Because their masters may be honest men?
How will it lessen your own guilt,
If you keep silence.
THE WOMAN: By force, the smoky torch of violence,
We shall not find the way.
Strangely you lead us to the promised land—
The ancient land of human slavery!
If fate thrusts you into these times,
Allotting power
To you to overpower those,
Despairing,
Who yearn for you as a new Savior,
Then I shall know
This fate hates man.
THE NAMELESS: The Masses count, not man.
No, you are not our heroine, our leader!
Each carries his infirmities of origin;
And you birthmarks of your class—
Weakness and self-deception.
THE WOMAN: No, you do not love people!
THE NAMELESS: Our Cause comes first.
I love the people that shall be,
I love the future.
THE WOMAN: People come first.
You sacrifice to dogmas,
The people that are now.
THE NAMELESS: Our Cause demands their sacrifice.
But you betray the Masses, you betray
The Cause.
You must decide today.
Who wavers, helps our masters—
The masters who oppress and starve us—
Who wavers,

Is our foe.

THE WOMAN: If I took but one human life,
I should betray the Masses.
Who acts may only sacrifice himself.
Hear me: no man may kill men for a cause.
Unholy every cause that needs to kill.
Whoever calls for blood of men,
Is Moloch.
So God was Moloch,
The State Moloch,
And the Masses—
Moloch.

THE NAMELESS: Then who is holy?

THE WOMAN: One day . . .
Community . . .
Free people, freely working together.
Mankind, fulfilling its measure of deeds
Freely.
Work. People.

THE NAMELESS: You lack the courage
To take upon yourself
Action—hard action.
Only by ruthless action
Can this free people
Come to be.
Atone then, by your death.
Perhaps your death is useful to us.

THE WOMAN: I live eternally.

THE NAMELESS: You live too soon.

(The NAMELESS *leaves the cell.)*

THE WOMAN: And you lived yesterday;
You live today;
Tomorrow you will die.
But I—
Turning and circling—
I
Come into being
Eternally.
I shall become

Cleaner, more guiltless,
I shall become
Mankind.

(The PRIEST *enters.)*

THE PRIEST: I come to help you in your last hours.
   The Church does not deny her care
   Even to you.
THE WOMAN: Who sent you?
THE PRIEST: The state officials
   Instructed me to come.
THE WOMAN: Where were you on the day of sentence?
   Go.
THE PRIEST: God forgives even you.
   I know your case.
   Mankind is good, you dreamed.
   So you committed nameless crimes
   Against the sanctity of State and order.
   Mankind is evil from the first.
THE WOMAN: Mankind gropes toward goodness.
THE PRIEST: A lie of decadence,
   Born of decay, despair and flight,
   Protected by the waxen shell
   Of borrowed faith
   And threatened with bad conscience!
   Believe me, men do not
   Even aspire.
THE WOMAN: Men grope for goodness.
   Even their evil doings wear the mask
   Of goodness.
THE PRIEST: Peoples become, peoples decay,
   The earth knows no millennium.
THE WOMAN: I believe!
THE PRIEST: Remember:
   Greed of power and greed of lust—
   These are the rhythms of life.
THE WOMAN: I believe!!
THE PRIEST: The world is endless and unchanging change of
   forms,
   Mankind is helpless, God is his one deliverance.
THE WOMAN: I believe!!!

But I am cold . . . go, now,
Go!

(The PRIEST *leaves the cell. The* OFFICER *enters.)*

THE OFFICER: Here is your sentence.
  In spite of mitigating circumstances,
  Your crime against the State
  Must be atoned.
THE WOMAN: So you will have me shot?
THE OFFICER *[as if giving words of command]:* Orders are
  orders and obedience obedience.
  The welfare of the State. Peace. Order.
  The duty of a soldier.
THE WOMAN: And of a man?
THE OFFICER: All conversation is forbidden
  By my orders.
THE WOMAN: I am ready.

(The OFFICER *and the* WOMAN *go out. For some seconds the cell
remains empty. Two Female Prisoners in convicts' clothes steal in
and stand by the door.)*

FIRST PRISONER: Did you see the officer?
  What a golden uniform!
SECOND PRISONER: I saw the coffin—in the washroom—
  A yellow box:

(The FIRST PRISONER *sees some bread on the table and pounces
upon it.)*

FIRST PRISONER: Bread there!
  I'm hungry! hungry! hungry!
SECOND PRISONER: Bread for me, for me—
  Bread for me!
FIRST PRISONER: A looking-glass! Fine!
  Hide it. Evenings in my cell.
SECOND PRISONER: Silk scarf!
  Bare breast and silk scarf!
  Hide it! Evenings in my cell!

*(The harsh rattle of a volley bursts into the cell. The Prisoners
spread their hands wide in fright. The* FIRST PRISONER *takes the*

mirror from her pocket hastily and lays it back on the table. She falls on her knees and sobs out:)

FIRST PRISONER: Sister, why do we do such things?

(Her arms hang into space with an immense helplessness. The SECOND PRISONER takes the silk scarf from her pocket and hastily lays it back on the bed.)

SECOND PRISONER: Sister, why do we do such things?

(SECOND PRISONER breaks down, hiding her head in her lap.)

(The stage closes.)

Translated by Vera Mendel

GAS I

A Play in Five Acts

and

GAS II

A Play in Three Acts

by Georg Kaiser

Gas I

A Play in Five Acts

Characters

The Gentleman in White
The Billionaire's Son
The Daughter
The Officer
The Engineer
First Gentleman in Black
Second Gentleman in Black
Third Gentleman in Black
Fourth Gentleman in Black
Fifth Gentleman in Black

Government Commissioner
The Clerk
First Workman
Second Workman
Third Workman
The Girl
The Woman
The Mother
The Captain
A Machine-gun Detachment,
    Workmen, Workwomen

Act 1

A vast square room, all in white, the office of the BILLIONAIRE'S SON. The rear wall is composed entirely of glass in large squares. The walls to right and left are covered from floor to ceiling with great charts bearing statistics, scales, and diagrams in black and white. To the left is a spacious desk and an armchair of austere design, a second armchair at the side. A smaller desk to the right. Visible through the glass wall in a murky violet light, the steep

*close-thronged shapes of great chimney stacks from which flame
and smoke pour in horizontal lines.*

Faint bursts of music come and go.

A young CLERK *at the smaller desk to the right.*

Enter noiselessly the GENTLEMAN IN WHITE, *a strange, whimsi-
cal, phantom figure, entirely in white, including a chalk-white face.
He shuts the door noiselessly, surveys the room, tiptoes toward the
Clerk, touches him upon the shoulder.*

GENTLEMAN IN WHITE: Music?

THE CLERK *turns up a startled face to him.*

GENTLEMAN IN WHITE *listens to sounds from overhead, and
nods:* Valse.

CLERK: How do you happen—?

GENTLEMAN IN WHITE: Quite casually. A certain noiselessness—
achieved by rubber soles. *(He seats himself in chair before desk
and crosses his legs.)* The Chief?—busy? Upstairs?

CLERK: What do you wish?

GENTLEMAN IN WHITE: A dancing party?

CLERK *(in growing haste and confusion)*: There's a wedding—
overhead.

GENTLEMAN IN WHITE *(with pointing finger)*: The Chief—or—?

CLERK: The Daughter—and the Officer.

GENTLEMAN IN WHITE: Then, of course, he can't be seen at present—the Chief?

CLERK: We have no chief—*here*—

GENTLEMAN IN WHITE *(switching round)*: Interesting! Assuming
that you are not too deeply engaged in delicate calculations—
the wage schedules there—?

CLERK: We have no wage schedules—*here!*

GENTLEMAN IN WHITE: That piles up the interest. That touches
the core of things. *(Pointing through the window.)* This gigantic
establishment going full blast—and no chief—no wage
schedules—?

CLERK: We work—and we share!

GENTLEMAN IN WHITE *(pointing to the wall)*: The diagrams? *(Rising and reading the tables.)* Three divisions. Up to thirty years,
Scale One. Up to forty years, Scale Two. Over forty, Scale Three.

A simple bit of arithmetic. Profit-sharing according to age. *(To Clerk.)* An invention of your Chief?—who refuses to be a chief?

CLERK: Because he does not wish to be richer than others!

GENTLEMAN IN WHITE: Was he ever rich?

CLERK: He is the son of the Billionaire!

GENTLEMAN IN WHITE *(smiling)*: So he advanced to the very periphery of wealth and then returned to its center—to its core—. And you work?

CLERK: Every man works to his utmost!

GENTLEMAN IN WHITE: Because you get your share of the total earnings?

CLERK: Yes—and that's why we work harder here than anywhere else on earth!

GENTLEMAN IN WHITE: I suppose you produce something worth such an effort?

CLERK: Gas!

THE GENTLEMAN IN WHITE *blows through his hollowed hand.*

CLERK *(excited)*: Haven't you heard of the Gas we produce?

THE GENTLEMAN IN WHITE *also shows excitement.*

CLERK: Coal-and-water power are out of date. This new source of energy drives millions of machines at super-speed. We furnish the power. Our Gas feeds the industry of the entire world!

GENTLEMAN IN WHITE *(at window)*: Day and night—fire and smoke?

CLERK: We have attained the acme of our achievement!

GENTLEMAN IN WHITE *(returning)*: Because poverty is abolished?

CLERK: Our intensive efforts create—create!

GENTLEMAN IN WHITE: Because profits are shared?

CLERK: Gas!

GENTLEMAN IN WHITE: And suppose sometime the Gas—should—

CLERK: The work must go on—not a moment's pause! We are working for ourselves—not for the pockets of others. No loafing—no strikes. The work goes on without a pause. There will always be Gas!

GENTLEMAN IN WHITE: And suppose sometime the Gas should—explode?

THE CLERK *stares at him.*

GENTLEMAN IN WHITE: What then?

THE CLERK *is speechless.*

THE GENTLEMAN IN WHITE *breathes the words directly into his face.* The White Horror! *(Rising to full height and listening to sounds overhead.)* Music. *(Halting half-way to door.)* Valse.

(Trips out, silently.)

CLERK *(in growing consternation, finally seizes telephone, almost screaming)*: The Engineer! *(His eyes dart back and forth between the doors to right and left.)*

*(*THE ENGINEER *enters from right, wearing a frock coat.)*

ENGINEER: What—

(A WORKMAN *in white blouse comes in from the left, greatly excited.)*

CLERK *(pointing with outstretched arm at* WORKMAN*)*: There—!
ENGINEER *(to* WORKMAN*)*: Are you looking for me?
WORKMAN *(surprised)*: I was just coming to report to you.
ENGINEER *(to* CLERK*)*: But you had already telephoned me!
CLERK: Because—
ENGINEER: Did you receive a report?
CLERK *(shakes his head and points to* WORKMAN*)*: This man—
ENGINEER: Has just come.
CLERK: —was bound to come!
ENGINEER *(somehow disquieted)*: What has happened?
WORKMAN: The Gas in the sight tube shows color.
ENGINEER: Color!
WORKMAN: It is still only a tinge.
ENGINEER: Growing deeper?
WORKMAN: Visibly.
ENGINEER: What color?
WORKMAN: A light rose.
ENGINEER: Are you not mistaken?
WORKMAN: I have been watching it carefully.
ENGINEER: How long?
CLERK *(impulsively)*: Ten minutes?

WORKMAN: Yes.

ENGINEER: How do *you* know that?

CLERK: Wouldn't it be best to ring up—upstairs?

ENGINEER *(telephones)*: Engineer. Report from Central Station—sight-tube shows color. I'll inspect personally. *(To* WORKMAN*)*: Come along. *(Both go out.)*

CLERK *(suddenly throws up his arms, then runs out screaming)*: We're done for—we're done for! *(From the right the BIL-LIONAIRE'S SON—sixty years old—and the OFFICER in red uniform come in.)*

OFFICER: Is there any cause for serious alarm?

BILLIONAIRE'S SON: I am waiting for the Engineer's report. Nevertheless, I am glad you are both going. I wanted to say a word about the fortune which my daughter is bringing you.

(Takes a notebook out of his writing table.)

OFFICER: I thank you.

BILLIONAIRE'S SON: You need not thank me. It is her mother's money. It ought to be considerable. I have no mind for such things.

OFFICER: An officer is forced—

BILLIONAIRE'S SON: You love each other—I offered no objection.

OFFICER: I shall guard your daughter, whom you are confiding to my hands, as I would my own honor.

BILLIONAIRE'S SON *(opening book)*: Here is the amount of the funds and where they are deposited. Select an efficient banker and take his advice. That is most necessary.

OFFICER *(reads, then in amazement)*: We shall certainly require a banker to manage all this!

BILLIONAIRE'S SON: Because the capital is a large one? I did not mean it that way.

OFFICER: I do not understand.

BILLIONAIRE'S SON: What you have now you have for the entire future. You must not expect anything from me. Not now and not later. I shall leave nothing. My principles are sufficiently well known—they must also be familiar to you.

OFFICER: It is not likely that we—

BILLIONAIRE'S SON: No one can tell. As long as money is piled up, money will go, lost. Conditions based on money are always uncertain. I feel I must tell you this, so that later on I may feel no responsibility. You have married the daughter of a workman—I am nothing more. I will not conceal from you the fact that I would rather that my daughter's mother had not left her a fortune. But I exercise authority only in my own province, and I never attempt to force anyone into this. Not even my daughter.

(The DAUGHTER, *in traveling dress, comes in from the right.)*

DAUGHTER: Why must we hurry off this way?

OFFICER *(kissing her hand)*: How warm you still are from the dance!

BILLIONAIRE'S SON: I should not like the marriage festival to end in a discord. *(They start.)* The danger can be, no doubt, averted. But it demands every possible effort.

DAUGHTER *(at window)*: Below—in the works?

BILLIONAIRE'S SON: I should not find time to say good-bye— later on.

DAUGHTER: Is it so very serious?

OFFICER: Counter measures have been taken.

BILLIONAIRE'S SON *(taking* DAUGHTER'S *hand)*: Bon voyage. Be happy. Today you have laid aside my name. That is no loss. I am a man of plain tastes. I cannot approach the splendor of your new name. Must you and all you are be extinguished in me— now that you are going?

THE DAUGHTER *looks at him questioningly.*

OFFICER: How can you say that?

BILLIONAIRE'S SON: I cannot follow you in your world—a world of fallacies.

DAUGHTER: But I shall return.

BILLIONAIRE'S SON: It is not likely that I can wait for a real return. *(Abruptly.)* I shall now ask the guests to leave. *(He kisses her forehead. The* DAUGHTER *stands deeply moved. He clasps the* OFFICER'S *hand. The* OFFICER *leads the* DAUGHTER *out.)*

BILLIONAIRE'S SON *(telephones)*: Tell the people in the drawing room that a disturbance at the works necessitates bringing the festivities to a close. It is advisable to leave the vicinity as quickly as possible. *(The music ceases.)*

(Enter ENGINEER *from left. A working coat over his dress suit. He is deeply agitated.)*

ENGINEER *(gasping)*: Report from Central Station—Gas colors deeper every second. In a few minutes—at the same rate of progress—it will be—a deep red!

BILLIONAIRE'S SON: Is anything wrong with the engines?

ENGINEER: All working perfectly!

BILLIONAIRE'S SON: Any trouble with the ingredients?

ENGINEER: All ingredients, all!—tested before mixing!

BILLIONAIRE'S SON: Where does the fault lie?

ENGINEER *(shaking from top to toe)*: In—the formula!

BILLIONAIRE'S SON: Your formula—does not—work out?

ENGINEER: My formula—does not—work out!

BILLIONAIRE'S SON: Are you sure?

ENGINEER: Yes! *Now!*

BILLIONAIRE'S SON: Have you found the mistake?

ENGINEER: No!

BILLIONAIRE'S SON: Can't you find it?

ENGINEER: The calculation is—correct!

BILLIONAIRE'S SON: And yet the sight tubes show color?

THE ENGINEER *throws himself into chair before desk and jerks his hand across sheet of paper.*

BILLIONAIRE'S SON: Have the alarms been set going?

ENGINEER *(without pausing in his work)*: All the bells are pounding away.

BILLIONAIRE'S SON: Is there enough time to clear the works?

ENGINEER: The lorries are whizzing from door to door.

BILLIONAIRE'S SON: In good order?

ENGINEER: In perfect order!

BILLIONAIRE'S SON *(in terrible agitation)*: Will all get out?

ENGINEER *(leaping to his feet, standing erect before him)*: I have done my duty—the formula is clear—without a flaw!

BILLIONAIRE'S SON *(stunned)*: You cannot find the error?

ENGINEER: Nobody can find it. Nobody! No brain could reckon more carefully. I've made the final calculation!

BILLIONAIRE'S SON: And it does not work out?

ENGINEER: It works out—and does not work out. We have reached the limit—works out and does not work out. Figures fail us—works out—yet does not work out. The thing sums itself up, and then turns against us—works out and does not work out!

BILLIONAIRE'S SON: The Gas—?!

ENGINEER: It is bleeding in the sight tube! Flooding past the formula—going red in the sight glass. Floating out of the formula—taking the bit in its own teeth. I have done my duty. My head is quite clear. The impossible is going to take place—it cannot come—yet it is coming!

BILLIONAIRE'S SON (*feeling for a chair*): We are helpless—delivered up to—

ENGINEER: The explosion!

(*A terrible sibilance tears asunder the silence without. A grinding thunder bursts—the smokestacks crack and fall. A silence, empty and smokeless, ensues. The great glass windows rattle into the room in a cascade of fragments.*)

BILLIONAIRE'S SON (*flattened against the wall—in a toneless voice*): The earth swayed—

ENGINEER: Pressure of millions of atmospheres—

BILLIONAIRE'S SON: All is silent—a grave.

ENGINEER: Immense radius of devastation—

BILLIONAIRE'S SON: Who is still living?

(*The door to left is flung open: a* WORKMAN—*naked—stained by the explosion—totters in.*)

WORKMAN: Report from Shed Eight—Central—white cat burst—red eyes torn open—yellow mouth gaping—humps up crackling back—grows round—snaps away girders—lifts up roof—bursts—sparks! sparks! (*Sitting down in the middle of floor and striking about him*): Chase away the cat—Shoo! Shoo!—smash her jaws—Shoo! Shoo!—bury her eyes—they flame—hammer down her back—hammer it down—thousands of fists! It's swelling, swelling—growing fat—fatter—Gas out of every crack—every tube! (*Once more half erecting himself*): Report from Central—the white cat has—exploded! (*He collapses and lies prone.*)

BILLIONAIRE'S SON *goes to him.*

THE WORKMAN *gropes with his hand.*

BILLIONAIRE'S SON *takes his hand.*

WORKMAN (*with a cry*): Mother! (*Dies.*)

BILLIONAIRE'S SON (*bending low above him*): Oh man! Oh mankind!

Act 2

The same room. A green jalousie or blind has been let down over the great window. In front of this stands a long drafting table covered with drawings.

The young CLERK—*with hair which has now grown snow white—at his table, inactive.*

The BILLIONAIRE'S SON *is leaning against the drafting table.*

BILLIONAIRE'S SON: How long since it happened?

CLERK: Just seventeen days ago today.

BILLIONAIRE'S SON *(turning and looking at the window)*: Formerly great sheds stood there and thrust smokestacks against the heavens—belching a fiery breath. That was what we used to see behind this green shutter—not so?

CLERK: Everything pulverized to dust—in a few minutes.

BILLIONAIRE'S SON: Are you sure it did not take place a thousand years ago?

CLERK: I shall never forget that day!

BILLIONAIRE'S SON: Perhaps this day is already too far distant for you?

THE CLERK *looks at him questioningly.*

BILLIONAIRE'S SON: That is to say—when you look at your hair?

CLERK: I was beside myself—it was almost hallucination. I felt it in my bones that it was coming. I saw Horror—saw it bodily. And that was worse—than what really happened! And I grew white before it really happened.

BILLIONAIRE'S SON *(nodding)*: The White Horror—this was necessary in order to give us impetus—a powerful impetus—to fling us forward for a thousand years! Seventeen days, you say? Seventeen days full of peace and quiet.

CLERK *(in a matter-of-fact manner)*: The workmen still persist in their refusal.

BILLIONAIRE'S SON: And I cannot employ them. The works have been levelled to the ground.

CLERK: They will not take up work before—

BILLIONAIRE'S SON: Before I give my permission.

CLERK *(nonplussed)*: Are you postponing the rebuilding?

BILLIONAIRE'S SON *(shaking his head)*: I am not postponing it—

CLERK: You are always at work upon the drawings.

BILLIONAIRE'S SON (*bending over the drafting table*): I am measuring—and coloring—

CLERK: The whole world is in urgent need of Gas—the demand is imperative. The supplies will soon be exhausted. If the Gas should—come to an end—!

BILLIONAIRE'S SON (*quickly erecting himself*): Then I hold the fate of the world in my hands.

CLERK: You must grant the demands of the workmen—or else the most terrible catastrophe of all will come!

BILLIONAIRE'S SON (*walks toward him and strokes his hair*): A catastrophe you call it?—you youthful whitehead? *You* should have had your warning. It was terrible enough when everything went up in thunder about us here. Do you wish to return to the White Horror? Are your fingers itching to play at the same old game? Can't you be anything but a Clerk?

CLERK: I have my calling.

BILLIONAIRE'S SON: Don't you feel the call—for something more important?

CLERK: I must earn my living.

BILLIONAIRE'S SON: And what if this particular "must" should be done away with?

CLERK: I am a Clerk.

BILLIONAIRE'S SON: From the crown of your head to the sole of your feet?

CLERK: I—am a Clerk.

BILLIONAIRE'S SON: Because you have always been a Clerk?

CLERK: It is—my calling.

BILLIONAIRE'S SON (*smiling*): Ah, it has buried you deep indeed. The strata of society are carried upon you—layer by layer. Nothing less than an exploding volcano will bring you to the surface—nothing less than this can teach you to rise.

THREE WORKMEN *enter from the left.*

BILLIONAIRE'S SON (*addressing them*): Have you once more come stamping through the debris? I have not yet been able to send you my reply. The thing is still taking shape—I am up to the ears in sketches and calculations—look here! But I can make you a definite proposal if you will grant me a final time limit. Are you willing?

FIRST WORKMAN: The excitement—

BILLIONAIRE'S SON: I understand. There were many victims—I do not dare to think of how many victims the accident claimed. *(Clasping his head with his hands.)* And yet I must keep them clearly before me. My decision will then be clear. Speak.

FIRST WORKMAN: We are merely making the same demand which we have always made.

BILLIONAIRE'S SON: I know what it is. I am revolving it in my mind. I am taking it as the basis of my—*(Abruptly.)* I am supposed to send away the Engineer?

FIRST WORKMAN: There is still time—today.

BILLIONAIRE'S SON: And tomorrow?

FIRST WORKMAN: Tomorrow we would refuse to take up work for a period of twenty weeks.

BILLIONAIRE'S SON: Leaving the wreckage lie?

FIRST WORKMAN: In case of a settlement the works could be set going again—in twenty weeks.

SECOND WORKMAN: The world's supply of Gas will not last longer than twenty weeks.

THIRD WORKMAN: There will be a worldwide holiday.

BILLIONAIRE'S SON: . . . Why should I let the Engineer go? *(The Workmen are silent.)* Where lies his fault? Did the safety appliances fail to work? Even in a slight degree? Were the alarm signals incomplete? In making concessions to you, I must also be just to him. That is no more than right.

THIRD WORKMAN: The Gas exploded.

BILLIONAIRE'S SON: Was it his fault? No. The formula was correct. It is still correct.

FIRST WORKMAN: The explosion came.

BILLIONAIRE'S SON: According to its own laws. Not his.

SECOND WORKMAN: He made the formula.

BILLIONAIRE'S SON: No man could make a safer one!

(The three WORKMEN are silent.)

FIRST WORKMAN: The Engineer must go!

SECOND WORKMAN: He must go today!

THIRD WORKMAN: His going must be announced at once!

FIRST WORKMAN: We must take this announcement back with us.

BILLIONAIRE'S SON: *Must* you have your sacrifice? Is that everything? Do you think that you can thereby silence the dead who call aloud in you? Do you think that you can strangle that which clamors in your blood? Can you hide a field of corpses under new corpses? Are you entangled in this horrible lust for revenge after all the horrors which have been? Is this the fruit of the fiery tree which rained pitch and brimstone upon us?

FIRST WORKMAN: There is also this—we can no longer be responsible for the attitude of the workers.

SECOND WORKMAN: There is a fermentation—which is growing.

THIRD WORKMAN: There will be an outbreak.

BILLIONAIRE'S SON *(violently)*: Tell them—all, all of them—that they have ears to hear and a brain to reason with. The thing passed beyond the limits of the human. The brain of the Engineer had calculated everything to the utmost. But beyond this there rule forces which suffer no rule. The flaw lies in eternity. Impossible to find by mortal means. The formula tallies—yet the Gas explodes. Can you not understand?

FIRST WORKMAN: We have our orders.

BILLIONAIRE'S SON: Will you also assume the responsibility?

FIRST WORKMAN: For what?

BILLIONAIRE'S SON: If I grant your demand—if I let the Engineer go—and you return to work—

FIRST WORKMAN: We'll pledge ourselves to that.

BILLIONAIRE'S SON: And you will make Gas?

SECOND AND THIRD WORKMAN: Gas!

BILLIONAIRE'S SON: The formula will be used?

FIRST WORKMAN *(hesitating)*: If it is correct—

BILLIONAIRE'S SON: Incontrovertibly so!

SECOND WORKMAN: It is correct and—

BILLIONAIRE'S SON: And the Gas exploded.

(The three WORKMEN *are silent.)*

BILLIONAIRE'S SON: And, therefore, must not the Engineer remain?

(The three WORKMEN *stare in front of them.)*

BILLIONAIRE'S SON: Is not my refusal a safeguard against horror? Am I not keeping a door shut, a door behind which hell is smoldering? A door which leaves no way open to life? It is like a burning cul-de-sac. Who would go into a cul-de-sac? and lose sight of his goal? Who would be such a fool as to batter his forehead against the last wall and say: I have reached the end. He has reached the end, it is true, but this end is Annihilation. Turn back! turn back! you have heard the warning thundered from the heavens—it rent the air and came crashing down upon us. Turn back! turn back!

FIRST WORKMAN (*erecting himself*): We must work!

SECOND WORKMAN: And our work is here!

THIRD WORKMAN: We are workers!

BILLIONAIRE'S SON: You are workers—indefatigably so. Caught up in the maelstrom of the ultimate effort. Immeasurably enthusiastic over all this. (*Pointing to the charts and tables.*) There we have the mad chase—all the diagrams. Your work—and your wages in the hollow of your hands. That cheers you up—that spurs you on beyond even profit—that makes you work for work's sake. It is like an outbreak of fever, and it clouds the senses. Work—work—a wedge that is driven forward and which bores because it bores. To what end? I bore because I bore—I was a borer—I am a borer—and I remain a borer! Doesn't this make you shiver? Shiver at thought of the mutilation you inflict upon yourselves? You living, sentient, wonderful beings—you manifold ones—you human beings?!

FIRST WORKMAN: We must take back a clear reply.

BILLIONAIRE'S SON: I have given you one. But you do not yet understand. And it is also new to me—to me who feels my way so slowly and carefully.

SECOND WORKMAN: Is the Engineer going?

BILLIONAIRE'S SON: He is going.

THIRD WORKMAN: Today?

BILLIONAIRE'S SON: He is not going!

FIRST WORKMAN: We do not understand.

BILLIONAIRE'S SON: He goes—and he remains—the Engineer must become a matter of utter indifference to us.

SECOND WORKMAN: What does this mean?

BILLIONAIRE'S SON: That is still a small and precious secret of mine. I shall reveal it to you—later on. Look at those plans—I did not finish them—because the help I need is not yet at hand—and this help I can obtain only from the man who is and is not your enemy.

FIRST WORKMAN: May we give a definite answer to our fellows out there?

BILLIONAIRE'S SON: Whatever you please. I will carry out every-thing—and more than you can promise your fellows out there. So now you may depart—in contentment.

(*The three* WORKMEN *go out.*)

BILLIONAIRE'S SON *bends over the drawings on the drafting table.*

CLERK (*leaping up from his chair, hurriedly*): I—am going!

BILLIONAIRE'S SON *rising to an erect position.*

CLERK: I am—out of work.
BILLIONAIRE'S SON: For the present.
CLERK: But there will be no change!
BILLIONAIRE'S SON: Visions again? But of a somewhat darker shade this time? No mirage with a green oasis rising from the desert? Prophecy, my young prophetic friend. You have a most peculiar gift. I am curious to hear your prophecies.
CLERK: I—there is nothing more to write about.
BILLIONAIRE'S SON: Can nothing tempt you? Are you not eager for health? Would you not like to work with both hands, instead of this right hand of yours which does nothing but write? you with the lamed left?
CLERK: I—am going!
BILLIONAIRE'S SON: Whither?
CLERK: To the others!
BILLIONAIRE'S SON: Gather together and growl before the gates. The wheels are still spinning in your breasts—the urge is still too great. It will require time before inertia can set in. And then I'll admit you all.

CLERK *goes out to the right.*

BILLIONAIRE'S SON *once more at the drafting table. Enter Engineer from the left.*

BILLIONAIRE'S SON (*looks up and regards him quizzically*): No damage? in body or clothes?

ENGINEER *looks at him questioningly.*

BILLIONAIRE'S SON: Are you not the scapegoat who is to be im-paled on his own horns? Haven't they beaten you yet?
ENGINEER: I heard them hissing.

BILLIONAIRE'S SON: That was only the signal for the bleeding sacrifice—the slaughter takes place tomorrow.

ENGINEER: I know that I am free of carelessness—or incapacity.

BILLIONAIRE'S SON: But they are after your scalp.

ENGINEER: These people ought to be shown—

BILLIONAIRE'S SON: . . . That a proof is clear and yet is not clear.

ENGINEER: I cannot leave—it would be like a confession of guilt—

BILLIONAIRE'S SON: Could I not discharge you?

ENGINEER: No! For you would then brand me with the mark—which makes me an outcast.

BILLIONAIRE'S SON: One must suffer for many.

ENGINEER (excitedly): Yes—if one would serve the advantage of the many. But where is the advantage here? Take this man or that man and put him in my place—the formula remains valid—must remain so. He must reckon with human reason, and human reason reckons only in this way. Or you must make Gas by means of a weaker formula.

BILLIONAIRE'S SON: Do you believe in a weaker formula?

ENGINEER: All the machinery of the world would have to be rebuilt.

BILLIONAIRE'S SON: That would not prevent its coming to pass.

ENGINEER: Facing the necessity of an inferior motive power—

BILLIONAIRE'S SON: The machines might be stopped—but not men.

ENGINEER: But after they have learned the danger?

BILLIONAIRE'S SON: And no matter if they were blown up ten times, they would establish themselves in the burning zone for the eleventh time.

ENGINEER: An explosion such as this—

BILLIONAIRE'S SON: Will bring them to their senses, you think? Has it had any influence upon the fever which makes them rave? They are already clamoring out there: hand the Engineer over to us—and then we'll speed on again—out of one explosion into another explosion.

ENGINEER: And, therefore, my leaving is senseless.

BILLIONAIRE'S SON (smiling craftily): It would be an unparalleled stupidity! They would merely come jumping into the witches' cauldron once more—the rogues. The gates must be blocked, and I intend to use you for that purpose. I am powerful, now that I am going to keep you by me.

ENGINEER *(stroking his forehead)*: But, what are you going—

BILLIONAIRE'S SON: Come here. *(He takes him to the drafting table.)* Do you see this? Sketches—rough sketches. The first draft of a new project. Merely hints of something big, something momentous—the first sketches.

ENGINEER: What is that?

BILLIONAIRE'S SON: Don't you recognize the land?

ENGINEER: The plant?

BILLIONAIRE'S SON: Has been leveled to the ground.

ENGINEER: Are these the new sheds?

BILLIONAIRE'S SON: What! of such ridiculous dimensions!

ENGINEER: Are these yards?

BILLIONAIRE'S SON: The colored circles?

ENGINEER: Are these railway tracks?

BILLIONAIRE'S SON: These green lines? *(The Engineer stares at the plans.)* Can't you guess? Have you no suspicions? You sly duck! You feeder on figures! Are you puzzled by this many-colored riddle? You are blind—color-blind from the eternal monotony of your doings—up to this very day. Now a new day is born to greet you, and smiles upon you like springtime. Open your eyes and let them sweep over this domain. The varicolored earth is all about you *(pointing to the plans.)* The green lines—streets bordered by trees. The red, the yellow, the blue circles—open spaces full of flowering plants, sprouting from smooth lawns. The squares—houses, human dwellings with a small holding of land—shelters. Mighty streets go forth here—penetrating, conquering other domains, great roads trodden by pilgrims, our pilgrims, who shall preach simplicity—to us—to all!

(His gestures are grandiose.)

ENGINEER *(puzzled)*: Do you intend to rebuild the plant—somewhere?—

BILLIONAIRE'S SON: It buried itself. It reached its apex and then collapsed. And that is why we are discharged—you and I and all the others—discharged with clear consciences. We went our way to the very end without fear—and now we turn aside. It is no more than our right—our honest right.

ENGINEER: The reconstruction—is doubtful?

BILLIONAIRE'S SON *(patting the plans with his hand)*: The decision is here and it is *against* reconstruction.

ENGINEER: And the Gas—which can be made only here?

BILLIONAIRE'S SON: The Gas exploded.

ENGINEER: The workmen?

BILLIONAIRE'S SON: Homesteaders—each on his patch of green.

ENGINEER: That—is—impossible!

BILLIONAIRE'S SON: Do you object to my plans? I told you that they were incomplete. I have counted upon you to help me carry them out. I am counting greatly upon your help. There is no other man so capable of carrying out a big project as yourself. I have the deepest confidence in you. Shall we proceed to work?

(He draws up a stool to the drafting table and sits down.)

ENGINEER *(making a few steps backward)*: But I am an Engineer!

BILLIONAIRE'S SON: You will find excellent use for your capacities here.

ENGINEER: That is not—my branch.

BILLIONAIRE'S SON: All branches are united in this.

ENGINEER: I cannot undertake such a task.

BILLIONAIRE'S SON: Is it too difficult for you?

ENGINEER: Too—pitiful!

BILLIONAIRE'S SON *(rising)*: That do you say? You think this trivial—you with your genius for figures! Are you the slave of your calculations? Are you fettered to those girders which you constructed? Have you delivered up your arms and legs, your blood and your senses to this frame which you devised? Are you a diagram covered with a skin? *(He reaches out for him.)* Where are *you*? Your human warmth? your beating pulse? your sense of shame?!

ENGINEER: If I cannot be occupied—in my own line—

BILLIONAIRE'S SON: Your hands should muzzle your mouth—for it is talking murder.

ENGINEER: . . . Then I must ask for my dismissal.

BILLIONAIRE'S SON *(supporting himself against the table)*: No! *that* will bring back the others. The road would be clear and they would come storming back, and build up their hell again— and the fever will continue to rage. Help me! stay by me! Work here with me—here where I am working.

ENGINEER: I am dismissed!

BILLIONAIRE'S SON *regards him speechlessly.*

ENGINEER *goes out to the right.*

BILLIONAIRE'S SON *(strong at last)*: Then I must force, must force you—every one of you!

Act 3

An oval room. There is a high wainscot of white-enameled wood. In this there are two invisible doors, two at the rear—one to the left. In the center there is a small round table covered with a green cloth. This is surrounded by six chairs, close together.

The OFFICER *enters from the left—in a military cape. He can scarcely control his emotion. He looks for the doors, taps parts of the wainscot.*

The BILLIONAIRE'S SON *enters from the left, to the rear.*

OFFICER *(turning swiftly about and advancing)*: Am I disturbing you?

BILLIONAIRE'S SON *(astonished)*: Have you two come back?

OFFICER: No, I've come back alone.

BILLIONAIRE'S SON: Where is your wife?

OFFICER: She—was not able to accompany me.

BILLIONAIRE'S SON: Is she ill—my daughter?

OFFICER: She—does not know I've come here!

BILLIONAIRE'S SON *(nodding)*: The looks of things here are certainly far from edifying. The paternal foundation is now only a mass of ruins. Would you like to have a look round?

OFFICER *(hastily)*: The catastrophe must have been terrible. I suppose the rebuilding is going ahead at a good pace?

BILLIONAIRE'S SON: Have you noticed anything of the sort going on?

OFFICER: It is natural—and you must be immensely busy.

BILLIONAIRE'S SON *(shaking his head)*: My time—

OFFICER: You are more than busy. The work is more than you can manage. *(Pointing to the table.)* There is going to be a meeting. I am sorry to be forced to disturb you. *(Suddenly, almost abruptly)*. But I must ask you to give me a little of your time—now!

BILLIONAIRE'S SON: All things are equally important to me.

OFFICER: I thank you for your willingness to hear me. The matter concerns me—concerns my salvation, my rescue—

BILLIONAIRE'S SON: Salvation? rescue? from what?

OFFICER: From being cashiered from the regiment—in disgrace.

BILLIONAIRE'S SON: Why?

OFFICER: I've contracted debts—at cards—debts of honor. And I must pay them by tomorrow noon.

BILLIONAIRE'S SON: Can't you pay them?

OFFICER: No!

BILLIONAIRE'S SON: If it is necessary—draw upon your fortune— your wife's dowry.

OFFICER: That—no longer exists.

BILLIONAIRE'S SON: What has become of it?

OFFICER (*excitedly*): I played and I lost. I tried to cover the losses and began to speculate. The speculations were a failure and involved great losses. I increased my stakes at the table beyond my means—and if I cannot pay—I—must—blow—out—my brains!

BILLIONAIRE'S SON (*after a pause*): And so your final way leads you to me?

OFFICER: It cost me a great effort to come here—to you—who has confided in me, and whom I have deceived. But despair drives me to you. I deserve your reproaches—all the blame you can pour upon me is just blame. I have nothing to say in my defense.

BILLIONAIRE'S SON: I do not reproach you.

OFFICER (*reaching for his hand*): I am shamed by your goodness— your forgiveness. I swear that—once I get out of this safely—I—

BILLIONAIRE'S SON: I do not wish you to swear—

OFFICER: Then I will pledge myself—

BILLIONAIRE'S SON: Because I cannot do you a service—

OFFICER (*stares at him*): Will you not—

BILLIONAIRE'S SON: I cannot help—even though I would. I told you at the time that you were marrying the daughter of a workman. I am that workman. I hid nothing from you. I gave you a clear idea of everything.

OFFICER: Means are everywhere at your disposal!

BILLIONAIRE'S SON: No.

OFFICER: A word from you—and every bank is at your service.

BILLIONAIRE'S SON: No longer today.

OFFICER: The great plant—surely that will be working again in a few weeks—

BILLIONAIRE'S SON: It will be standing still!

OFFICER: Still—?

BILLIONAIRE'S SON: Yes, I have come to other conclusions. Will you help me? I need help—much help. The great stronghold of error cannot be toppled over by one man alone—a thousand hands must help to shake it.

OFFICER *(bewildered)*: You will not help—?

BILLIONAIRE'S SON: I am myself in need. A good wind brings you hither. You are a debtor—as I am a debtor. And we are both guiltless. But now lips are loosened and accusations pour forth—accusations against all of us.

OFFICER *(clutching his head with his hands)*: I—can—not—think—

BILLIONAIRE'S SON: Take off that gaudy uniform and put aside your sword. You are a good man—for did not my daughter become your wife? You are sound at heart. Whence came this shadow? Whence all that hides and covers up your real self? How did you succumb to this temptation for show?

OFFICER: What!—you expect me to give up my career as an officer—?

BILLIONAIRE'S SON: Confess your fault—and prove your guiltlessness. See that you win the eyes and ears of men—see that your voice carries farther and farther. I myself cannot realize myself—I remain disguised for life in this coat. And so the currents of the great forces in me are turned awry—turned into a canal full of deeds undone—because one deed still threatens—a deed which will bring annihilation in its train. I would save those who would bring about something which can only bring about ruin.

OFFICER *(suppressing a groan)*: Can—you help me?

BILLIONAIRE'S SON: Yes!

OFFICER: Then give me—!

BILLIONAIRE'S SON: That which *you* give me I could never pay for.

OFFICER: My period of grace is expiring.

BILLIONAIRE'S SON: No, it will go on for ever.

OFFICER: Money!

BILLIONAIRE'S SON: Ought I to cheat you with money—cheat you out of your real self?

OFFICER *(in desperation)*: I must leave the Service—I shall be struck off the Rolls—I—

BILLIONAIRE'S SON *(leading him toward the door with his arm about his shoulder)*: Yes, no doubt there will be a sensation, should I abandon you. You, my son-in-law, and I with the most abundant means at my disposal. And yet I did nothing, they will say. That will arouse their attention—they will become most attentive listeners. I need good listeners . . . and you will help me to get them. That will be your service. And praise shall be ours—even without my recognition. But my recognition will not fail.

(The OFFICER *goes out.)*

BILLIONAIRE'S SON *steps up to the table, passes his hand over the green cloth—nods—and then goes out behind to the left.*

*(*THE FIRST GENTLEMAN IN BLACK *enters from the left. A massive head with short bristles of grey hair rises above the closely buttoned black frock coat.)*

THE SECOND GENTLEMAN IN BLACK *enters—he is bald—and his costume, like that of all following him, resembles that of the First.*

SECOND GENTLEMAN IN BLACK: How are things at your place?
FIRST GENTLEMAN IN BLACK: Not a finger moving.
SECOND GENTLEMAN IN BLACK: The same thing at my place.

(Enter THIRD GENTLEMAN IN BLACK—*with blond pointed beard.)*

THIRD GENTLEMAN IN BLACK *(to the First)*: How are things at your place?
FIRST GENTLEMAN IN BLACK: Not a finger moving.
THIRD GENTLEMAN IN BLACK *(to Second)*: And with you?

SECOND GENTLEMAN IN BLACK *shakes his head.*

THIRD GENTLEMAN IN BLACK: The same with me.

(The FOURTH *and the* FIFTH GENTLEMAN IN BLACK *enter—two brothers closely resembling each other, about thirty.)*

FOURTH GENTLEMAN IN BLACK *(to the First)*: How are things at your place?
FIFTH GENTLEMAN IN BLACK *(to Second)*: How are things with you?
THIRD GENTLEMAN IN BLACK *(to both)*: How are things with you?
FOURTH AND FIFTH GENTLEMEN IN BLACK: Not a finger moving!
FIRST GENTLEMAN IN BLACK: The same with us.

SECOND GENTLEMAN IN BLACK: This is the most tremendous stoppage of work I have ever experienced.

FIFTH GENTLEMAN IN BLACK: And what is the cause?

THIRD GENTLEMAN IN BLACK: Our workmen are striking in sympathy with these men here.

FIFTH GENTLEMAN IN BLACK: Why are they striking?

SECOND GENTLEMAN IN BLACK: Because the Engineer has not been discharged.

FIFTH GENTLEMAN IN BLACK: Why is he kept on?

SECOND GENTLEMAN IN BLACK: Yes, why?

FOURTH GENTLEMAN IN BLACK: Because of a mere whim!

THIRD GENTLEMAN IN BLACK: Just so!

FIRST GENTLEMAN IN BLACK: There may be another reason. A reason based on principle. They demand the dismissal of the Engineer—that gives them something to fight about—furnishes a difficulty—a stumbling-block. If the workers make demands upon us—we must oppose these demands—unconditionally. That has been the case here—and, therefore, the Engineer keeps his post!

THIRD GENTLEMAN IN BLACK: But you forget that he is not one of us.

FOURTH GENTLEMAN IN BLACK: It is another whim—of our friends—just like the first.

SECOND GENTLEMAN IN BLACK: And just as dangerous as the other. You will see!

SECOND GENTLEMAN IN BLACK: It is to be hoped that it is not more dangerous!

THIRD GENTLEMAN IN BLACK: I am of the opinion it could not be worse.

SECOND GENTLEMAN IN BLACK: This one affair causes us enough trouble!

FOURTH GENTLEMAN IN BLACK: The whole body of workers has its eyes on these works!

FIFTH GENTLEMAN IN BLACK: This sharing of profits with everybody causes unrest in all the other syndicates.

SECOND GENTLEMAN IN BLACK: An ulcer which ought to be burnt out!

THIRD GENTLEMAN IN BLACK: With fire and brimstone!

FIRST GENTLEMAN IN BLACK: But you must not overlook the results which have been attained on the basis of this method. The sharing of profits has brought about the highest intensification of production, and this has brought about the most powerful of all products—Gas!

SECOND GENTLEMAN IN BLACK: Yes—Gas!

THIRD GENTLEMAN IN BLACK: Gas!

FIFTH GENTLEMAN IN BLACK: At any rate we need Gas.

FOURTH GENTLEMAN IN BLACK: Under all circumstances.

THIRD GENTLEMAN IN BLACK: We must present our demand: the dismissal of the Engineer.

SECOND GENTLEMAN IN BLACK: Quite independently of the workmen!

FIFTH GENTLEMAN IN BLACK: Quite independently of the workmen.

FOURTH GENTLEMAN IN BLACK: That saves our faces!

THIRD GENTLEMAN IN BLACK: Have you got the order of business?

FOURTH GENTLEMAN IN BLACK (*at the table*): Nothing on hand here.

FIRST GENTLEMAN IN BLACK: We have only this point to consider. Are we of one mind?

(*The other* GENTLEMEN IN BLACK *shake his hand in agreement.*)

(*Enter the* SON OF THE BILLIONAIRE *from the left to the rear. He points to the chairs upon which the* GENTLEMEN IN BLACK *quickly seat themselves. The* SON OF THE BILLIONAIRE *seats himself last, between the* FOURTH *and* FIFTH GENTLEMEN IN BLACK.)

FIFTH GENTLEMAN IN BLACK: Who will take down the minutes?

BILLIONAIRE'S SON: No, no, let there be no minutes.

THIRD GENTLEMAN IN BLACK: A meeting and no minutes!

BILLIONAIRE'S SON: Yes, yes, we'll have an open discussion.

FIRST GENTLEMAN IN BLACK: Considering the importance of the matter I hold it as absolutely necessary that—in all cases our independence of a similar demand by the Workmen be—

SECOND GENTLEMAN IN BLACK: I move that the minutes of the meeting be published!

THIRD GENTLEMAN IN BLACK: Let us vote upon that.

FIRST GENTLEMAN IN BLACK: Those who are for—

(*The* GENTLEMEN IN BLACK *each fling up an arm with a vigorous gesture.*)

BILLIONAIRE'S SON *(forcing down the arms of the* FOURTH *and* FIFTH GENTLEMEN IN BLACK)*:* Not all against one—that would make me too powerful. That would be coercing you—and I wish only to persuade you.

FIRST GENTLEMAN IN BLACK: If our negotiations—

BILLIONAIRE'S SON: Do you wish to negotiate with me? Are you the workmen? Are you not the masters? The employers?

THIRD GENTLEMAN IN BLACK: You have invited us without drawing up the order of business for the day. We conclude from this that you wish us to draw up this order ourselves. That, surely, is a just conclusion. We have agreed and are unanimous upon one point.

SECOND GENTLEMAN IN BLACK: I think the discussion will be brief, and that we had better return to our own plants.

FOURTH GENTLEMAN IN BLACK: It is high time that we begin work once more.

FIFTH GENTLEMAN IN BLACK: The first nightshift will begin work this evening.

THIRD GENTLEMAN IN BLACK: There are losses which can never be made good.

BILLIONAIRE'S SON: Losses? You have had losses? What have *you* lost?

THE GENTLEMEN IN BLACK *(together)*: No work is going on—the plants are lying still—the workmen are on strike!

BILLIONAIRE'S SON *(lifting up a hand)*: I know; they are holding funeral exercises. Surely they have good reason. Were not thousands—burned?

FIRST GENTLEMAN IN BLACK: The strike is quite a different motive.

BILLIONAIRE'S SON: No, no! You must not listen to their speeches. These are senseless. What would you say when I tell you that they demand the dismissal of the Engineer? Isn't that a sign of their muddled minds? No, they do not know out there what they are doing.

THE GENTLEMEN IN BLACK *look at him in perplexity.*

BILLIONAIRE'S SON: Is the Engineer guilty, and must he do penance by resigning? Was his formula bad? It stood the test before—and it stands the test now. Upon what pretext could I send him away?

SECOND GENTLEMAN IN BLACK *(nodding)*: The formula has been tested—

THIRD GENTLEMAN IN BLACK *(also nodding)*: Its validity has been proved—

FOURTH GENTLEMAN IN BLACK *(also nodding)*: It is the formula—

FIFTH GENTLEMAN IN BLACK *(also nodding)*: For Gas!

BILLIONAIRE'S SON: Do you really realize this?

FIRST GENTLEMAN IN BLACK: And for that reason it may be applied by any Engineer.

SECOND GENTLEMAN IN BLACK: This or that one.

FOURTH GENTLEMAN IN BLACK: The Engineer is a mere side issue.

FIFTH GENTLEMAN IN BLACK: A new Engineer—and the same old formula!

THIRD GENTLEMAN IN BLACK: And thereby the strike comes to an end.

FIRST GENTLEMAN IN BLACK: We are assembled here to present our demands—the dismissal of the Engineer!

BILLIONAIRE'S SON *(staring)*: —Have you forgotten—you are still deaf—is the thunder and the crashing no longer rolling in your ears—are you no longer shaken upon your seats?—are you paralyzed?

SECOND GENTLEMAN IN BLACK: The catastrophe is a dark page—

FOURTH GENTLEMAN IN BLACK: We book it to profit and loss—

FIFTH GENTLEMAN IN BLACK: And turn over a new leaf!

BILLIONAIRE'S SON: The same formula!?

FIRST GENTLEMAN IN BLACK: We hope—

SECOND GENTLEMAN IN BLACK: Naturally!

BILLIONAIRE'S SON: The same formula—?

THIRD GENTLEMAN IN BLACK: Perhaps there will be a longer interval between the—

FOURTH GENTLEMAN IN BLACK: One must gain experience!

BILLIONAIRE'S SON: Twice—thrice—?

FIFTH GENTLEMAN IN BLACK: We shall know when to expect the next—

SECOND GENTLEMAN IN BLACK: It is not likely that we shall live to see it.

BILLIONAIRE'S SON: I am to let them in—surrender—?

FIRST GENTLEMAN IN BLACK: After all, the industry of the entire world cannot be permitted to stand still.

THIRD GENTLEMAN IN BLACK: It is entirely dependent upon Gas!

BILLIONAIRE'S SON: Is it that? Am I the source of energy which sets all this in motion? Is my power as vast as that?

(The GENTLEMEN IN BLACK *regard him in amazement.)*

BILLIONAIRE'S SON: My voice is mighty—mightier than horror and joy! Does the choice between being and nonbeing depend upon my word? Does the yes or the no which my lips may speak determine life—or annihilation—? *(Lifting his hands.)* I say— no!—no!—no! A human being decides—as a human being only can decide, no!—no!—no!

(The GENTLEMEN IN BLACK *look at one another.)*

FOURTH GENTLEMAN IN BLACK: That—
FIFTH GENTLEMAN IN BLACK: —is—
THIRD GENTLEMAN IN BLACK: —really—
SECOND GENTLEMAN IN BLACK: What—is—the—
BILLIONAIRE'S SON: The wreckage lies there—and above the wreckage there is new soil—layer upon layer—the growth of the earth in a new garment—the eternal law of becoming.
FIRST GENTLEMAN IN BLACK: What does this mean?
BILLIONAIRE'S SON: Never again shall smokestacks belch here! Never again shall machines pound and hammer. Never again shall the cry of the doomed be mingled with the—unavoid-able—explosion.
SECOND GENTLEMAN IN BLACK: The plant—
THIRD GENTLEMAN IN BLACK: The reconstruction—
FIRST GENTLEMAN IN BLACK: Gas?
BILLIONAIRE'S SON: No reconstruction!—no plant!—no Gas! I will not take the responsibility upon myself—no man can take it upon himself!
FIRST GENTLEMAN IN BLACK: We are—
THIRD GENTLEMAN IN BLACK: —to do without—
FIFTH GENTLEMAN IN BLACK: —Gas?
BILLIONAIRE'S SON: Without human sacrifices!
SECOND GENTLEMAN IN BLACK: We have established everything upon a basis—
THE OTHER GENTLEMAN IN BLACK: —of Gas!
BILLIONAIRE'S SON: Invent a better Gas—or make shift with an inferior one!
FIRST GENTLEMAN IN BLACK: This is monstrous. We unqualifiedly reject all such imputations. What does it mean?—nothing less than a transformation of our entire plants—

FOURTH GENTLEMAN IN BLACK: The costs would be ruinous!

THIRD GENTLEMAN IN BLACK: It is not a matter of costs—even if these should bankrupt some of us. What I ask is this: shall the production of the world be reduced?

FIFTH GENTLEMAN IN BLACK: And that is why you must produce Gas. It is your duty. Now, if we had not had your Gas—

SECOND GENTLEMAN IN BLACK: You have brought about the highest development of modern mechanics. And now you must continue to supply Gas!

FIRST GENTLEMAN IN BLACK: By means of your advanced and fruitful methods which give your workmen a share in the profits, you have achieved this great finality—Gas. And that is why we tolerated this method—and now we demand Gas!

BILLIONAIRE'S SON: The method is indeed fruitful—as I have discovered. But I have merely gone these ways a little sooner than yourselves. Sometime or other you must all follow—the wages of all to be shared by all.

FIFTH GENTLEMAN IN BLACK: This formula should not have been invented—if there was any likelihood that the making of Gas was to be suspended sometime or other!

BILLIONAIRE'S SON: The invention was necessary—for the fever for work possessed the world. It raged blindly, and flooded all the frontiers of life.

FIRST GENTLEMAN IN BLACK: A reduction of the speed to which we have been accustomed could not be enforced.

BILLIONAIRE'S SON: No I do not counsel a return to a feebler, slower movement. We must go on—leaving only the finished, perfect thing behind us—or we should be unworthy of our task. We must not succumb to cowardice. We are men—human beings imbued with a mighty courage. Have we not once more shown this courage? Did we not bravely exhaust every possibility?—It was only after we saw dead men by the thousands lying about us, that we struck out for new fields. Have we not once more tested the elements of our power and driven it to extremes merely to know how much power we enjoyed—to fetter the whole—to fetter mankind? Surely our pilgrimage goes toward mankind—epoch upon epoch—one epoch closes today so that the other may open—perhaps the last of all.

SECOND GENTLEMAN IN BLACK: ... Do you really intend to stop all production?

BILLIONAIRE'S SON: Man is the measure for me—and the needs that uphold him.

THIRD GENTLEMAN IN BLACK: We have other needs.

BILLIONAIRE'S SON: As long as we exhaust man in other ways.

FOURTH GENTLEMAN IN BLACK: Do you wish to gull us?

FIFTH GENTLEMAN IN BLACK: With pamphlets?

BILLIONAIRE'S SON: I will set an example—establish it on my own land—there will be small domains for all of us in the midst of green promenades.

FIRST GENTLEMAN IN BLACK: What! you are going to cut up the most valuable tract of land in the world—for *such* a purpose!

BILLIONAIRE'S SON: The purpose—is Man!

THIRD GENTLEMAN IN BLACK: You must have command of great means, for the world takes account only of—money.

BILLIONAIRE'S SON: Our former profits will suffice for such a period as will be necessary before our new enterprise can take root and grow.

FOURTH GENTLEMAN IN BLACK: You would have to wait long before you found any imitators!

BILLIONAIRE'S SON: And what if there should be no Gas for you?

(The GENTLEMEN IN BLACK *are silent.)*

BILLIONAIRE'S SON: I could force you—as you see—but I do not wish to force you. It would offend you—and I have need of your help. Here we are—six of us seated about this table—let us say the six of us get up and go forth, and our voices become a sextuple thunder which all men must hear. The dullest, deafest ear would hear our message, under this sixfold pressure. You are the great ones of the earth—Labor's Great Gentlemen in Black— arise and come forth and we shall proclaim that the fullness of time has fulfilled itself—and tell it again and again to them who will not understand, because the whirlwind which shook them until yesterday is still in their blood. Arise—go forth!!

FIRST GENTLEMAN IN BLACK *(after a pause, during which he looks about the table, exchanging glances)*: Are we unanimous? *(The* GENTLEMEN IN BLACK *fling up their right hands.)* We will set a time limit—until this evening. If we are not informed by then that the Engineer has been dismissed, we shall apply to the Government. We bid you good day.

(*The* GENTLEMEN IN BLACK *go out.*)

BILLIONAIRE'S SON (*seated at the table, rubbing his hand slowly across the green cloth, murmuring*): No—no—no—no—no—!

(*Enter the* OFFICER *in extreme perturbation—from the left.*)

OFFICER (*unbuckling his sword and about to lay it on the table. But he halts, and feverishly buckles the sword on again*): I—cannot—do—it—I—cannot! (*He draws a revolver, places it against his breast, stalks slowly out, step by step. As the door closes, a shot is heard.*)

BILLIONAIRE'S SON (*rising, staring toward the door*): The world is out of joint—let others force it back again!

Act 4

A great circular hall of concrete, the upper part vague and nebulous. From the cupola of this hall a cone of light from a hidden arc lamp falls through dusk and dust, a mysterious illumination.

In the center, directly under this lamp, there is a steep, small, pulpitlike platform of iron, with two winding stairs.

WORKMEN *are assembled, there are many women. Stillness reigns. The* SPEAKERS *in alternation appear suddenly upon the platform, almost as from a trap-door.*

VOICES (*rapidly swelling*): Who?

GIRL (*with upraised arms*): I!

(*Stillness.*)

GIRL: I'll tell you of my brother!—I no longer knew I had a brother. Someone left the house in the morning and came home at night—and slept. Or he left the house at night and came back in the morning—and slept. One of his hands was large—the other small. The large hand never slept. It kept making the same movement—day and night. This hand ate up his body and sucked up all his strength. This hand grew to be the whole man!—What was left of my brother? My brother who used to play beside me—who made sand-castles with his two hands?—He plunged into work. And this work needed only one hand—one hand that lifted and depressed the lever—minute after minute—up and down, to the very second! He never missed a stroke—the lever was always true—always exact. And he stood in front of it and served it like a dead man. He never made a mistake—never missed a count. His hand obeyed his head and his head belonged to his hand!—And that was all that was left of my brother—Was this really all that was left?—Then one day at noon—*It* came! Rivers of fire shot out of every crack and cranny! And the explosion ate up the hand of my brother. And so my brother gave up his all!—Is that too little?—Did my brother dicker about the price when they hired his hand to lift that lever? Did he not suppress all that had made him my brother—and turned him into a mere hand?—And did he not at last pay for his hand too?—Is the pay too little—to ask for the Engineer?—My brother is my voice—do not work before the Engineer is forced to leave!—Do not work—you hear my brother's voice! *(Bending over toward them.)*

GIRL *(crowding up from below)*: And it is *my* brother's voice!

*(*THE GIRL *descends into the* CROWD. *Stillness.)*

VOICES *(swelling forth anew)*: Who?

(A MOTHER *stands on the platform.)*

MOTHER: I!

(Stillness.)

MOTHER: A Mother's son was ground to pieces by the explosion! What is a son? What was it the fire killed? My son?—I did not know my son any more—for I had buried him long ago—the first morning that he went to the works.—Are two eyes that had a fixed stare from looking at the sight tube—are they a son?— Where was my child—that I had born with a mouth to laugh— with limbs to play? My child—that threw its arms about my neck and kissed me from behind? My child?—I am a Mother, and know that what is born in pain is lost in sorrow. I am a Mother—I do not groan over this. I stifle the cry on my lips—I choke it down. I am a Mother—I do not strike—I do not ac- cuse—not I—it is my child that calls—here! I gave it birth— and now it comes back into my womb—dead!—from Mother to Mother! I have my son again! I feel his throbbing in my blood! I feel him tearing at my tongue—I feel him crying, crying: Mother! Where have you been so long? Mother! You were not by me—Mother! You left me alone so soon—Mother! You did not smash the sight tube—and it was no longer than a finger and as thin as a fly's wing.—Why did he not crush it himself— one touch had done it.—Why was his will so weak—and all his strength gone into his staring eyes? Why did the flames put out his eyes? Why? Why? Must he do everything—and demand nothing? What does it all mean compared to his loss? Here, look! Mother—and there, look! The Engineer!

(WOMEN *crowd closely about the foot of the platform.*)

WOMEN: It is our son!

MOTHER: Mothers and Mothers and Mothers you!—sons cry out in you—do not strangle their cries; stay away from the works— stay away from the works—there is the Engineer.

WOMEN: Stay away from the works!

MOTHER (*descends from the platform and mingles with the* WOMEN).

(*Stillness.*)

VOICES (*loudly*): Who?

WOMAN (*upon the platform*): I!

(*Stillness.*)

WOMAN: We had our wedding—one day. A piano played—it was in the afternoon. Everybody danced about the rooms. A whole day was ours—morning—noon—and night. My man, my fine big man, was with me one whole day. One day from morning till night. His life lasted a whole day!—Is that too much? Because a day has morning—and noon—and evening? And the night? Is that too long for a man's life?—It is wonderfully long—twenty-four hours—and a wedding! A wedding and twenty-four hours—and a piano—and dancing—don't these make up a life? What does a man expect? To live *two* whole days? What a time!—an eternity! The sun would grow tired of shining upon him! We only get a wedding once—but the iron car rolls on for ever. Forward and backward—backward—and forward—and the man goes with it—always with it—because the man is part of the foot. Only his foot is important—his foot operates the block switch—making the car go and halt—and the foot works,

works almost without the man that travels with it. If only the foot were not so closely tied to the man! The man would have a chance to live—but his foot pins him to the car which rolls back and rolls forward—day after day—with the man fastened by the foot. But then the explosion came! Why was my husband burned alive? Why the whole man? And not only the foot which was the most important part of my man? Why must my man be burned, body and limbs, because of a foot?—Because foot and body and limbs were all part of him, because the foot will not work without the man. The foot cannot work alone—it needs my man.—Is this plant like my man—who lived only one day—his wedding day—and died a whole life long?—Are not old worn-out pieces replaced with new?—and the works go on as before?—Is not every man a mere part, interchangeable with other parts—and the works go on?—Do not fight for the man at the lever—do not fight for the man at the sight tube—do not fight for the man on the iron car—the Engineer blocks the way—the Engineer blocks the way!

WOMEN *(about the platform)*: Not for our men!

GIRLS: Not for our brothers!

MOTHERS: Not for our sons!

(THE WOMAN leaves the platform. The WORKMAN appears on the platform.)

WORKMAN: Girls—I am your brother. I have sworn it—and I am your brother. I have sworn—and I am burned as he was burned. I am lying under the ashes and dust—until you send me back to the lever—in place of your brother—who was blown up.—Here is his hand—broad and stiff, for gripping a jerking lever.—This hand has had its earnings—they lay in the hollow of it—and this hand carried them home. And this hand never counted the wages—there they lay in the drawer—and filled the boxes—and became worthless. What can a hand buy—now that this hand has lost its motive power—your brother? What can a hand wish—desire? A single hand—and all the savings in the box?—That hand has been paid for—but not your brother!—He has been burned alive—and has, therefore, become alive—and now he is crying for his wages—: give us the Engineer—give us the Engineer!

WORKMEN *(around the platform)*: We are your brothers!

(The WORKMAN *descends among them.)*

WORKMAN *(already standing on the platform):* Mother—I am your son!—he has grown alive again—for the sake of his eyes—those eyes that stared so because of the sight tube—he has grown alive again. Your son lives again—in me—breathing and speaking! Mother—I sacrificed myself for a sight tube as long as a finger—Mother—I gave myself for the sake of the sight tube—Mother—I died all over my whole body—and all that remained alive in me were my two eyes! I poured my wages upon the table before you—you did not catch the coin in your apron—it rolled upon the floor—Mother—you no longer bend down to pick it up! Do not pick it up—do not pile it into stacks—you cannot build a house for your son with such columns! He lives in a glass capsule, narrow and poisonous—in the sight tube—Read the tables in the office and see if you can find the price of a Mother—for my blood and the blood of my Mother—for it was blood that these eyes drank at the sight tube. Count up your earnings, the premiums, the profits we share—are they enough to pay for a Mother and a Mother's son? The eyes fixed upon the sight tube brought their profit—but the son came out of it with empty hands. Ought he not charge Heaven and Earth with this great debt? Is he not willing to accept a mere trifle in payment for this debt? What is this worth in comparison with his sacrifice? The Engineer? Only the Engineer! and my eyes look past the Mother and stare at the sight tube—only the Engineer—only the Engineer!

WORKMAN *(below the platform):* I am a son!

*(*WORKMAN *on platform descends among them.)*

WORKMAN *(now on platform):* Woman—your wedding day will come once more! That day—with its morning, its noon, and its evening will be yours once more! It will be *the* day—and all the other days that follow it will not seem like days at all. Your husband will go rolling back and forth again on the iron car—forward and backward—a man attached to a foot that operates a switch!—Why don't you laugh—you whose whole life is crammed into a single day!—a man and a woman with a whole day between them—is it not a waste of time while the iron car is whizzing to and fro?—Doesn't the dancing foot feel for the switch block even in the dance?—Can the piano shut out the sound of the iron wheels grinding the tracks?—No, not a single day belongs to you—or to your man!—the iron car keeps rolling, and the foot controls it, and the beat of it holds the man. Can a drop out of a bucket grow into a river—can one day out of a thousand days make up a life? Do not be deceived by the profits: no real profits could be spent in one day!—You have your profits—but you do not live! What good to you are profits— profits made by the foot—profits which make a man poor in living?—You have lost time—and so you have lost life—you have lost everything—time and life—and you should spit upon these gains which are worthless in the face of what you have lost! Cry out your losses—fill your mouths with fury and curses, cry out: We have lost time and life—shout!—shout!—shout! Shout your demand—shout your will—shout what you want—shout if only to prove you have a voice—shout merely to shout—the Engineer!

WORKMEN (*throughout the entire hall*): Shout! shout!!

(*The* WORKMAN *leaves the platform.*)

WORKMAN (*on the platform*): Girls and Girls—we promise you! Women and Women—we promise you!—Mothers and Mothers—we promise you—not one of us will drive a spade into the rubbish—not one of us will lay a brick—not one of us drive home a rivet in steel—Our resolve remains unshakable—the Works will never go up—unless they give us a new Engineer! Come and crowd this hall every day—Brothers and brothers— Sons and sons—Husbands and husbands—each as determined as the other—and let there be one unbendable will in the assemblies—up with your right hands—out with the oath—no Gas— if this Engineer remains!

ALL MEN, ALL WOMEN: No Gas!—if this Engineer remains!

(WORKMAN *leaves the platform.*)

STRANGE WORKMAN: Our resolutions tally with yours—I am sent here by the men of our plant—and the plant is standing still! We are waiting, we are with you—until you give us the word to take up work again. Count upon us—state your demands!

ALL MEN, ALL WOMEN: The Engineer!!

(STRANGE WORKMAN *leaves the platform. Another* STRANGE WORKMAN *ascends it.)*

STRANGE WORKMAN: I am a stranger to you. I hail from a distant factory. I bring you this message—we have laid down our work because you are on strike. We are with you to the last. Hold out—stand firm—force your demands—for you speak in the name of all—you are responsible for all!

ALL MEN, ALL WOMEN: The Engineer!!

*(*STRANGE WORKMAN *leaves the platform.)*

WORKMAN *(on platform)*: We shout, but our shouts do not cause this hall to explode. Our shouts go thundering into the vault up there and echo from blocks of concrete, but they do not go ringing out into the world.—Out! out of the hall!—make for the house—his house—thunder your cries at him who still keeps on the Engineer! —Form ranks!—march across the waste of ashes— go to him—he cannot hear us here—he cannot hear us here!

ALL MEN, ALL WOMEN: On to the house!!—he cannot hear us here!!

(The CROWD *pushes tumultuously toward the doors. A stormy babble of voices.)*

VOICE OF BILLIONAIRE'S SON: I hear you—here!

(A deathly silence.)

VOICE OF BILLIONAIRE'S SON: I am here—in this hall—I have heard you!

(A buzzing and craning of necks among the crowd.)

VOICE OF BILLIONAIRE'S SON: I will answer you—here in this very hall!

(Great excitement and movement.)

VOICE OF BILLIONAIRE'S SON: You shall listen to me now!

(A path is cleared for him.)

CLERK *(leaping upon the platform)*: Don't let him speak!—Don't let him come up!—Crowd together—don't make room!—Run!!

run out of the hall!—run to the works!—Run!—and clean up
the rubbish—put up the scaffolds—rebuild the plant!—Don't
listen to him!—Don't listen to him—Don't listen to him! Run!—
run!!—I'll run ahead—back to my desk!—I must write—
write!—write!

(Rushes off platform.)

BILLIONAIRE'S SON *(on platform)*: I have been in the hall from the
very beginning. You could not see me, because I shouted with
you. Girl, I was a brother to you—Woman, I was a husband to
you—Mother, I was a son to you. Every cry that passed your
lips passed my own! And now I am here. Here I stand—stand
above you—because I must state the final demand which you
cannot state. You make a demand, but your demand is only a
sand-grain of the mountain of demands you must make. You
scream and scold about a trifle. What is the Engineer? What is
he to you? What can he be to you—you who have come through
the fiery furnace? What can he be to you who have passed
through annihilation? What can the Engineer be to you? It is
only a cry of yours, a word that means nothing, an echoing
word!—I know the Engineer is like a red rag to you—the sight
of him brings back the horror to you, the mere sight of him. The
Engineer and the explosion are one—the formula could not keep
the Gas in check—this Engineer controlled this formula—and
this formula brought on the explosion. You think that you can
put out the explosion only after you have chased away the Engineer. And that is why you cry out against him.—Do you not
know that the formula tallies? That it tallies, that it is correct to
the very limits of calculation? You know this—yet you cry out
against the Engineer!

VOICES *(sullenly)*: The Engineer!

BILLIONAIRE'S SON: Your cry comes from a deeper source! Your
demand comprises much more than you demand! I urge you to
demand more!

(Silence.)

BILLIONAIRE'S SON: What was there so terrible about the explosion? What did it burn up—what did it rend apart? Did it go
booming and hissing over one of you—one of you who was not
already mutilated before the explosion? Girl—your brother—

was he whole?—Mother—your son, was he whole?—Woman—your man—was he whole? Was there a single man in all the works who was whole and sound? What havoc could the explosion wreak upon you?—You who were shattered before the walls fell—you who were bleeding from many wounds before the crash came—you who were cripples—with one foot—with one hand—with two burning eyes in a dead skull—can the Engineer make this good? Can any demand make this good again? I tell you—demand more!—demand more!

GIRLS, WOMEN, MOTHERS (*shrilly*): My brother!—my son!—my husband!

BILLIONAIRE'S SON: Brother and Brothers—Son and Sons—Man and Men—the call goes forth, the summons soars up from this hall—over the wreckage—over the avalanches that buried brother and brothers—son and sons—man and men—and it comes circling back into your hearts—demand to be yourselves!

(Silence.)

BILLIONAIRE'S SON: Demand!—and I will fulfill!—You are men—you represent Humanity—in the son, in the brother—in the husband! A thousand ties bind you to all about you. Now you are parts—each is a perfect unit in the great Commonwealth. The whole is like a body—a great, living body. Deliver yourselves from confusion—heal yourselves!—you that have been wounded—be human, human, human!

(Silence.)

BILLIONAIRE'S SON: Demand!—and I will fulfill! Brother—you are a man—you are Man. That hand of yours which clutched the lever shall cripple you no longer!—Son, you are a man—your eyes shall leave the sight tube and gaze into the blue distances! Husband, you are a man—your day shall be the day of all the days you shall live!

(Silence.)

BILLIONAIRE'S SON: Space is yours—and all that life can give within this space—it is Earth—it is your home. You are human beings in the great house of Earth. Every wonder is known to you—your will opens the way to all things!—In you the heavens reflect themselves and the surface of the Earth is covered with the garment of many-colored grasses—as with a flood. The day's work is great and full of gladness and full of many new inventions. But you are not inventions—you are perfected even now—complete—from this new beginning onward. You have achieved a greater humanity—after this last shift you are done with the task to which you had been pledged!—You have completed the shift, toiled to the very extreme—the dead have sanctified the ground—you, that part of you, lies buried!

(Silence.)

BILLIONAIRE'S SON: All that you demand—I will grant—tomorrow you shall be free human beings—in all their fullness and unity! Pastures broad and green shall be your new domains. The settlement shall cover the ashes and the wreckage which now cover the land. You are dismissed from bondage and from profit-making. You are settlers—with only simple needs and with the highest rewards—you are men—Men!

(Silence.)

BILLIONAIRE'S SON: Come out of the hall—come, walk upon the new homesteads—take measure of the land! No great effort is needed—but all creation waits—limitless—vast! Come out of the hall—come into the open!

(He leaves the platform.)

(Silence.)

(The ENGINEER *stands upon the platform.)*

A VOICE *(shrilly)*: The Engineer!

ENGINEER: I am here!—Listen to me: I will bow to your will—I will go. I will take upon me the great shame which will be branded upon my brow—if I should go. I will take upon me all the curses which go howling up against me—and my departure shall be the confession of my monstrous guilt. I will be guilty—as you wish!—I will go—so that you may return to the works!—The way is free—it leads back to the works!

BILLIONAIRE'S SON *(from below)*: Come out of the hall!—and build up the colony!

ENGINEER: Stay here!—stay here in this hall!—my voice is big enough for all of you—here you can hear me thunder!

BILLIONAIRE'S SON: Come out of the hall!

ENGINEER: Stay in the hall—refuse to be frauds!

(Growls and murmurs.)

BILLIONAIRE'S SON: Hatred is still at work here—outside the winds will sweep it away.

ENGINEER: You cheat the very shame with which you would scorch me. I am going—and you must go—back to work!

BILLIONAIRE'S SON: Fling open the doors—out!—into the daylight!

ENGINEER: You must go back to the works.—Do not pile fraud upon fraud—do not betray yourselves. Face the victory you have won—the victory that crowns you—Gas!—It is *your* work which creates these miracles in steel. Power, infinite power, throbs in the machines which you set going—Gas!—*You* give speed to the trains which go thundering your triumphs over bridges which *you* rivet. *You* launch leviathans upon the seas, and *you* divide the seas into tracks which *your* compasses decree! You build steep and trembling towers into the air which goes singing about the antennae from which the sparks speak to all the world! *You* lift motors from the earth and these go howling through the air out of sheer fury against the annihilation of their weight! You who are by nature so defenseless that any animal may attack and destroy you—you who are vulnerable in every pore of your skin—you are the victors of the world!

(Profound silence.)

BILLIONAIRE'S SON *(at the foot of the platform, pointing at the ENGINEER)*: He is once more showing you the pretty picture book—of your childhood days. He would tempt you with memories. But you are no longer children—for *now* you have become adult!

ENGINEER: You are heroes in soot and sweat.—You are heroes at the lever—at the sight tube—at the switch block. You persist grandly, immovably, amidst the lashing of the pulleys and the thumping and thundering of the pistons!—And even the greatest ordeal of all cannot appall you for long—the explosion!

BILLIONAIRE'S SON: Come out of the hall!

ENGINEER: Where would you go?—would you leave your kingdom and enter a sheepfold? Go pottering from early till late in the tiny quadrangle of your farms? Plant paltry weeds with those hands of yours—hands that created towering forces? And your passion for work—shall it serve merely to nourish you—and no longer create?

BILLIONAIRE'S SON: Come out 'of the hall!

ENGINEER: Here you are rulers—in these works where the motive power of the whole world is born—you create Gas! There is your rule, your mastery—the empire you have established—shift upon shift—day and night—full of feverish work! Would you barter this power for the blade of grass that sprouts as it will?—Here you are rulers—there you are—peasants!

A VOICE (crying): Peasants!

OTHER VOICES: Peasants!

MORE VOICES: Peasants!

ALL MEN, ALL WOMEN (a torrent of shouts and upflung fists): Peasants!!!

    ENGINEER stands there in a triumphant attitude.

BILLIONAIRE'S SON (at foot of the platform): Will you listen to him—or to me?

ALL MEN, ALL WOMEN: To the Engineer!!

ENGINEER: The Explosion has *not* sapped your courage! Who gives in to Fear?

BILLIONAIRE'S SON: I do not wish you to fear.—Is it not I who make the greater demands upon your courage?—Do I not ask you to realize—Man? How can you become peasants again—after you have been workmen?—Do we not expect you to climb still higher? The peasant in you has been overcome—and now the Workman must be overcome—and Man must be the goal! This mission thrusts you forward—not backward. Have you not ripened—after this last experience? How far could you still go—working with your hands—working in shifts?—Are your thundering trains, and vaulting bridges and flying motors sufficient recompense for your fever? No, you would laugh at the miserable wages!—Are you tempted by the rich profits which we share? But you waste these again—as you waste yourselves!—The fever is in you—a madness of toil, which brings forth nothing. It is you that the fever eats. It is not your house that you build! You are not the wardens—you sit in the cells! You are pent about by walls, and these walls are the work of your own hands. Come forth! I say, come forth! You are heroes—who do not fear the new adventure! You do not fear to go to the end of the road—terror cannot palsy your steps! The road has come to an end—exalt your courage with fresh courage—Man has arrived!!

ENGINEER: You would be peasants, slaves to grubbing toil!

BILLIONAIRE'S SON: You are men—in all your Wholeness and all your Oneness!

ENGINEER: Petty needs will mock your rightful claims!

BILLIONAIRE'S SON: All that you hope for you shall receive!

ENGINEER: Your days would be lost in sloth!

BILLIONAIRE'S SON: You are working at a timeless task!

ENGINEER: Not a single invention could take form!

BILLIONAIRE'S SON: You are honorably discharged—you are promoted—to human beings!—

ENGINEER (holding a revolver over his head): Shout—and let destruction come!

BILLIONAIRE'S SON: Leave destruction and come forth to the consummation—of Humanity!

ENGINEER: Shout!—and your shout shall destroy me—but go back to work!

(The muzzle is at his temple. Silence.)

ENGINEER: Dare the word!

VOICE (suddenly): The Engineer shall lead us!

VOICES AND VOICES: The Engineer shall lead us!

ALL MEN, ALL WOMEN: The Engineer shall lead us!

ENGINEER: Come out of the hall!!—back to the works!—from Explosion to Explosion!!—Gas!!

ALL WOMEN, ALL MEN: Gas!!

(The ENGINEER leaves the platform. Broad doors are flung open. The WORKERS stream out.)

BILLIONAIRE'S SON (tottering upon the platform): Do not strike down your brother Man! You shall not manufacture cripples! You, Brother, are more than a hand! You, Son, are more than a pair of eyes!—You, Husband, live longer than one day!—You are eternal creatures—and perfect from the very beginning!—do not let the days mutilate you, nor dumb mechanical movements of the hand—be greater, be greedy for the higher thing—in yourselves—in yourselves!!

(Empty hall.)

BILLIONAIRE'S SON *(summoning up all his strength)*: I have seen man—I must protect him against himself!

Act 5

A wall of brick or concrete, partly shattered and blackened by the explosion. A wide iron gate, thrown from its hinges, in the center of this wall. A waste of rubbish.
    Outside the gate a soldier with rifle and fixed bayonet.
    The BILLIONAIRE'S SON *with a bandage about his head, standing in the shelter of the wall.*
    An OFFICER, *a* CAPTAIN, *in waiting attitude, in the center.*

BILLIONAIRE'S SON: It is all a horrible mistake. I must speak—I must explain.

CAPTAIN: They met you with a volley of stones.

BILLIONAIRE'S SON: They would not do it a second time—when they see that they have injured me.

CAPTAIN: I would not be so sure of that.

BILLIONAIRE'S SON: The sight of the soldiers angers them. That is the real reason.

CAPTAIN: You sought this shelter yourself.

BILLIONAIRE'S SON: Not for myself. I wanted to shut off the works. I could do that in three or four words.

CAPTAIN: They won't let you speak even one word.

BILLIONAIRE'S SON: But surely they would not attack me—when I want to justify myself!

CAPTAIN: Keep close to the wall!

BILLIONAIRE'S SON: Will you escort me out?

CAPTAIN: No.

BILLIONAIRE'S SON: No?

CAPTAIN: They might also attack me—and I would be obliged to open fire.

BILLIONAIRE'S SON: No, no, not that!—I must wait then, until they come to their senses!

(The SOLDIER *before the gate is relieved by another* SOLDIER. *Cries and clamor from thousands of throats.)*

BILLIONAIRE'S SON: What are they shouting for now?

CAPTAIN: The sentry is being relieved.

BILLIONAIRE'S SON: This confusion is terrible! Can't they understand what I am after? They are my brethren--I am merely older, more mature—and must keep my hand over them!

(Enter the GOVERNMENT COMMISSIONER *from the right.)*

GOVERNMENT COMMISSIONER *(at the gate, peering out)*: The situation looks serious! *(To the* CAPTAIN*)*: Are you prepared for all emergencies?

CAPTAIN: Machine guns.

(The tumult without has arisen afresh and continues until the Government Commissioner moves away from the gate.)

GOVERNMENT COMMISSIONER *(to* BILLIONAIRE'S SON, *lifting his top hat, and looking for papers in his portfolio)*: The extraordinary and dangerous developments in your works have compelled the Government to discuss the situation with you. May I present my authorization?

BILLIONAIRE'S SON *(taking the paper, reading, looking up)*: Full powers?

GOVERNMENT COMMISSIONER: Under certain conditions. Shall we proceed to negotiations—here?

BILLIONAIRE'S SON: I shall not leave this place.

GOVERNMENT COMMISSIONER *(putting the paper back into his portfolio, taking out another)*: The events which have led up to this strike may, no doubt, be summarized as follows:—After the catastrophe the workmen refused to take up the rebuilding of the plant because certain conditions which they had made were not accepted by you, these conditions involving the discharge of the Engineer.

BILLIONAIRE'S SON: That would not have prevented fresh catastrophes!

GOVERNMENT COMMISSIONER: The Government can recognize only facts.

BILLIONAIRE'S SON: But the explosion is certain to occur again—there is only this formula—only this—or no Gas!

GOVERNMENT COMMISSIONER: Future eventualities cannot be accepted as evidence. The condition imposed by the Workmen was rejected by you. As a consequence the Workmen continue the strike—which has now spread to neighboring works, and is extending itself from day to day.

BILLIONAIRE'S SON: Yes. Yes!

GOVERNMENT COMMISSIONER: In the meantime the Engineer has offered his resignation at a meeting of the Workmen. A sudden change of feeling on the part of the Workmen induced them to drop their demand, and now they wish the Engineer to remain.

BILLIONAIRE'S SON: Yes!

GOVERNMENT COMMISSIONER: The cause of the strike has thereby been done away with, and the Workmen are willing to take up work again.

BILLIONAIRE'S SON: As you see—they are clamoring to get in.

GOVERNMENT COMMISSIONER: But now you have issued an order forbidding them to return. You declare that you could not possibly render yourself responsible for the production of Gas!

BILLIONAIRE'S SON: No—for the destruction of human life!

GOVERNMENT COMMISSIONER: The Government is fully cognizant of the uncommon severity of the misfortune which has regrettably taken place.

BILLIONAIRE'S SON: That says little.

GOVERNMENT COMMISSIONER: The number of victims has called forth the greatest sympathy. The Government is preparing a vote of condolence in Parliament. The Government is of the opinion that in making this proclamation in so conspicuous a place it has done full justice to you and to the Workmen.

BILLIONAIRE'S SON: Yes. The Government has no power beyond this. The rest will be my task.

GOVERNMENT COMMISSIONER: It is with the gravest concern that the Government has heard of your further intentions of permanently keeping the works from being rebuilt.

BILLIONAIRE'S SON: You must not doubt my powers—I will carry out my plans!

GOVERNMENT COMMISSIONER (*drawing forth a new paper*): A conference as to how this danger may best be averted has already taken place.

BILLIONIARE'S SON: Give me a few soldiers—and give me a guarantee that I shall be heard—out there!

.

GOVERNMENT COMMISSIONER: The danger involved in a stoppage of the production of Gas has induced the Government to make you a confidential communication.

BILLIONAIRE'S SON *(staring at him)*: You—demand—Gas?!

GOVERNMENT COMMISSIONER: The whole armament industry is operating upon a basis of Gas. The lack of this motive-power would inflict great damage upon the manufacture of war material. And a war is imminent. Our program of armaments cannot be carried out without this supply of energy. It is this solemn contingency which forces the Government to declare that it cannot any longer tolerate a delay in the delivery of Gas to the armament plants!

BILLIONAIRE'S SON: Am—I—not—my—own—master—on—my—own—ground?

GOVERNMENT COMMISSIONER: The Government is impelled by a sincere desire to come to an understanding with you. It is prepared to further the reconstruction by every means in its power. Toward this end it has ordered four hundred motor-lorries, with tools and workmen—they will be here in the course of the hour. The clearance of the wreckage can be taken in hand at once.

BILLIONAIRE'S SON: —To make weapons—to be used against human beings?!

GOVERNMENT COMMISSIONER: I trust that you will treat my communication with the utmost secrecy.

BILLIONAIRE'S SON: I—I will bellow it out—I will look for confidants in every nook and corner!

GOVERNMENT COMMISSIONER: I can well understand your excitement. But the Government is face to face with a grim necessity.

BILLIONAIRE'S SON: Do not blaspheme! It is Man alone who is necessary!—Why must you inflict new wounds upon him—we find it so hard to cure the old!—Let me talk to them—I must go—

(At the gate. He is greeted with howls.)

CAPTAIN *(pulling him back)*: You will unloose the storm!

BILLIONAIRE'S SON *(tottering against the wall)*: —Are we all mad?—

GOVERNMENT COMMISSIONER: It is important that the Government should know whether or not you intend to persist in your refusal to let the Workmen recommence work?

BILLIONAIRE'S SON: Now—more than ever, I regard it as my duty—to refuse!

GOVERNMENT COMMISSIONER: You persist in your former refusal?

BILLIONAIRE'S SON: As long as I can breathe and speak!

GOVERNMENT COMMISSIONER: I must then make use of the power imposed in me by the Government. In view of the danger which threatens the defense of the Realm, the Government is obliged to dispossess you of your works for the time being and to carry on the manufacture of Gas under Government control. The reconstruction of the works will take place at the expense of the Government and will be taken in hand at once. We trust that we may count upon you making no attempt at resistance. We should greatly regret being forced to adopt more rigorous measures against you!—Captain, open the gates—I wish to communicate the essential points to the Workmen.

(At the gate. A stormy tumult breaks loose.)

CAPTAIN: Stand back!—stones!

GOVERNMENT COMMISSIONER *(retreating to the shelter of the wall)*: This is incredible!

(The uproar continues.)

GOVERNMENT COMMISSIONER: These people simply hinder—

BILLIONAIRE'S SON: I do not fear them—

(At the gate. The uproar at its maximum.)

BILLIONAIRE'S SON *holds up his arms on high.*

(The surge of the tumult draws nearer.)

CAPTAIN *(shouting to the* GOVERNMENT COMMISSIONER*)*: They are coming!

(Goes through the gate—issues orders toward the left. A machine-gun detachment comes and takes up position. The CAPTAIN *stands, holding his naked sword over his head, prepared to give the signal.)*

(Deep silence.)

GOVERNMENT COMMISSIONER *(close to the* BILLIONAIRE'S SON*)*: Why won't you forestall this bloodshed?!

BILLIONAIRE'S SON *stands as though stunned.*

GOVERNMENT COMMISSIONER: Here *(he hands him his white handkerchief)*. They will understand this sign. Wave this white flag!

BILLIONAIRE'S SON *obeys mechanically.*

GOVERNMENT COMMISSIONER: You see—that works! They are dropping their stones! *(To the* CAPTAIN*)*: Throw the gates wide open! *(Soldiers throw open the gates.)* Withdraw the cordon! *(The* CAPTAIN *and the machine-gun detachment withdraw. To the* BILLIONAIRE'S SON*)*: I will go tell them at what point the lorries will deliver the tools. I'll lead the people there myself!

(Goes through the gate. Soon after high, clear shouts and cheers are heard without—these grow rapidly fainter.)

(Silence.)

BILLIONAIRE'S SON *sinks upon a heap of debris).*

(Enter the DAUGHTER—*in black.)*

DAUGHTER *goes up to him—puts her arms about his shoulders.*

BILLIONAIRE'S SON *looks up in surprise.*

DAUGHTER: Do you not know me?
BILLIONAIRE'S SON: Daughter!—in black!
DAUGHTER: My husband is dead.
BILLIONAIRE'S SON: Have you come to reproach me—Will you, too, cast a stone upon me?
DAUGHTER *(shakes her head)*: Are you all alone here?
BILLIONAIRE'S SON: Yes, I am alone at last—like all men who wish to give themselves to all men!
DAUGHTER *(touching the bandage about his forehead)*: Did they strike you?
BILLIONAIRE'S SON: They struck me—struck me, too. There are bolts that rebound and wound both—the archer and the target.
DAUGHTER: Is all danger over?
BILLIONAIRE'S SON: Are men born? Born of women—men who do not scream nor make horrible threats? Has time lost count of itself—and thrust Mankind into the light? What does Man look like?
DAUGHTER: Tell me!

BILLIONAIRE'S SON: I have lost all memory of Man. What was he like? *(He takes her hands.)* Here are hands—and growing to these—*(taking her by the arms)*—are limbs, members—and the body unites them—parts that are active, parts of the whole, and all a part of life—!

DAUGHTER: Tell me!

BILLIONAIRE'S SON: The torrent rages too hideously—it overflows the banks. Cannot a dam be built which will hold in the flood? Cannot this raging be bounded, cannot it be used to water the barren places of the Earth and convert them into pastures of peaceful green? Is there no halting?! *(He draws his DAUGHTER close to him.)* Tell me, where can I find Man? When will he make his appearance—when will he announce his name—Man? When will he understand himself? And plant the Tree of his Knowledge of Himself? When will he rid himself of the primal curse?—when will he re-create the creation which he has ruined—Man?—Was I not happy in having had a glimpse of him and his coming?—Did I not behold him clearly with all the symbols of his fullness of power—silent, yet speaking the tongue that all the world understands?—Man! Was Man not close to me—Mankind? Can Man be extinguished—must he not come again and again—now that at least one man has seen his face? Must he not arrive—tomorrow or the day after tomorrow—every day—every hour? Am I not a witness for him—and for his lineage and his advent.—Do I not know him—his bold, beautiful face? Can I doubt any longer?!

DAUGHTER *(sinking on her knees before him)*: I will give him birth!

Translated by Herman Scheffauer

Gas II

A Play in Three Acts

Characters

The Billionaire Worker	The Chief Engineer
Figures in blue:	*Figures in yellow:*
First	First
Second	Second
Third	Third
Fourth	Fourth
Fifth	Fifth
Sixth	Sixth
Seventh	Seventh

Workers: Men, Women, Old Men, Old Women, Youths, and Girls

The action takes place in the same country as that of Gas I, *but a generation later.*

Act 1

Concrete Hall. Light falls in dusty beams from arc lamp. From misty height of dome dense wires run horizontally to iron platform, thence diagonally distributed to small iron tables—three right, three left. Red Wires to the left, green to the right. At each table a FIGURE IN BLUE—*seated, stiffly, uniformed—gazing into glass pane in the table which, lighting up, reflects its color on the face above it, red to the left, green to the right. Across and further down, a longer iron table checkered like a chessboard with green and red plugs—operated by the* FIRST FIGURE IN BLUE. *For a time, silence.*

SECOND FIGURE IN BLUE *(at red pane):* Report from third fighting sector—enemy concentration preparing.

(Pane dark.)

FIRST FIGURE IN BLUE *(switches red plug).*

FIFTH FIGURE IN BLUE *(at green pane):* Report from third works—production one lot below contract.

(Pane dark.)

FIRST FIGURE IN BLUE *(switches green plug).*

THIRD FIGURE IN BLUE *(at red pane):* Report from second fighting sector—enemy concentration preparing.

(Pane dark.)

FIRST FIGURE IN BLUE *(switches red plug).*

SIXTH FIGURE IN BLUE *(at green pane):* Report from second works—production one lot below contract.

(Pane dark.)

FIRST FIGURE IN BLUE *(switches green plug).*

FOURTH FIGURE IN BLUE *(at red pane):* Report from first fighting sector—enemy concentration preparing.

(Pane dark.)

FIRST FIGURE IN BLUE *(switches red plug).*

SEVENTH FIGURE IN BLUE *(at green pane):* Report from first works—production two lots below contract.

(Pane dark.)

FIRST FIGURE IN BLUE *(switches green plug).*

(Silence.)

SECOND FIGURE IN BLUE *(at red pane):* Report from third fighting sector—enemy sweeping forward.

(Pane dark.)

FIRST FIGURE IN BLUE *(switches red plug).*

FIFTH FIGURE IN BLUE *(at green pane):* Report from third works—production three lots below contract.

(Pane dark.)

First Figure in Blue *(switches green plug).*

Third Figure in Blue *(at red pane):* Report from second fighting sector—enemy sweeping forward.

(Pane dark.)

First Figure in Blue *(switches red plug).*

Sixth Figure in Blue *(at green pane):* Report from second works—production five lots below contract.

(Pane dark.)

First Figure in Blue *(switches green plug).*

Fourth Figure in Blue *(at red pane):* Report from first fighting sector—enemy sweeping forward.

First Figure in Blue *(switches red plug).*

Seventh Figure in Blue *(at green pane):* Report from third fighting sector—enemy breaking through.

(Pane dark.)

First Figure in Blue *(switches green plug).*

(Silence.)

Second Figure in Blue *(at red pane):* Report from third fighting sector—enemy breaking through.

(Pane dark.)

First Figure in Blue *(switches red plug).*

Fifth Figure in Blue *(at green pane):* Report from third works—production nine lots below contract.

(Pane dark.)

First Figure in Blue *(switches green plug).*

Third Figure in Blue *(at red pane):* Report from second fighting sector—enemy breaking through.

First Figure in Blue *(switches red plug).*

Sᴇxᴛʜ Fɪɢᴜʀᴇ ɪɴ Bʟᴜᴇ *(at green pane):* Report from second works—production eleven lots below contract.

(Pane dark.)

Fɪʀsᴛ Fɪɢᴜʀᴇ ɪɴ Bʟᴜᴇ *(switches green plug).*

Fᴏᴜʀᴛʜ Fɪɢᴜʀᴇ ɪɴ Bʟᴜᴇ *(at red pane):* Report from first fighting sector—enemy breaking through.

(Pane dark.)

Fɪʀsᴛ Fɪɢᴜʀᴇ ɪɴ Bʟᴜᴇ *(switches red plug).*

Sᴇᴠᴇɴᴛʜ Fɪɢᴜʀᴇ ɪɴ Bʟᴜᴇ *(at green pane):* Report from first works—production twelve lots below contract.

(Pane dark.)

Fɪʀsᴛ Fɪɢᴜʀᴇ ɪɴ Bʟᴜᴇ *(into telephone by him):* The Chief Engineer!

Tʜᴇ Cʜɪᴇғ Eɴɢɪɴᴇᴇʀ *(comes in: aged in petrification of fanatical working energy, gaunt profile, white streak in hair, white smock).*

Fɪʀsᴛ Fɪɢᴜʀᴇ ɪɴ Bʟᴜᴇ: Control stations report less production of Gas. *Is* defaults against *Must* by twelve lots.

Cʜɪᴇғ Eɴɢɪɴᴇᴇʀ: Collapse of workers at pressure gauges, at switch gears, at levers.

Fɪʀsᴛ Fɪɢᴜʀᴇ ɪɴ Bʟᴜᴇ: Why no substitutes?

Cʜɪᴇғ Eɴɢɪɴᴇᴇʀ: Each shift combed of each superfluous man or woman.

Fɪʀsᴛ Fɪɢᴜʀᴇ ɪɴ Bʟᴜᴇ: Disease?

Cʜɪᴇғ Eɴɢɪɴᴇᴇʀ: Then without visible sign.

Fɪʀsᴛ Fɪɢᴜʀᴇ ɪɴ Bʟᴜᴇ: Delivery of food unhindered?

Cʜɪᴇғ Eɴɢɪɴᴇᴇʀ: Supply continuous, variety, plenty.

Fɪʀsᴛ Fɪɢᴜʀᴇ ɪɴ Bʟᴜᴇ: Disappointment over payment out of profits to be shared?

Cʜɪᴇғ Eɴɢɪɴᴇᴇʀ: Already profits in net cash stuff wide even boys' pockets.

Fɪʀsᴛ Fɪɢᴜʀᴇ ɪɴ Bʟᴜᴇ: Then how do you account for . . . the discrepancy?

Cʜɪᴇғ Eɴɢɪɴᴇᴇʀ: Movement creates its own law. Excessive repetition of single action blunts the onspurring will to work. Gas is no longer a goal—purpose vanished in the little motion which repeated and repeated became purposeless, part without whole.

Planless the man at his tool—the work withdrew ever farther out of sight as the man slipped day by day ever deeper into sameness and monotony. Wheel by wheel in whirring hum yet never cogged within next wheel and next wheel. Motion roaring upward into emptiness and, unresisted, hurtling down to earth again.

FIRST FIGURE IN BLUE: Can you discover no means by which to assure production?

CHIEF ENGINEER: New masses of workers to the machines.

FIRST FIGURE IN BLUE: Not to be found after sevenfold siftings.

CHIEF ENGINEER: Children are already on full time.

FIRST FIGURE IN BLUE: Then what?

CHIEF ENGINEER: Upleaping increase of gas deficit.

FIRST FIGURE IN BLUE (pointing to table): Do you see this? Calculation of attack and defense comparison of force on either side.

CHIEF ENGINEER: Red dominates.

FIRST FIGURE IN BLUE: Enemy spreads.

CHIEF ENGINEER: Green recedes.

FIRST FIGURE IN BLUE: Gas withholds defense. (CHIEF ENGINEER silent.) This table works out the sum. We lack numbers, but our technical equipment is superior. That balances the outcome. So long as we maintain our technical strength. . . . With the impetus of the Gas which we alone produce, our technical force far exceeds the enemy's. One lot of Gas short of what is calculated here—and we lose our chance of salvation more completely than we have lost it already.

CHIEF ENGINEER (staring): Then the possibility of our crushing the enemy is no longer . . . ?

FIRST FIGURE IN BLUE: Chimera now!

CHIEF ENGINEER: The end?

FIRST FIGURE IN BLUE: At best a draw with both sides checkmate. (CHIEF ENGINEER catches at table for support.) It simplifies the issue. It fell out the only possible way. Fight and downfall. Attack and resistance to the last on either side. Adversary against adversary to the last drop of blood, and they fall together. The enfeebled remnant that remains soon vanishes. None escape from that annihilation. (strongly.) This is knowledge only we possess!

CHIEF ENGINEER (pulling himself together): Then what?

FIRST FIGURE IN BLUE: Increase in production of Gas without consideration of man, woman, or child. No more shifts—let one shift overlap the other without release. Every last hand mobilized from collapse to collapse. No rest, no respite. Let the last dead hand fall from the lever, the last dead foot slip off the switch pedal, the last glazed eye turn sightless from the pressure gauge— let this table here show: the last enemy wiped off the face of the earth, our last fighter dead at his post.

CHIEF ENGINEER *(tensely):* I will fulfill that order.

FIRST FIGURE IN BLUE *(stretching out his hand):* In with us, into the tunnel that has no exit.

CHIEF ENGINEER *(taking his hand):* Gas!

(He goes. Outside nearby, high, shrill sirens, others farther off— fainter—silence.)

FIRST FIGURE IN BLUE *(into telephone):* The Billionaire Worker. *(he comes—middle twenties—worker's dress, shaved head, barefoot.)* Is this your shift?

BILLIONAIRE WORKER: No, but the relay summons has just sounded.

FIRST FIGURE IN BLUE: Prematurely.

BILLIONAIRE WORKER: You must have been forced into that decision.

FIRST FIGURE IN BLUE: Under what compulsion?

BILLIONAIRE WORKER: No worker can manage the earlier shift.

FIRST FIGURE IN BLUE: What is your advice?

BILLIONAIRE WORKER: What value has my advice here?

FIRST FIGURE IN BLUE: You heard—I put the question to you.

BILLIONAIRE WORKER: You can inform yourself by asking any worker in the factories.

FIRST FIGURE IN BLUE: I ask no worker—I want my information from the chief.

BILLIONAIRE WORKER: What chief?

FIRST FIGURE IN BLUE *(looking at him intently):* The one who stands before me.

BILLIONAIRE WORKER: Is this your abdication?

FIRST FIGURE IN BLUE: The new task demands redoubled strength. The chief and we unite our efforts.

BILLIONAIRE WORKER: What do you want of us?

FIRST FIGURE IN BLUE: Gas with tenfold energy.

BILLIONAIRE WORKER *(with a shrug):* You decide the production.

FIRST FIGURE IN BLUE: That does not suffice. The workers are slack. They're soft—orders would run to water in their brains instead of stiffening them to action.

BILLIONAIRE WORKER: Make your punishments harder.

FIRST FIGURE IN BLUE: And take them off their work. . . .

BILLIONAIRE WORKER: Can none be spared?

FIRST FIGURE IN BLUE: From the last great spending of our forces? No. Annihilation on both sides—but annihilation!

BILLIONAIRE WORKER (*flinches, recovers himself*): What do you want of me?

FIRST FIGURE IN BLUE: To send through the whole works a galvanizing current. Fanaticize them for the final ruin. Hate and pride can kindle a fever to heat the coldest veins for once—night will become day in the struggle to reach the goal that blood-red beacon lights.

BILLIONAIRE WORKER: Is that the goal?

FIRST FIGURE IN BLUE: Which your voice shall announce. Go amongst them in all the shops—let your words sound amidst the roar of the pistons and the hum of turning belts—overcome that din with your shout to arms that shows them the goal and lends meaning to their effort. Hands will grasp levers with new strength—feet tighten on the switch pedals—eyes clear at the pressure gauges. The floodgates of work shall open wide and Gas overpower power.

BILLIONAIRE WORKER (*very calm*): I am due for punishment if I miss my shift.

FIRST FIGURE IN BLUE: You are no longer a worker.

BILLIONAIRE WORKER: You have no power to dismiss any worker in this factory.

FIRST FIGURE IN BLUE: I lay you under special contract.

BILLIONAIRE WORKER: I decline to accept it.

FIRST FIGURE IN BLUE: Do you wish to make conditions?

BILLIONAIRE WORKER: I repeat the only one which is the one my mother and my mother's father demanded: set this factory free.

FIRST FIGURE IN BLUE (*fiercely*): Your grandfather and your mother protested against the production of Gas. Therefore it became necessary to use force in the works. Otherwise our preparations for this war would have come to a standstill.

BILLIONAIRE WORKER: Therefore their implacable refusal.

First Figure in Blue: We are engaged in a war such as no party was ever involved in before.

Billionaire Worker: I have obeyed every order in silence.

First Figure in Blue: The time has come now for you to speak.

Billionaire Worker: Against myself and against my mother?

First Figure in Blue: For the workers who want Gas. After the explosion they came back—they rebuilt the factory—they stayed in the shops in spite of danger that hourly threatened. They bowed in willingness before their master, whose name then was Gas, whose name today is downfall if a voice they will heed will make it known to them. Yours is that voice—at your "yes" the "yes" of thousands will light the train of fire for the ultimate destruction. Come over to us, and the half-dead will spring to life again throughout these works.

Billionaire Worker: I defend the legacy of my grandfather.

First Figure in Blue: The workers themselves laughed his plans to scorn.

Billionaire Worker: The form for people will manifest itself.

First Figure in Blue: For others who survive. There is no future for us.

Billionaire Worker: There is always a way out.

First Figure in Blue: Do you seek one without us?

Billionaire Worker: With you and within you.

First Figure in Blue (*after a moment's reflection*): We shall achieve by punishment the output we require.

(*He makes a gesture of dismissal. The* Billionaire Worker *goes. Silence.*)

Second Figure in Blue (*at red pane*): Report from third fighting-sector—enemy pressure irresistible.

(*Pane dark.*)

First Figure in Blue (*switches red plug*).

Third Figure in Blue (*at red pane*): Report from second fighting-sector—enemy pressure irresistible.

(*Pane dark.*)

First Figure in Blue (*switches red plug*).

FOURTH FIGURE IN BLUE *(at red pane.)* Report from first fighting-sector—enemy pressure irresistible.

(Pane dark.)

FIRST FIGURE IN BLUE *(springs up):* No report from the factories?

CHIEF ENGINEER *(enters hastily).*

CHIEF ENGINEER: Turmoil everywhere! Shift-changes hitched! Relief gang and gang on duty cease to cog! For the first time a gap opens in a system that has been flawless all the years. The pendulum swings wild! The machine has stalled.

FIRST FIGURE IN BLUE: Your organization?

CHIEF ENGINEER: Announced by sirens! Answered by the gang on duty with laying-down of tools—and by the relief gang with ignoring it.

FIRST FIGURE IN BLUE: Is anyone inciting them to resist?

CHIEF ENGINEER: Not a wheel-minder among them! It's the machine that is running wild—and it's running wild because its works are moving to a different rhythm. The new distribution of time has disturbed the old pace and drags it down to seconds which suffice for remembrance to remember themselves! Lightning flashes in heads and illuminates the path they have been driven along these years upon years! The tumult becomes a face grinning its hideousness into their horror-frozen minds!

FIRST FIGURE IN BLUE: Then—strike?

CHIEF ENGINEER: What is that?

FIRST FIGURE IN BLUE: Are they leaving switch gear, lever, observation dial?

CHIEF ENGINEER: Already happenings of the past! Standstill turned into movement!

FIRST FIGURE IN BLUE: Commotion?

CHIEF ENGINEER: Flaming through the shops! Not a voice—not a cry—no eloquence! Silence of ice—gazing before them—or stealing a glance at the next man who does likewise at his neighbor, and so on from partner to partner! It is out of their eyes it's coming—this thing that is on its way to shatter us to bits—this tempest!

FIRST FIGURE IN BLUE: A cordon round the shops—anyone attempting to leave to be stopped at the gates!

CHIEF ENGINEER: Is there still time?

FIFTH FIGURE IN BLUE *(at green pane):* Report from third works. . . .

CHIEF ENGINEER *(goes to him—reading off):* Work stands still—workers leaving shops!

FIRST FIGURE IN BLUE: Lock the others in.

SIXTH FIGURE IN BLUE *(at green pane):* Report from second works. . . .

CHIEF ENGINEER: Work stands still. . . .

SEVENTH FIGURE IN BLUE *(at green pane.)* Report from first works. . . .

CHIEF ENGINEER: Workers leaving shops!

FIRST FIGURE IN BLUE: Alarm throughout the works!

CHIEF ENGINEER: Too late! We're crushed under the weight of their numbers. See it towering fearfully over us, the wave about to break. We have brought it towering over our heads—they come and we are here!

FIRST FIGURE IN BLUE: Are they through?

CHIEF ENGINEER: In inevitable march. The line presses back upon the place we drove them from. There the storm gathers, there, when it breaks, it shall strike us—if we are here for the striking.

FIRST FIGURE IN BLUE *(flinging the plugs together in disorder):* The calculation did not come out—there was a remainder!

(He goes out with the CHIEF ENGINEER *and the* FIGURES IN BLUE. *The hall remains empty. Then an ever-swelling crowd of people emerge in a circle against the dim gray walls—men young and middle-aged, old men, boys, in gray workers' clothes, shorn-headed and barefoot; women, young and middle-aged, old women, girls, in the same clothes, barefoot, with gray kerchiefs close round their hair. A short distance from the tables the dead, silent, forward-pressing, movement, stops still. The outbreak comes in a great flood—silent—yet full of haste. The tables are overturned and passed from hand to hand until they vanish into the shadowy edge of the hall; the wires from platform to tables, from dome to platform, are torn away. Then utter silence. The women pull the kerchiefs off their heads and begin to smooth their hair.)*

ALL *(looking at one another—in a great shout):* No Gas!!

Act 2

Concrete hall. Dimmer light from the arc lamps. Hall full.

VOICES *(rising clear through a murmurous swell):* What of us?

GIRL *(on the platform—spreading her hair):* Morning for us—day with a morning so filled with joy in light that it postpones the noon! Radiance streams from that morning, dawning as no morning dawned for us before. We open eyes of awe upon that wider vision, chaos of light in white and many colors ... the wonder passes and is retrospect. Morning for me leads my lover to me by the hand.

YOUNG WORKER *(beside girl on the platform):* Morning for you and me and our fulfillment. Empty were being and seeking from day to day, neither yours nor mine until this bright morning. Now the locked waters flow once more, tide strong against the shore, riotous with color, loud with wedding joy!

GIRL *(embracing him):* Morning for you!

YOUNG WORKER *(holding her):* Morning for you.

GIRLS AND YOUNG WORKERS *(pressing about the platform—embracing):* Morning for us.

VOICES OF THE OTHERS: More for us!

WOMAN *(on the platform):* Noon for us. Out of that beginning I had not yet drawn the arc that sweeps toward the height—it crept flat along the ground. Between man and wife nothing lay behind the morning—the dead husk rustled, riveting but not uniting. Now it showers out of the brightness, and the rainbow shines overhead. The clouds flaunt gold, they vanish in fire of glory the sky around, raining beneficence, warming and nourishing the dead-brittle crust. Man and wife at noon, one life, one breath, absorbed and welded, indistinguishable. Demands shall be answered, last and first, the answer rings forth with a noonday clamor through the blue noon over us.

MAN *(beside her on the platform):* Noon streams from you, driving a swarm of blue-rimmed clouds. Noon spread over me like a tent of permanence—bounding the space where I am yours. No exit to seduce where nothing serves—no will that defies where nothing signifies—the syllable is breathed and understanding outreaches further words where both command. Desire grew bold, immeasurable—body binds body, mated—our law is the doubling of being and being unabated, forbidding nothing, allowing nothing, for oneness knows neither pleading nor resistance and is indivisible in Man and Woman at noon.

WOMAN *(reaching out her hands):* Noon for you!

MAN *(taking them):* Noon for you!

MEN AND WOMEN *(round the platform, seeking one another's hands):* Noon for us!

(MAN *and* WOMAN *down from platform.*)

VOICES OF OTHERS: More for us!

OLD WOMAN *(on the platform):* Evening for us. Once to be still after the day's round, feet quiet in their shoes. What were morning and noon to me? No difference to me between the noon and the morning. One and the same and all the same pattern of bitter labor, slipping by like muddy trickling water over bumps in a stream bed we can't see the bottom of. That was morning and noon for us. . . . Was I alone? Was no one by me in the beginning and after? Was I so quite alone? Did I go under with only myself, reach out my hand only for my own other hand to save me from sinking, sinking? Had I died lonely even then? . . . Evening brings life, adding all the lost hours to the hours that shall be. Time is dealt out to a new measure—I hold out my two hands and join them about nothingness—for it pours out of them—dazzled I look and see the treasure before me which noon and morning hid and evening reveals.

OLD MAN *(beside her on the platform):* For us the evening. Rest from the aimless, driven haste; trees and shade for us now. Where whirls the tumult? Where are they hurrying? Drowsy birds twitter in the branches—wind soughs, rustles. Day ebbs away. Is it late? Morning is forcing and crowding without peace, without end. Was there loss? The curve of a lip can extravagantly bestow. You suffered no want, I promised myself nothing—and our evening discloses a plenty we shall never exhaust. *(Leads her with him down from the platform.)*

OLD MEN AND WOMEN *(moving toward them—supporting one another):* Evening for us!

VOICES OF THE OTHERS: More for us!

A VOICE: What of us?

SOME VOICES: More for us!!

OTHER VOICES: What of us?

A WAVE OF VOICES: More for us!

A COUNTER-WAVE OF VOICES: What of us?!

VOICES UPON VOICES *(in flood and counter-flood):* More for us!! What of us?! *(Ending in a great cry. Silence.)*

A Voice: The Billionaire Worker!

ALL THE VOICES TOGETHER *(swelling—uniting—triumphing)*: The Billionaire Worker!! *(Silence.)*

BILLIONAIRE WORKER *(ascends the platform)*: I stand here, yours. Above you only by these steps I climb with my feet. *(On the platform.)* No mind more deep-thinking—no mouth more eloquent before you. You call to morning and to evening and to noon—and make the speakable articulate with words forever relevant. For you, Young Girl, the morning, dawn, and beginning of your life—and your sisters' here and your sisters' yet to come. That is primeval law! For you, Youth, the fire of early day, beating in blood and pulsing with the first embrace—and in your brothers' here and in your brothers' yet to come. That is primeval law! For you, Woman, day big with noon, season of all fulfillment—and for all these women about you and all who are yet to come. That is primeval law! For you, Man, the high stars' brand of mighty noon—and for all these men about you and all who are yet to come. That is primeval law! For you, old men and old women, evening falling on shoulders, into laps, out of shadow and calm airs—lulling into the night that shall receive your sleep without cry, without fear. That is primeval law! *(Stronger.)* Day is about you again—day and its fullness, morning and noon and evening. Law is restored and shines out from new tablets. You have come home again—out of bondage—returned to the ultimate duties of life.

VOICES: What of us?

BILLIONAIRE WORKER: Proclaim yourselves in your self-recognition—under bitterest oppression crushed to earth—penned in slavery like beasts for the slaughter—you shall be heard! Your experience shall be your seal and oath—this is no child's play. Let your cry be heard—a truth of truths—in a great YES!

VOICES UPON VOICES: What of us?

BILLIONAIRE WORKER: Report yourselves in your unfolding! Your discovery would turn to sacrilege were you to hide what you have found. Silence would set a stain upon your souls, black and terrible, never to be effaced. The air in this house of yours will turn foul if you bar your windows shut and keep that light from shining on the streets without. You would stand cursed in that instant and forever damned!

ALL THE VOICES TOGETHER: What of us?!

BILLIONAIRE WORKER: Spread your tidings abroad! Send your cry forth out of this hall over all the world. Spare no labor—it shall be your last. Give of your treasure: it is inexhaustible and will return tenfold. Roll the dome clear!

(Silence.)

VOICES UPON VOICES: Roll the dome clear!

ALL THE VOICES TOGETHER: Roll the dome clear!

BILLIONAIRE WORKER: Stretch the wire that shall flash your message around the earth's circle!

VOICES: Stretch the wire!

VOICES UPON VOICES: Stretch the wire!

ALL THE VOICES TOGETHER: Stretch the wire!

BILLIONAIRE WORKER: Send out the signal of truth to all the world's fighters!

VOICES: Send out the signal!

VOICES UPON VOICES: Send out the signal!

ALL THE VOICES TOGETHER: Send out the signal!

YOUNG WORKER *(on the platform—arms raised to the dome):* We shall clear the dome!

(Silence.)

VOICE *(above):* We in the dome!

VOICES *(below):* Roll the dome clear!

VOICE *(above):* Rust clogs the grooves!

VOICES *(below):* Loosen the rivets!

VOICE *(above):* Mightily pressing. . . .

VOICES *(below):* Break down the girders!

VOICE *(above):* Plates giving way!

VOICES *(below):* Widen the gap!

VOICE *(above):* Now the dome moves!

ALL THE VOICES TOGETHER *(below):* Roll the dome clear!

(A broad beam of light falls suddenly from dome to ground, and remains there erect like a shining column. Dazzled silence—all faces raised.)

BILLIONAIRE WORKER *(calling upward):* Speed up the work without slacking.

VOICE *(above):* The wire hangs plumb.

BILLIONAIRE WORKER: Make haste to be done.

VOICE *(above):* Wireless at summit, here in good order.

BILLIONAIRE WORKER: Flash what I call!

VOICE *(above):* We stand by.

BILLIONAIRE WORKER: Send out the rally: hands have ceased from their work—hands have quit their slaving for destruction—hands are free to take the pressure of all hands in ours which now rest. No Gas!

VOICE *(above):* Hands have ceased their work—hands are free to take the pressure of all hands in ours which now rest. No Gas!

ALL THE VOICES TOGETHER *(below):* No Gas!!

BILLIONAIRE WORKER: Stand by for the answer!

VOICES *(below):* Tell us the answer!

(Silence.)

VOICE *(above):* Answer fails!

(Silence.)

BILLIONAIRE WORKER: Send a new call: Tumult in blood subsided—fever fell cool—sight came to eyes that look up to greet you—shift-changing turned to abidance of being—No Gas!

ALL THE VOICES TOGETHER *(below):* No Gas!!

BILLIONAIRE WORKER: Watch for the answer!

VOICES UPON VOICES *(below):* Call down the answer!

BILLIONAIRE WORKER: Keep good watch for the answer!

(Silence.)

VOICE *(above):* Answer fails!

(Silence.)

BILLIONAIRE WORKER: Urge a reply: Land melted into land—frontiers into the all—the farthest are neighbors—joining with you we disperse among you, divided in oneness, one in division. No Gas!

VOICE *(above, repeating):* Land melted into land—frontiers into the all—the farthest are neighbors—joining with you we disperse among you, divided in oneness, one in division—no Gas!

ALL THE VOICES TOGETHER *(below):* No Gas!!

BILLIONAIRE WORKER: Take the answer right!

ALL THE VOICES TOGETHER *(below):* Shout us the answer!

BILLIONAIRE WORKER: Take it up accurately to the last syllable.

(Silence.)

VOICE *(above):* Answer fails!

(Dead silence.)

VOICE *(from farthest rim of the crowd):* Strangers!
VOICES UPON VOICES: The Yellow Ones!
ALL THE VOICES TOGETHER: The Enemy!!

(They fall back, making way for seven FIGURES IN YELLOW *who pass between them into the center of the hall.* BILLIONAIRE WORKER *staggers from the platform.)*

FIRST FIGURE IN YELLOW: A hitch in the reckoning. A rift in the game. Yours threw the cards down, we overtrumped. Enter our losses into your books. *(Silence.)* The power of the Gas you produce will serve our needs. Your work shall pay your debt but never liquidate it. Gas is our fuel. *(Silence.)* The works pass from your disposal to our commands. We scrap the schedule of your sharings. Proceeds shall concentrate out of your many hands into our few—wages for you in the minimum measure for maintenance of strength. *(Silence.)* From this hour these works resume the production of Gas. You entered this hall as a crowd, you leave it as shifts—back to your service, shift succeeding shift. We are the users of Gas and demand it—the Chief Engineer is the maker of Gas and shall answer to us. *(CHIEF ENGINEER comes.)* The Chief Engineer stands in power over you to order and punish. *(Silence. To the* CHIEF ENGINEER.*)* Set the hall to rights.

CHIEF ENGINEER *(calls upward):* Roll the dome shut. *(The sunlight diminishes and is gone.)* Set up the tables. *(With noiseless and rapid obedience tables are reached over the heads of the crowd and set up in the center.)* Stretch the wires. *(Swiftly, dully, wires are stretched from where they hang perpendicular from the dome diagonally to the tables as before.)* Recharge the lamps. *(Dusty light beams from arc lamps.)* To the shops, forward! *(Wordless melting away toward the edge of the hall—vanishment.)*

(Six FIGURES IN YELLOW *sit down at the tables.* FIRST FIGURE IN YELLOW *arranges the plugs at the switch-board.* CHIEF ENGINEER *waits.)*

FIRST FIGURE IN YELLOW *(to the* CHIEF ENGINEER*):* Gas! (CHIEF ENGINEER *off.)*

Act 3

Cement hall. Dusty light beams from arc lamp. At the tables the seven FIGURES IN YELLOW. *Silence.*

SECOND FIGURE IN YELLOW *(at red pane):* Report from requisitions headquarters—two quotas more required for third district.

(Pane dark.)

FIRST FIGURE IN YELLOW *(switches red plug).*

FIFTH FIGURE IN YELLOW *(at green pane):* Report from third works: Production one lot below contract.

(Pane dark.)

FIRST FIGURE IN YELLOW *(switches green plug).*

THIRD FIGURE IN YELLOW *(at red pane):* Report from requisitions headquarters: Three quotas more required for second district.

(Pane dark.)

FIRST FIGURE IN YELLOW *(switches red plug).*

SIXTH FIGURE IN YELLOW *(at green pane):* Report from second works: Production one lot below contract.

(Pane dark.)

FIRST FIGURE IN YELLOW *(switches green plug).*

FOURTH FIGURE IN YELLOW *(at red pane):* Report from requisitions headquarters: Four quotas more required for first district.

(Pane dark.)

FIRST FIGURE IN YELLOW *(switches red plug).*

SEVENTH FIGURE IN YELLOW *(at green pane):* Report from first works: Production two lots under contract.

(Pane dark.)

FIRST FIGURE IN YELLOW *(switches green plug.)*

(Silence.)

SECOND FIGURE IN YELLOW *(at red pane)*: Report from requisitions headquarters: Five quotas more required for third district.

(Pane dark.)

FIRST FIGURE IN YELLOW *(switches red plug)*.

FIFTH FIGURE IN YELLOW *(at green pane)*: Report from third works: Production six lots under contract.

(Pane dark.)

FIRST FIGURE IN YELLOW *(switches green plug)*.

THIRD FIGURE IN YELLOW *(at red pane)*: Report from requisitions headquarters: Eight quotas more required for second district.

(Pane dark.)

FIRST FIGURE IN YELLOW *(switches red plug)*.

SIXTH FIGURE IN YELLOW *(at green pane)*: Report from second works: Production ten lots under contract.

(Pane dark.)

FIRST FIGURE IN YELLOW *(switches green plug)*.

FOURTH FIGURE IN YELLOW *(at red pane)*: Report from requisitions headquarters: Eleven quotas more required for first district.

(Pane dark.)

FIRST FIGURE IN YELLOW *(switches red plug)*.

SEVENTH FIGURE IN YELLOW *(at green pane)*: Report from first works: Production twelve lots under contract.

(Pane dark.)

FIRST FIGURE IN YELLOW *(springs up—telephones)*: The Chief Engineer! *(CHIEF ENGINEER comes—without haste)*: Check-up stations; verify decreased production of gas. *Is* defaults against *Must* by twelve lots.

CHIEF ENGINEER *(calmly)*: Are you astonished?

FIRST FIGURE IN YELLOW: Does personal opinion enter?

CHIEF ENGINEER *(shrugging shoulders)*: If you can deny yourself.

First Figure in Yellow: Automaton as all are here.

Chief Engineer: The automata in the shops are moving fast with accessory sounds.

First Figure in Yellow: Buzzing what?

Chief Engineer: "Not for me."

First Figure in Yellow: Meaning?

Chief Engineer: This hand lifting lever—not for me. This foot pressing switch pedal—not for me. These eyes watching pressure gauge—not for me.

First Figure in Yellow: Do you know your responsibility?

Chief Engineer: Gas.

First Figure in Yellow: You will be held to account for every minus in delivery.

Chief Engineer *(peculiarly):* I am prepared—for the reckoning.

First Figure in Yellow: You applied your powers?

Chief Engineer *(as before):* Not yet.

First Figure in Yellow: You inflicted no punishments?

Chief Engineer: Upon whom?

First Figure in Yellow: The hand that falters at the lever—the foot that misses the switch pedal—the eyes that blink before the pressure gauge.

Chief Engineer: And take every man, woman, and child off the shift.

First Figure in Yellow: All resisting?

Chief Engineer: We weaken from shift to shift.

First Figure in Yellow: Then what next?

Chief Engineer: Gas!

First Figure in Yellow: Why did you not flog the first that flagged?

Chief Engineer: No.

First Figure in Yellow: Did you doubt its spread, having begun?

Chief Engineer: No.

First Figure in Yellow: Why did you conceal these occurrences?

Chief Engineer: I did so.

First Figure in Yellow: Are you supporting the revolt?

Chief Engineer: With all my power.

Fifth Figure in Yellow *(at green pane):* Report from third works: production . . .

CHIEF ENGINEER (*triumphantly*): Stopped!

SIXTH FIGURE IN YELLOW (*at green pane*): Report from first works: production . . .

CHIEF ENGINEER: Stopped!

(*The* FIGURES IN YELLOW *leave their tables.*)

FIRST FIGURE IN YELLOW: Who . . . ?

CHIEF ENGINEER: My orders! As I left to come here. With my power behind them, conferred by yourself. The obedient obey. No more hands lifting levers—for others. No more feet pressing switch pedals—for others. No more eyes watching pressure gauges—for others. Hand falls, fist clenches against you—foot withdraws, poises to run against you—eyes turn away, dart glances against you. Gas for us—Gas against you!

FIRST FIGURE IN YELLOW: Do you overlook the consequences?

CHIEF ENGINEER: None for us.

FIRST FIGURE IN YELLOW: Batteries surround the works.

CHIEF ENGINEER: In triple circle.

FIRST FIGURE IN YELLOW: Primed for the first sign of rebellion.

CHIEF ENGINEER: Rebellion rages!

FIRST FIGURE IN YELLOW: The works to the last man, into the dust with one volley.

CHIEF ENGINEER: Are you sure?

FIRST FIGURE IN YELLOW: We await your report of resumption of work within minimum delay. (*He signs to the* FIGURES IN YELLOW—*they leave together.*)

CHIEF ENGINEER (*at front table—telephones*): Leave all shops—meeting in the hall.

(*Crowd entrance—shoving accumulation toward center—full hall.*)

VOICE (*at last—shrill, frightened*): Who has turned us off?

CHIEF ENGINEER: Those who fill this place with crowding pressure to limit of its walls. Those who left lever, switch block, and gauge glass in the lurch. Those who were serf-silence and will now be freemen voice.

VOICES UPON VOICES: Who has turned us off?

CHIEF ENGINEER: Those whose hands double to fists defying. Those whose feet rush to the attack. Those whose eyes take in the measure of the slave-master.

ALL THE VOICES TOGETHER: Who has turned us off?

CHIEF ENGINEER: Your command is your destiny. Your word is your law. Yesterday, rented slaves—masters today.

(*Silence.*)

VOICE: What of us?

CHIEF ENGINEER: Release from debt and deeper debt. Backs pull straight after burden and yoke. Strangling compulsion relaxed.

VOICES UPON VOICES: What of us?

CHIEF ENGINEER: Up from the knees. Weakness grows strong. Fear soars to fight.

ALL THE VOICES TOGETHER: What of us?

CHIEF ENGINEER: Unleash the slinking rage in you. Unleash the hatred that cringed in you. Unleash the poison that oozed in you. Repay!

VOICES: Have we power?

CHIEF ENGINEER: Pushed from shadow into light. Purple for your rags. Nothingness raised to affluence.

VOICES UPON VOICES: Have we power?

CHIEF ENGINEER: Beyond all measure. No weapon can strike with the force of your arms raised to strike. No shot is deadlier than the breath of your lungs. You are on the march, conquerors, before ever you reach the field.

ALL THE VOICES TOGETHER: Have we power?

CHIEF ENGINEER: The battle is yours without the loss of a knuckle-joint. In less than half a day, the day is yours. Where is the means to victory more terrible than yours? Poison Gas! (*He takes a red globe out of his pocket.*) My discovery for you. Beasts of burden you, and I too—and the shame devoured me for all of us. Not for a second did I lose sight of my goal, to destroy our whip-masters—at last I reached it—the formula that frees: hatred and shame were its ingredients. In a skin-thin glass— victory: that swells and eats away flesh from legs, bleaches stiff bones. (*Silence.*) There is no looking on the power of annihilation with impunity. Reason leaves, and madness enters the brain of the beholder who sees living men turned to bleached skeletons before his very eyes. Resistance screams itself down out of the mouth of the first inquisitive one who rashly rushes hither, crying out world's end and massacre! (*Silence.*) This is the decisive hour for time everlasting—decide, and you are the victors. Set the example—hurl your ball from the top of the dome—aim at the

lines waiting to aim at you—meet onslaught with onslaught—
hurl your balls!
VOICES: Poison Gas.
CHIEF ENGINEER: Be avengers!
VOICES UPON VOICES: Poison Gas!
CHIEF ENGINEER: Be fighters!
ALL THE VOICES TOGETHER: Poison Gas!
CHIEF ENGINEER: Be conquerors!

*(Young workers crowd on to the steps of the platform—hands
out-stretched for the globe. BILLIONAIRE WORKER pushes his way
through them past their uplifted arms.)*

BILLIONAIRE WORKER: Don't touch that globe. Reject that temp-
tation. Do not destroy your power with the hurling of the balls.
VOICES: The Billionaire Worker!
BILLIONAIRE WORKER: Do not follow those orders. Do not aim in
the dark. Do no mean and paltry trafficking.
VOICES UPON VOICES: The Billionaire Worker!
BILLIONAIRE WORKER: Protect your privileges. Know your means
of conquest. Build upon rock the house that shall stand un-
shaken forever.
ALL THE VOICES TOGETHER: The Billionaire Worker!!

*(The young workers have fallen away from the steps. The BILLION-
AIRE WORKER ascends further.)*

BILLIONAIRE WORKER: Spread your sight to span the new that
began in the old. Beginning meets end, new truth, truth revealed.
All ages debouch in your age, endlessly repeating. Your need is
not discovery—your fulfillment not experiment and proof. Your
lot is in the wheel thousands of years revolving—purifying your
decisions with sorting and sorting. *(Silence.)* No road of many
turnings leads to perfection as the street that is opening for you
now. Yours the gain—your tables ran over. Riches were piled up
all round you. *(Silence.)* But it scattered away like sand children
play with on the beach. The rising of a wind retards nothing—
you cannot stop springs black with the birth of earth-disturbing
tempest. Momentum of release met you and flung you to the
ground. A deep fall. The tower of your own height buried you!
(Silence.) You were reckoned great before—you shall be greater
now—as martyrs. *(Silence.)* The unslaked passion left you—day-

labor. Endlessly satiating the nameless other replaced it. Not tables and shifts and dismissals feed it; but its own coin that pays never more, never less. *(Silence.)* Pay with the counterfeit they demand of you. Cheat the cheater with his own spurious currency's dull ring. Your work brings nothing to maturity—do it. Their currency is falling—convert it. Martyrs in the works— freemen in yourselves. *(Silence.)* Build up the kingdom. Not with the burden of new discoveries—distance does not intimidate. Hard upon the ungrudging promise crowd the first-fruits—law long and long since, piled on law—preparations ripe, time out of mind—use your existence to which all reverts—build to the last stronghold the kingdom which is in yourselves. *(Silence. The* BILLIONAIRE WORKER *on the platform.)* You shall dare what generations and generations have bred in you. You exiled one of yourselves, and wisely—over green pastures he decoyed you here before me. Not from outside can you protect the greatness within you—you cannot pen it in with colony and colony—*your kingdom is not of this world!!* *(Silence.)* Face the stranger—pay him his interest—leave him his wage—shovel him his gains—suffer his demands—ignore the spine bleeding in your skin—Be your Kingdom! *(Breathing silence.)*

CHIEF ENGINEER *(at the foot of the steps):* Treachery spits in your faces in that cry—do you not hear it? Have you no tongues to downcry it? Have you forgotten the pledge of your surging voices raised to me?

BILLIONAIRE WORKER: Deliver yourselves within yourselves!

CHIEF ENGINEER: What will remain to you once dispossessed? Your necks for the bloody spurring of the lash—yourselves for defilement, laughing you to scorn—a cattle team misused. And drudgery for ever, a whimgin cranking you eternally round and round, wearing and bearing you down. To be racked with chastisement when your limbs break under you. Those are your terms of hire.

BILLIONAIRE WORKER: Let the kingdom arise, which shall reign in you almighty.

CHIEF ENGINEER: Let the power fall low which exploits you now. Yours the gain—without the bending of a finger. Gas the magician works for you. You use your victory as the victors of yesterday showed you to.

BILLIONAIRE WORKER: Deliver yourselves in the endurance of serfdom which cannot touch the kingdom within.

CHIEF ENGINEER: Think of the tribute that will fall to you. No place on the world's globe but will be your debtor, no ships hold but will carry freight for you, no bridge but whose arch bears supplies for you, no wire but flashes your commands from pole to pole. Your will is world empire.

BILLIONAIRE WORKER: The voice speaks again—the light that tempts and dazzles shines out again.

CHIEF ENGINEER: Give your purpose voice that it may bind you implacably.

BILLIONAIRE WORKER: Decide for the way of humility.

CHIEF ENGINEER: Strike a bargain with your term and the bombardment!

BILLIONAIRE WORKER: Return to your places, perform your services—they are the lesser part.

CHIEF ENGINEER *(on the platform):* Take aim and cast the single throw which gives you victory!

BILLIONAIRE WORKER: Return!

CHIEF ENGINEER *(holding the globe high).* Dominion!

BILLIONAIRE WORKER: Found the kingdom!

CHIEF ENGINEER: Ignite the Gas that kills!!

(Silence.)

BILLIONAIRE WORKER: Be silent and listen how heaven and earth both hold their breath before your decision which shall seal the fate of the world.

(Silence.)

VOICES: The Gas that kills!

VOICES UPON VOICES: The Gas that kills!

ALL THE VOICES TOGETHER: The Gas that kills!!

CHIEF ENGINEER *(victorious):* Ours the power! Ours the world! Aim the bomb—hasten the throw—they shall not shoot! . . . Who volunteers?

YOUNG WORKERS *(storming on to the platform):* I!

CHIEF ENGINEER: Have a care of this ball—it is dangerous.

BILLIONAIRE WORKER *(restraining the young workers—turning to the* CHIEF ENGINEER): I am the rightful one—I have priority.

ALL THE VOICES TOGETHER: The Billionaire Worker!! *(The* CHIEF
ENGINEER *gives him the bomb.)*

BILLIONAIRE WORKER *(on the platform—bomb upraised over his
head):* My blood's blood beat for our conversion. My thirst
slaked itself at the thirst of mother and mother's father. Our
voices might have waked the wilderness—Our voices could wake
the wilderness—men's ears are deaf. I am vindicated! I can fulfill!
*(He throws the bomb into the air—it falls and smashes with a
frail clatter. Silence.)*

CHIEF ENGINEER: The Gas that kills!

ALL THE VOICES: The Gas that kills!

*(Paralyzed silence. Bombardment thunders from without.
Darkness, and vast crash of collapsing walls. Silence. Light comes
gradually. The hall a shambles of cement slabs lying on top of
one another like broken gravestones—the skeletons of the workers
already bleached jut out amongst them. FIGURE IN YELLOW—hel-
meted, telephone at head, hastens toward the wreckage, unrolling
wire.)*

FIGURE IN YELLOW *(stops—stares wildly—shrieks into telephone):* Report of effect of bombardment—Turn your bullets on
yourselves—exterminate yourselves—the dead crowd out of
their graves—day of judgment—*dies irae—solvet—in favil. . . .*

*(His shot shatters the rest. In the mist-gray distance sheaves of
flaming bombs bursting together—clearly in self-extermination.)*

Translated by Winifred Katzin

Bibliography

Primary Sources

Benn, Gottfried. *Ithaka*. Trans. J. M. Ritchie. *Expressionist Texts by Oskar Kokoschka, August Stramm, Georg Kaiser, Gottfried Benn, Ernst Toller, Walter Hasenclever, Lothar Schreyer*. Ed. Mel Gordon. New York: PAJ Publications, 1986, 37–45

Hasenclever, Walter. *The Son*. Trans. Henry Marx. *Expressionist Texts*, 95–153

Kaiser, Georg. *From Morning to Midnight*. Trans. James M. Ritchie. *Five Plays*. Ed. James M. Ritchie. 2 vols. London: Calder and Boyars, 1970, I, 17–73

———. *Gas I. A Play in Five Acts*. Trans. Herman Scheffauer. New York: Frederick Ungar, 1957

———. *Gas II. A Play in Three Acts*. Trans. Winifred Katzin. New York: Frederick Ungar, 1963

Kokoschka, Oskar. *Murderer, the Women's Hope*. Trans. Michael Hamburger. *An Anthology of German Expressionist Drama: A Prelude to the Absurd*. Ed. Walter H. Sokel. Garden City, N.Y.: Doubleday & Co., Inc., 1963, 17–21

Sternheim, Carl. *The Bloomers*. Trans. M. A. McHaffie. *Five Plays*. Ed. James M. Ritchie. London: Calder and Boyars, 1970, 77–144

Stramm, August. *Sancta Susanna*. Trans. Henry Marx. *Expressionist Texts*, 37–45

Toller, Ernst. *Masses and Man*. Trans. Vera Mendel. *Seven Plays*. New York: Liveright, 1936, 107–54

German Versions of the Plays

Benn, Gottfried. *Gesammelte Werke*. Ed. Dieter Wellershoff. Four vols. Stuttgart: Klett-Cotta, 1958–61

Denkler, Horst, Ed. *Einakter und kleine Dramen des Expressionismus*. Reclams Universal Bibliothek. Stuttgart: Philipp Reclam jun., 1968 [Contains Gottfried Benn's *Ithaka*, Oskar Kokoschka's *Mörder*,

Hoffnung der Frauen, and plays by Johannes R. Becher, Georg Britting, Alfred Brust, Alfred Döblin, Ivan Goll, Walter Hasenclever, Hanns Johst, Franz Jung, Georg Kaiser, Hermann Kasack, Wassily Kandinsky, Friedrich Koffka, Reinhard Sorge, Franz Werfel]

Hasenclever, Walter. *Sämtliche Werke*. Eds. Dieter Breuer and Bernd Witt. Five vols. Die Mainzer Reihe 70. Mainz: v. Hase & Koehler, 1990

———. *Gedichte, Dramen, Prosa*. Ed. Kurt Pinthus. Reinbek: Rowohlt, 1963

———. *Der Sohn. Ein Drama in fünf Akten*. Reclams Universal Bibliothek. Stuttgart: Philipp Reclam jun., 1990

Kaiser, Georg. *Werke*. Ed. Walther Huder. Six vols. Frankfurt a. M./Berlin/Wien: Propyläen, 1970–72

———. *Von morgens bis mitternachts*. Ed. Walther Huder. Reclams Universal-Bibliothek. Stuttgart: Philipp Reclam jun., 1994

Kokoschka, Oskar. *Das schriftliche Werk*. Ed. Heinz Spielmann. Four vols. Hamburg: Hans Christians, 1973–76

Sternheim, Carl. *Gesamtwerk*. Ed. Wilhelm Emrich. Ten vols. Neuwied/Berlin: Luchterhand, 1963 ff.

Stramm, August. *Das Werk*. Ed. René Radrizzani. Wiesbaden: Limes, 1963

Rühle, Günther. *Zeit und Theater. Vom Kaiserreich zur Republik 1913–1925*. Vol. 1. Berlin: Propyläen, 1973 [Contains Walter Hasenclever's *Der Sohn*, Georg Kaiser's *Gas* plays, and plays by Arnolt Bronnen, Reinhard Goering, Hans Henny Jahn, Paul Kornfeld, Ludwig Rubiner, Reinhard Sorge, Carl Sternheim, Ernst Toller, Fritz von Unruh]

Toller, Ernst. *Gesammelte Werke*. Eds. John M. Spalek and Wolfgang Frühwald. Six vols. Munich: Hanser, 1978–79

Schondorff, Joachim ed. *Deutsches Theater des Expressionismus*. Munich: Langen-Müller, 1962 [Contains Georg Kaiser's *Von morgens bis mitternachts* and plays by Ernst Barlach, Reinhard Goering, Hans Henny Jahn, Else Lasker-Schüler, Frank Wedekind]

Toller, Ernst. *Masse Mensch. Ein Stück aus der sozialen Revolution des 20. Jahrhunderts*. Stuttgart: Philipp Reclam jun., 1979

Expressionist Plays in English Translation

Gordon, Mel, Ed. *Expressionist Texts by Oskar Kokoschka, August Stramm, Georg Kaiser, Gottfried Benn, Ernst Toller, Walter Hasenclever, Lothar Schreyer*. New York: PAJ Publications, 1986

Kaiser, Georg. *Five Plays*. Ed. J. M. Ritchie. Two vols. London: Calder and Boyars, 1970

Ritchie, J. M., Ed. *Seven Expressionist Plays: Kokoschka to Barlach*. London: Calder and Boyars, 1968. [Plays by Ernst Barlach, Alfred Brust,

Ivan Goll, Franz Kafka, Georg Kaiser, Oskar Kokoschka, August Stramm

——. *Vision and Aftermath. Four Expressionist War Plays.* London: Calder and Boyars, 1969. [Plays by Reinhard Goering, Walter Hasenclever, Carl Hauptmann, Ernst Toller]

Sokel, Walter H., Ed. *An Anthology of German Expressionist Drama: A Prelude to the Absurd.* Garden City, N.Y.: Doubleday & Co., Inc., 1963. [Plays by Bertolt Brecht, Ivan Goll, Walter Hasenclever, Georg Kaiser, Oskar Kokoschka, Rolf Lauckner, Reinhard Sorge, Carl Sternheim]

Sternheim, Carl. *Scenes from the Heroic Life of the Middle Classes: Five Plays.* Ed. J. M. Ritchie. London: Calder and Boyars, 1970

Toller, Ernst. *Seven Plays.* New York: Liveright, 1936

Secondary Sources

Bauland, P. *The Hooded Eagle: Modern German Drama on the New York Stage.* Syracuse: Syracuse University Press, 1968

Benson, Renate. *German Expressionist Drama: Ernst Toller and Georg Kaiser.* London: Macmillan, 1984

Dedner, Burghard. *Carl Sternheim.* Boston: G. K. Hall, 1982

Denkler, Horst. *Drama des Expressionismus. Programm—Spieltext—Theater.* Munich: Fink, 1967

Durzak, Manfred. *Das expressionistische Drama.* Two vols. Munich: Nymphenburger, 1978–79

Garten, H. F. *Modern Gereman Drama.* London: Methuen, 1959

Hill, Claude and Ralph Ley. *The Drama of German Expressionism: A German–English Bibliography.* Chapel Hill: University of North Carolina Press, 1960

Ihering, Herbert. *Von Reinhard bis Brecht. Vier Jahrzehnte Theater und Film.* Three vols. Berlin: Aufbau, 1958–61

Kaes, Anton. *Expressionismus in Amerika. Rezeption und Innovation.* Tübingen: Niemeyer, 1975

Kenworthy, B. J. *Georg Kaiser.* Oxford: Blackwell, 1957

Krispyn, Egbert. *Style and Society in German Literary Expressionism.* Gainesville: University of Florida Press, 1964

Meisel, Victor H., Ed. *Voices of German Expressionism.* Englewood Cliffs, N.J.: Prentice-Hall, Inc., 1970

Mennemeier, Franz Norbert. *Modernes Deutsches Drama. Kritiken und Charakteristiken.* Vol. 1: 1910–33. Munich: Fink, 1973

Myers, Bernard S. *The German Expressionists: A Generation in Revolt.* New York: Praeger, 1966

Pascal, Roy. *From Naturalism to Expressionism: German Literature and Society 1880–1918.* London: Weidenfeld and Nicholson, 1973

Perkins, Geoffrey C., Ed. *Contemporary Theory of Expressionism.* Bern/ Frankfurt a. M.: Lang, 1974

Pittock, Malcolm. *Ernst Toller.* Boston: Twayne, 1979

Raabe, Paul, Ed. *The Era of German Expressionism.* Trans. J. M. Ritchie. London: Calder and Boyars, 1974

Ritchie, J. M. *German Expressionist Drama.* Boston: Twayne, 1976

Rühle, Günther. *Theater für die Republik 1917–1933. Im Spiegel der Kritik.* Frankfurt a. M.: S. Fischer, 1967

Samuel, Richard and Thomas R. Hinton, *Expressionism in German Life, Literature, and the Theatre (1910–1924).* Cambridge: W. Hoffer & Sons, 1939

Schürer, Ernst. *Georg Kaiser.* New York: Twayne, 1971

———. *Georg Kaiser. Von morgens bis mitternachts. Erläuterungen und Dokumente.* Stuttgart: Philipp Reclam jun., 1975

Sokel, Walter H. *The Writer in Extremis.* Stanford: Stanford University Press, 1959

Spalek, John M. *Ernst Toller and His Critics: A Bibliography.* Charlottesville: University of Virginia Press, 1968

Szondi, Peter. *Theorie des modernen Dramas.* Frankfurt a. M.: Suhrkamp, 1956

Tyson, Peter K. *The Reception of Georg Kaiser (1915–1945): Text and Analysis.* Two vols. New York: Lang, 1984

Vietta, Silvio and Hans-Georg Kemper. *Expressionismus.* Munich: Fink, 1975

Webb, Benjamin. *The Demise of the "New Man": An Analysis of Ten Plays from Late German Expressionism.* Göppingen: Kümmerle, 1973

Weisstein, Ulrich (Hg.) *Expressionism as an International Literary Phenomenon.* Paris: Didier, 1973

Willet, John. *Expressionism.* London: Weidenfeld and Nicholson, 1970

Acknowledgments

Every reasonable effort has been made to locate the owners of rights to previously published works printed here. We gratefully acknowledge permission to reprint the following material:

Grateful acknowledgment is made to Michael Hamburger for permission to reprint his translation of *Murderer the Women's Hope* by Oskar Kokoschka.

August Stramm, *Sancta Susanna,* translated by Henry Marx, from *Expressionist Texts,* edited by Mel Gordon, Copyright 1986 by PAJ Publications, pages 39–45. Reprinted by permission of the Johns Hopkins University Press.

Ithaka by Gottfried Benn. Permission granted by Klett-Cotta © J. G. Cotta'sche Buchhandlung Nachfolger GmbH, Stuttgart. The German text is printed in: *Gesammelte Werke in vier Bänden.* Ed. by Dieter Wellershoff. Volume 2: *Prosa und Szenen.* Klett-Cotta, Stuttgart 1959, 9th edition 1995.

Ithaka by Gottfried Benn © 1972 by Oswald Wolff Publishers, by kind permission of Berg Publishers Ltd., Oxford, UK.

The Bloomers by Carl Sternheim, translated by M. A. McHaffie, from *Carl Sternheim Plays: Scenes of the Heroic Life of the Middle Classes,* Calder & Boyars, London. Copyright English translation © Calder & Boyars 1970. Reprinted by permission of The Calder Educational Trust, London. *From Morning to Midnight* by Georg Kaiser, translated by J. M. Ritchie, from *Georg Kaiser Plays, Volume 1,* John Calder (Publishers) Ltd., London 1985. Copyright English translation © John Calder (Publishers) Ltd., 1971, 1985. Reprinted by permission of The Calder Educational Trust, London.

Walter Hasenclever, *The Son*, translated by Henry Marx, from *Expressionist Texts*, edited by Mel Gordon, Copyright 1986 by PAJ Publications, pages 97–153. Reprinted by permission of the Johns Hopkins University Press.

Walter Hasenclever, *Der Sohn*, by permission of © Akademie der Wissenschaften und der Literatur, Mainz, Germany.

LaVergne, TN USA
19 August 2010

193865LV00002B/143/A